Claude Lévi-Strauss

Garland Reference Library of the Humanities (Vol. 72)

Claude Lévi-Strauss and His Critics
An International Bibliography of Criticism (1950-1976)
Followed by a Bibliography of the Writings of Claude Lévi-Strauss

François H. Lapointe
and
Claire C. Lapointe

Garland Publishing, Inc., New York & London

1977

Copyright © 1977
by François H. Lapointe
and
Claire C. Lapointe

All Rights Reserved

Library of Congress Cataloging in Publication Data

Lapointe, François
   Claude Lévi-Strauss and his critics ; an international bibliography of criticism (1950-1976)

   (Garland reference library of the humanities ; v. 72)
   Includes index.
   1. Lévi-Strauss, Claude--Bibliography. 2. Structural anthropology--Bibliography. I. Lapointe, Claire, joint author. II. Title.
Z8504.35.L36   [GN21.L4]   016.3012   76-24752
ISBN 0-8240-9925-7

Printed in the United States of America

TABLE OF CONTENTS

		Page
Introduction		1
I. PART ONE: Bibliography On Claude Lévi-Strauss		7
A. Section 1:	Books Devoted to Lévi-Strauss.	9
B. Section 2:	Dissertations.	19
C. Section 3:	General Presentation and Discussion	23
D. Section 4:	Studies Devoted to Individual Works of Claude Lévi-Strauss	33
	1. *Les Structures Elementaires de la Parenté (1949)*	35
	2. *Race et Histoire (1952; reedited 1967)*	40
	3. *Tristes Tropiques (1955)*	40
	4. *Anthropologie Structurale (1958)*	42
	5. *Leçon Inaugurale (1960)*.	44
	6. *La Geste D'Asdiwal (1959)*.	44
	7. *Le Totemisme Aujourd'hui (1962)*.	45
	8. *La Pensée Sauvage (1962)*	46
	9. *Les Chats (1962)*	50
	10. *Mythologiques I, II, III, IV*	51
	11. *Anthropologique Structurale Deux (1973)*.	63
E. Section 5:	Items Arranged by Proper Names	65
F. Section 6:	Items Arranged by Subjects	81
G. Section 7:	Appendix: Additional Items	163

vi   CONTENTS

II. PART TWO: Bibliography Of the Writings of
               Claude Lévi-Strauss. 175

    Index 209

INTRODUCTION

INTRODUCTION

Every epoch seems to need a leading figure and a leading movement. Existential phenomenology with Jean-Paul Sartre as its guru admirably fulfilled that role for many years after the Second World War, particularly in France. And it was no accident that circumstances happened to be favorable to Sartre. As Simone de Beauvoir points out in *Forces of Circumstances*, there existed, at least at first glance, a remarkable agreement between what Sartre was offering the public and what the public wanted.

But in the early 1960s there was a noticeable shift in the French intellectual mood, a shift toward structuralism, and the new leading figure was now Claude Lévi-Strauss who popularized the new intellectual fashion, structuralism. To insure the victory of structuralism, he felt compelled to challenge Sartre. The final chapter of *The Savage Mind* (1962) forcefully attacked Sartre's existential Marxism and initiated a new era of controversy that did not abate until May 1968.

For the past twenty years, Claude Lévi-Strauss has been the most influential anthropological theorist in France. He has attracted a large following in Europe and evoked wide interest in the United States. Standing in the mainstream of the French sociological school, he has carried Durkheim's and Mauss's theories to a totally new level of conceptualization.

Born in Brussels, Lévi-Strauss studied philosophy and law at the University of Paris. Finding these disciplines intellectually unstimulating he turned his attention to anthropology. In 1934 he accepted a post as professor of sociology at the University of São Paulo in Brazil. During this period he made several field trips in the Amazon and produced his first anthropological articles. At the beginning of World War II, he left France for America, where he met one of the masters of structuralism, Roman Jakobson, the phonologist, at the New School for Social Research in New York. This meeting fixed his future tasks: to apply the insights of structural linguistics to the study of society specifically to the kinship systems and mythologies of the primitives. His major publications began in 1949 with *The Elementary Structures of Kinship* in which he uncovered the structures through which women were exchanged in traditional societies.

But the popularity of Lévi-Strauss in France began not with *The Elementary Structures of Kinship*, but with the poetic, autobiographical travel and voyage report, *Tristes Tropiques*

(1955). Yet, the popular success of *Tristes Tropiques* was nothing compared with the intellectual success of *The Savage Mind* in 1962, an event marking the beginning of the era of structuralism. With the publication in 1964 of *The Raw and the Cooked*, Lévi-Strauss began his ambitious enterprise of classifying myths. That task having been completed with the publication of *L'Homme nu* (1973), Lévi-Strauss now addressed himself to *La Voie des masques*.

****

Although Lévi-Strauss's work has been widely read and reviewed, and has exerted a significant influence on contemporary thought, yet no comprehensive bibliography of the wide range of critical response to his writings has appeared to date. Since bibliography is an essential tool at some stage of most scholarly endeavors, we hope that this compilation of secondary materials will give scholars some assistance.

Bibliography always serves a utilitarian purpose. To compile as complete a collection of items as possible is one thing. To provide a useful arrangement of this collection is another thing. The major task of the bibliographer should be to bring order out of the chaos of alphabetic or chronological listing. After long deliberation, we have decided to distribute the material of this bibliography as follows. Part II contains a complete bibliography of the writings of Lévi-Strauss, including English translations, as well as translations into the major European languages. Part I is divided into seven sections. Section 1 contains books devoted to Lévi-Strauss (or almost exclusively so), including reviews, and the books are classified by language. Section 2 lists unpublished dissertations and theses, also indicating the entries, when available, in *Dissertation Abstracts International*. In Section 3, we have included works dealing with a general presentation and discussion of Lévi-Strauss's contributions. In Section 4, we have listed books and articles devoted to a single work of Lévi-Strauss, beginning with *Les Structures élémentaires de la parenté*, and concluding with *Anthropologie structurale deux*. In Section 5, we have listed other items by proper names. This section includes material in which Lévi-Strauss is being compared, or contrasted with major figures in anthropology, philosophy, literature or art. Section 6 lists items arranged by subject. Section 7 includes entries that arrived too late to be included in the body of the manuscript.

INTRODUCTION   5

The bibliography is intended to be as complete as is technically feasible. Our purpose is to provide an accurate, reasonably complete and useful arrangement of materials for those interested in Lévi-Strauss's work and life. Although no bibliography can claim to be exhaustive, every attempt at completeness and accuracy has been made. All of the standard reference works known to us were consulted, and many periodicals and books were searched individually. Items through June 1975 are included.

Although we have made every effort to compile an accurate, up-to-date, and reasonably complete bibliography, we are fully aware of the provisional nature of our work and feel no obligation to apologize for this. As is well known to bibliographers, publication constitutes a stage in the movement toward completeness, a more or less 'complete' starting point for further work. Our hope is that eventually we can come closer to our ideal of completeness in a supplementary volume, or a second edition, which will continue this one beyond 1976, and which will include earlier important items we were regrettably unable to include, as well as corrections of possible errors.

It is impossible in an extensive bibliography to remove all errors and make good all gaps of information. Since we intend to issue a supplementary volume, or a revised second edition, we urgently sollicit the help of those scholars who might use this bibliography. Please send us corrections, leads, and information. We would be pleased to hear from students of Lévi-Strauss, especially those in Scandanavia as well as Central and East Europe who are frustrated by our omissions.

I would like to take this opportunity to thank Professor Lévi-Strauss for his kindness in sending us information that made it possible to present an up-to-date bibliography of his writings.

                                        François and Claire Lapointe
                                        Tuskegee Institute, Alabama   36088
                                        U.S.A.

PART ONE

BIBLIOGRAPHY ON CLAUDE LEVI-STRAUSS

SECTION 1: BOOKS DEVOTED TO LEVI STRAUSS

1) BOOKS IN ENGLISH

1   Boon, James. *From Symbolism to structuralism. Lévi-strauss in a literary tradition.* Oxford: Basil Blackwell, 1971; New York: Harper & Row, 1972, xii-250p.

    Review:
2   Jonathan Culler, *Human Context-Le Domaine Humain*, vol. V, Spring 1973, pp. 238-245.

3   Richard Macksey, *Modern Language Notes*, vol. LXXXVII, 1973, p. 1338.

4   Charbonnier, Georges. *Conversations with Claude Lévi-Strauss.* Translated from the French by John and Doreen Weightman. London: Jonathan Cape, 1969.

    Review:
5   Annette Lavers, "No small talk," in *The Spectator*, vol. CCXXIII, no. 7363, August 9, 1969, pp. 179-180.

6   Edmund R. Leach, "The prejudices of Lévi-Strauss," *The Listener*, vol. LXXXII, no. 2105, July 31, 1969, pp. 156-157.

7   Gardner, Howard. *The Quest for mind: Piaget, Lévi-Strauss and the structuralist movement.* New York: Knopf, 1973.

8   Glucksmann, Miriam. *Structuralist analysis in contemporary social thought. A comparison of the theories of Claude Lévi-Strauss and Louis Althusser.* London: Routledge & Kegan Paul, 1974.

9   Hayes, Nelson E., and Hayes, Tanya, eds. *Claude Lévi-Strauss: The anthropologist as Hero.* Cambridge, Mass.: M.I.T. Press, 1970. Contains:
    1 - Gramont, Sanche de. "There are no superior societies," pp. 3-21.
    2 - Hughes, H. Stuart. "Structure and society," pp. 22-46.
    3 - Leach, Edmund R. "Lévi-Strauss in the Garden of Eden: An examination of some recent developments in the analysis of myth," pp. 47-60.
    4 - Huxley, Francis, "Which may never have existed," pp. 61-69.
    5 - Nutini, Hugo G. "Some considerations on the nature of social structure and model building: A critique of C. Lévi-Strauss and E. Leach," pp. 70-107.

BOOKS

> 6 - Scholte, Bob. "Epistemic paradigms: Some problems in cross-cultural research on social anthropological history and theory," pp. 108-122.
> 7 - Leach, Edmund R. "Brain-twister," pp. 123-132.
> 8 - Maybury-Lewis, D. "Science by association," pp. 133-139.
> 9 - Turnbull, Colin M. "The nature of reality," pp. 140-144.
> 10 - Scholte, Bob. "Lévi-Strauss's unfinished symphony: The analysis of myth," pp. 145-149.
> 11 - Mayburn-Lewis, D. "Science or bricolage?" pp. 150-163.
> 12 - Murphy, Robert F. "Connaissez-vous Lévi-Strauss?" pp. 164-169.
> 13 - Steiner, George. "Orpheus with his myths," pp. 170-183.
> 14 - Sontag, Susan. "The anthropologist as hero," pp. 184-196.
> 15 - Caws, Peter. "What is structuralism?" pp. 197-214.
> 16 - Zimmerman. Robert L. "Lévi-Strauss and the primitive," pp. 215-234.
> 17 - Abel, Lionel. "Sartre vs. Lévi-Strauss," pp. 235-246.

10 Josseling de Jong, J.P.B. de. *Lévi-Strauss's theory on kinship and marriage.* Mededelingen van het Rijksmuseum voor Volkenkunde, no. 10. Leiden: Brill, 1952.

11 Korn, Francis. *Elementary structures reconsidered. Lévi-Strauss on kinship.* Berkeley: University of California Press, 1973, 168p.

12 Korn, Francis, and Needham, Rodney. *Lévi-Strauss on the 'Elementary structures of kinship: A concordance to pagination.* London: Royal Anthropological Institute, 1969.

13 Leach, Edmund R., ed. *The Structural study of myth and totemism.* London: Tavistock Publications, 1967.

14 Leach, Edmund R. *Lévi-Strauss.* London: Fontana/Collins, 1970, 127p. 'Modern Masters'.

   Review:
15   Burton Bendow, "The instinct for order." *The Nation*, vol. CCXI, no. 22, December 28, 1970, pp. 692-694.

16   Godfrey Lienhardt. "Liaisons with Lévi-Strauss: Two new books by E. Leach." *The Listener*, vol. LXXXIII, no. 2144, April 30, 1970, pp. 589-590.

17   Moore, Tim. *Lévi-Strauss and the cultural sciences.* Birmingham (England), University Centre for Contemporary Cultural Studies. Occasional studies no. 4, 1971.

Review:
18   James Littlejohn. "The rules of the game." *New Statesman*, vol. LXXVII, no. 1985, March 28, 1969, p. 452.

19   Needham, Rodney. *Structure and sentiment. A test case in social anthropology.* Chicago: University of Chicago Press, 1962.

Review:
20   Floyd G. Lounsbury, *American Anthropologist*, vol. LXIV, 1962, pp. 1302-1310.

21   Paz, Octavio. *Claude Lévi-Strauss: An introduction.* Translated from the Spanish by J. S. Bernstein and Maxine Bernstein. London: Jonathan Cape, 1971, 109p. Another edition, Ithaca, N.Y.: Cornel University Press, 1970, 159p.

Review:
22   Edmund R. Leach. "A Mexican Virgil and the modern Inferno." *The Listener*, vol. LXXXVII, no. 2238, February 17, 1972, p. 218.

23   Rossi, Ino, ed. *The Unconscious in Culture. The structuralism of Claude Lévi-Strauss in perspective.* New York: E. P. Dutton and Co. Inc., 1974. Contains:
    Part One: THEORETICAL FOUNDATIONS OF STRUCTURALISM: INTRODUCTION
        A. *Theoretical Assumptions and their Historical Antededents*
            Intellectual antecedents of Lévi-Strauss' notion of unconscious by Ino Rossi, pp. 7-30.
            Lévi-Strauss' Use of Linguistics by Georges Mounin, pp. 31-52.
            Structuralism as Scientific Method, by Ino Rossi, pp. 60-105.
        B. *The Study of Kinship and Myth*
            Structure and History in *'The Elementary Structures of Kinship'*, by Ino Rossi, pp. 107-122.

Isomorphism and Symbolism as 'explanations' of Myths by Jacques Maquet, pp. 123-135.
Part Two: STRUCTURALISM IN ETHNOGRAPHY: INTRODUCTION
   A. *Criticism by Empirical Anthropologists*
      Lévi-Strauss' idea of Social Unconscious: the Problem of Elementary and Complex Structures in Gitksan Marriage Choice, by Alice Kasakoff, pp. 143-169.
      Dialectics and Contingency in 'The Story of Asdiwal': An Ethnographic note, by John W. Adams, pp. 170-178.
   B. *Support for the Structural Method by the Application of Lévi-Strauss' Techniques*
      Sacred Ritual vs. Unconscious: The Efficiency of Symbols and Structure in North Mexican Folk Saint's Cults and General Ceremonialism, by W. Ross Crumrine and Barbara Jane Macklin, pp. 179-197.
      The Structural Principle of Chinese World View, by Shin-pyo Kang, pp. 198-208.
   C. *Strengthening the Structural Method*
      Objects of Mediation: Myth and Praxis, by Erik Schwimmer, pp. 209-237.
      The Structural-Configurational Approach: A Methodological Outline, by Jan Pouwer, pp. 238-255.
      Comments to the essays of Part Two: The Practice of Structural Analysis, by Erik Schwimmer pp. 256-266.
Part Three: STRUCTURALISM AND CONTEMPORARY SOCIAL SCIENCES: INTRODUCTION, pp. 267-272
   A. *Critical Views*
      Structuralism as Epistemology of Closed Systems, by Anthony Wilden, pp. 273-290.
      Comments by Yvan Simonis, p. 291.
      The Myth of Structuralism, by Stanley Diamond, pp. 292-335.
      Beyond Structuralism: The Dialectics of the Diachronic and Synchronic Methods in the Human Sciences, by Lawrence Krader, pp. 336-361.
   B. *Positive Views*
      Two Ways of Approaching Concrete Reality: 'Group Dynamics' and Lévi-Strauss' Structuralism, by Yvan Simonis, pp. 363-388.
      Language, History, and the Logic of Inquiry in the Works of Lévi-Strauss and Sartre, by Lawrence Rosen, pp. 389-423.

Comments to the essays of Part Three: Structuralism as Ethno-logic, by Bob Scholte, pp. 424-454.
Epilogue: Towards a Constructive Dialogue by Ino Rossi, pp. 455-462.

2) BOOKS IN FRENCH

24 Backès-Clément, Catherine. *Lévi-Strauss ou la structure et le malheur.* Paris: Seghers, 1970, 1974, 190p. ('Philosophes de tous les temps', no. 66)

   Review:
25 L. Finas, "La pirogue et la spirale," in *Critique*, no. 294, November 1971, pp. 998-1008.

26 Roger Maria, in *Europe*, no. 539, March 1974, pp. 326-327.

27 Caruso, Paolo. *Entretiens avec Claude Lévi-Strauss, Michel Foucault, Jacques Lacan.* Paris: Editions du Seuil, 1970.

28 Charbonnier, Georges. *Entretiens avec Claude Lévi-Strauss.* Paris: Plon-Julliard, 1961, 160p. Union Générale d'Editions, 1969.

   Review:
29 M. Freedman, *American Anthropologist*, vol. LXIV, Fall 1962, pp. 208-209.

30 James Hamilton-Peterson. "Triste topique." *New Statesman*, vol. LXXVIII, no. 2003, August 1, 1969, p. 152.

31 Courtès, Jean. *Lévi-Strauss et les contraintes de la pensée mythique. Une lecture sémiotique des 'Mythologiques'.* Paris: Mame, 1973, 188p. (Univers sémiotiques).

32 Cressant, Pierre. *Lévi-Strauss.* (Psychothèque, 4). Paris: Editions Universitaires, 1970, 159p.

   Review:
33 Raymond Bellour. "Raymond Bellour a lu *Lévi-Strauss* de Pierre Cressant." *Le Magazine Littéraire*, no. 46, novembre 1970, p. 62.

BOOKS

34 Delfendahl, Bernard. *Le Clair et l'obscur. Critique de l'anthropologie savante, et défense de l'anthropologie amateur.* Paris: Editions Anthropos, 1973.

35 *Echanges et communications, I and II.* Mélanges offerts à Claude Lévi-Strauss à l'occasion de son 60e anniversaire, réunis par Jean Pouillon et Paul Maranda. La Haye-Paris: Mouton, 1970, 2 vol.

   Review:
36 M. De Grève, *Revue Belge de Philologie et d'Histoire*, vol. L, 1972, pp. 210-212.

37 Bob Scholte, *American Anthropologist*, vol. LXXV, 1973, pp. 1778-1781.

38 Fages, J.-B. *Comprendre Lévi-Strauss.* Toulouse: Privat, 1972, 130p.

39 Heusch, Luc de. *Pourquoi l'épouser? et autres essais.* Paris: Gallimard, 1971. Coll. 'Bibliothèque des sciences humaines'.

40 Leach, Edmund R. *Lévi-Strauss* (Coll. 'Les maîtres modernes, 3). Paris: Seghers, 1970, 192p. Translated from the English by Denis Verguin.

41 Marc-Lipiansky, Mireille. *Le structuralisme de Lévi-Strauss.* (Bibliothèque scientifique). Paris: Payot, 1973, 347p.

   Review:
42 A. Devyver, in *Revue Belge de Philosophie*, Lii, 1974, pp. 705-708.

43 Jean-D. Robert, in *Archives de Philosophie*, tome 38, cahier 1, janvier-mars, 1975, pp. 167-168.

44 Makarius, Raoul, et Laura Makarius. *Structuralisme ou Ethnologie. Pour une critique radicale de l'anthropologie de Lévi-Strauss.* Paris: Editions Anthropos, 1973, 373p.

45 Milet, André. *Pour ou contre le structuralisme. Claude Lévi-Strauss et son oeuvre.* Tournai: Editions du Centre diocésain de Documentation, 1968.

46 Paz, Octavio. *Deux transparents. Marcel Duchamp et Claude Lévi-Strauss.* Paris: Gallimard, 1970.

47 Review:
    Jean-Louis Ferrier, "L'ambassadeur et les transparents." *L'Express*, no. 1023, 15-21 février 1971, p. 67.

48 Simonis, Yvan. *Claude Lévi-Strauss ou la 'Passion de l'inceste'. Introduction au structuralisme*. Paris: Aubier-Montaigne, 1968, 380p. Coll. 'Recherches économiques et sociales'.

49 Review:
    Maurice Corvez, *Revue Thomiste*, tome LXVIII, 1968, pp. 457-462.

50 Jean Langlois, *Dialogue*, vol. IX, sp. 70, pp. 276-278.

51 Y. M., *Dialogue*, vol. VIII, 1969-1970, pp. 357-358.

52 Bob Scholte, *American Anthropologist*, vol. LXXI, 1969, pp. 503-505

3) BOOKS IN GERMAN

53 Dumasy, Annegret. *Restloses Erkennen. Die Diskussion über den Strukturalismus des Claude Lévi-Strauss in Frankreich* (Soziologische Schriften, v. 8). Berlin: Duncker & Humblot, 1972.

54 Gasché, Rodolphe. *Die hybride Wissenschaft. Zur Mutation d. Wissenschaftsbegriffs bei Emile Durkheim und im Strukturalismus von Claude Lévi-Strauss*. (Texte Metzler, 26). Stuttgart: Metzler, 1973.

55 Lepenies, Wolf, und Ritter, Hans H. eds. *Orte des Wilden Denkens. Zur Anthropologie von Claude Lévi-Strauss*. Herausgegeben von Wolf Lepenies und Hans H. Ritter. Frankfurt am Main: Suhrkamp, 1970. Contains:

   Lepenies, Wolf, & Hanns H. Ritter, "Einleitung," pp. 7-46.
   Leach, Edmund R. "Claude Lévi-Strauss, Philosoph und Antropolog," pp. 49-76.
   Fleischmann, Eugene. "Claude Lévi-Strauss über den menschlichen Geist," pp. 77-109.

BOOKS

    Ritter, Hanns H. "Claude Lévi-Strauss als Leser Rousseaus. Exkurse zu einer Quelle ethnologischer Reflexion," pp. 113-159.
    Lepenies, Wolf. "Lévi-Strauss und die strukturalistische Marx-Lecture," pp. 160-224.
    Nagel, Herbert. "Claude Lévi-Strauss als Leser Freuds," pp. 225-305.
    Gasché, Rodolphe. "Das wilde Denken und die Ökonomie der Repräsentation. Zum Verhältnis von Ferdinand de Saussure und Claude Lévi-Strauss," pp. 306-385.
    Derrida, Jacques. "La structure, le signe et le jeu dans le discours des sciences humaines" (German translation), pp. 387-463.

56 Schmidt, Alfred. *Der strukturalistische Angriff auf die Geschichte*. Frankfurt am Main: Suhrkamp, 1968.

4) BOOKS IN ITALIAN

57 Backès-Clément, Catherine. *Lévi-Strauss. La vita, il pensiero i testi esemplari*. Trad. di Donatella Guarnotta (I memorabili, 20). Milano: Accademia; Firenze: Sansoni, 1971, 254p. Translation of no. 24.

58 Caruso, Paolo. *Conversazioni con Claude Lévi-Strauss, Michel Foucault, Jacques Lacan*. A cura di Paolo Caruso. Milano: U. Mursia, 1969, 190p. (Il Camino. Pensiero e civiltà, 4).

59 Charbonnier, Georges. *Dialoghi Charbonnier-Claude Lévi-Strauss*. Milano: U. Mursia, 1970. Translation of no. 28.

    Review:
60   Riccardo Lanza. *"Dialoghi Charbonnier-Lévi-Strauss." Vita e Pensiero*, anno LI, no. 6, June 1968, pp. 529-535.

61 Mcravia, Sergio. *La ragione nascosta. Scienza e filosofia nel pensiero di Claude Lévi-Strauss*. (Saggi, 1). 2a ed. Firenze: G. C. Sansoni, 1972, 413p.

    Review:
62   M. Galzingna, *Rivista Critica di Storia della Filosofia*, XXVI, 1971, pp. 162-167.

63   Francesco Remotti, *Rivista di Filosofia*, LX, 1969,
        pp. 509-514.

64   Remotti, Francesco. *Lévi-Strauss. Struttura e storia.*
     Torino: G. Einaud, 1971, 367p. (Piccola biblioteca
     Einaudi, 1956).

        Review:
65   Marco Ravera. *Filosofia* (Torino), n.s. anno XXIII,
        fasc. 1, January 1972, pp. 73-75.

66   R. Radice, *Rivista di Filosofia Neo-Scolastica*, LXIV,
     1972, pp. 736-744.

67   Scarduelli, Pietro. *L'Analisi strutturale dei miti.*
     Pref. Enzo Paci. Milano: Celuc, 1971.

68   Schmidt, Alfred. *La negazione della storia. Strutturalismo
     e marxismo in Althusser e Lévi-Strauss.* Trad. Giancarlo
     Bosetti (Interventi, 8). Milano: Lampugnani Nigri, 1972,
     103p. Translation of 56.

                    5)   BOOKS IN SPANISH

69   Caruso, Paolo. *Conversaciones con Lévi-Strauss, Foucault y
     Lacan.* Trad. del italiano de F. Serra Cantarell (Argumen-
     tos, 5). Barcelona: Ed. Anagrama, 196, 130p.

70   Leach, Edmund R. *Lévi-Strauss, antropólogo y filósofo*
     [seguido de Cl. Lévi-Strauss: El oso y el barbero].
     Trad. del inglés por José R. Llobera (Col. Cuadernos
     anagrama, 2). Barcelona: Ed. Anagrama, 1970, 73p.

71   Montes, Santiago. *Claude Lévi-Strauss* (Un nuevo discurso
     del metodo). San Salvador: Ministero de Educación, 1971.

72   Paz, Octavio. *Claude Lévi-Strauss o el nuevo festin de
     Esopo.* [2. ed.] México: J. Mortíz, 1969, 134p. Serie
     del volador.

73   Pingaud, Bernard et al., ed. *Lévi-Strauss: Estructuralismo
     y dialéctica.* Buenos Aires: Paidos, 1968. [Translation
     of *L'Arc*, no. 26, 1965]. Contains:

        Bernard Pingaud: "Comment on devient structuraliste,"
        Luc de Heusch, "Situation et positions"

18 BOOKS

    Claude Lévi-Strauss, "Le triangle culinaire"
    Catherine Backès, "Du Miel aux Cendres,"
    Gérard Genette, "Structuralisme et critique littéraire"
    Célestin Deliège, "La musicologie devant le structuralisme"
    Jean Pouillon, "Sartre et Lévi-Strauss."
    NOTES, par Jean Guiart, J.-C. Gardin, Pierre Clastres.

6) BOOKS IN PORTUGUESE

74 Pingaud, Bernard et al. *Lévi-Strauss* (Texto original de *l'Arc* Documents). São Paulo: Ed. Documentos Ltda., 1968, 102p. [Contains same as 73]

75 Costa Lima, Luiz., ed. and trans., *O Estruturalismo de Lévi-Strauss*. Petropolis: Vozes, 1969. Contains:

    Luis Costa Lima, "Introducão," pp. 11-43.
    Andre Bonomi, "Implicacoes filosoficas na antropologia de Claude Lévi-Strauss," pp. 114-139 [From *Aut Aut* nos. 96-97, 1967].
    Enzo Paci, "Antropologia estrutural e fenomenologia," pp. 94-106 [from *Aut Aut*, July 1965, no. 88].
    Emilio Renzi, "Sobre a nocao do inconsciente em Lévi-Strauss," pp. 107-113 [from *Aut Aut*, no. 88, July 1965].
    Paul Ricoeur, "Strutura e hermeneutica," pp. 157-191 [From *Esprit*, no. 322, novembre 1963, pp. 596-627].
    Nicolas Ruwet, "Linguistica e ciencias do homem," pp. 78-93 [From *Esprit*, no. 322, novembre 1963, pp. 564-578].

SECTION 2: DISSERTATIONS

DOCTORAL DISSERTATIONS

76 Courtès, Joseph. Recherches sémiotiques sur les 'Mythologiques' de Lévi-Strauss, le vraisemblable de la démonstration. Thèse 3e cycle Paris III, 1971, 217ff, dactylographié.

77 De Ipola, Emilio Rafael. Le structuralisme ou l'histoire en exil, étude critique de l'oeuvre de Claude Lévi-Strauss. Thèse. Lettres. Nanterre, 1969, 283ff. multigraphié.

78 Lampo, Mireille. Le structuralisme de Lévi-Strauss. Thèse 3e cycle Paris X-Nanterre, 1971, 483ff. dactylographié.

79 Melhman, Jeffrey. A structural study of autobiography: Proust, Leiris, Sartre, Lévi-Strauss. Yale University, 1971. *Dissertation Abstracts*, XXXIII, no. 1, July 1972, p. 320-A.

80 Rossi, Ino. Theoretical foundations of Lévi-Strauss's structuralism: An exegetical interpretation and a critique. New School for Social Research. *Dissertation Abstracts*, XXXI, 1970, pp. 33-34-B.

81 Schintholzer, Birgit. Die Auflösung des Geschichtsbegriffs im Strukturalismus. Eine Studie zu Lévi-Strauss. Univ. Hamburg, 1973, 141p.

82 Scholte, Bob. The ethnology of anthropological traditions: A comparative study of Anglo-American commentaries on French structural anthropology. University of California at Berkeley, 1969. *Dissertation Abstracts*, XXX, no. 5, 1969, p. 2000.

83 Shalvey, Thomas J. The philosophical foundations of the role of the collective in the work of Lévi-Strauss. Georgetown University, 1970. *Dissertation Abstracts*, XXXI, no. 8, p. 4221-A.

84 Simonis, Yvan. Claude Lévi-Strauss ou la passion de l'inceste. Institut Catholique de Paris, 1967.

85 Van Haeperen, Joseph. Médiation et symbole. Articulation de la notion de symbole dans l'oeuvre de Claude Lévi-Strauss. Thèse de doctorat, 1971-1972. Université Catholique de Louvain.

86 Verstraeten, Pierre. Esquisse pour une critique de la
   raison structuraliste. Thèse de doctorat en philosophie,
   Université de Bruxelles, 1964.

SECTION 3: GENERAL PRESENTATION AND DISCUSSION

GENERAL PRESENTATION AND DISCUSSION

87 Aron, Raymond. "Le paradoxe du même et de l'autre," pp. 943-952 in no. 35.

88 Audiberti, Jacques. "Lettres à Lévi-Strauss." *L'Ouvre-boite, Cahiers Jacques Audiberti*, no. 4, 1975, pp. 11-19.

89 Backès-Clément, Catherine. "Réflexions sur Claude Lévi-Strauss." *La Nouvelle Critique*, no. 24, mai 1969.

90 Backès-Clément, Catherine. "Le voyageur, Balzac et Wagner." *Le Magazine Littéraire*, no. 58, novembre 1971, pp. 13-16.

91 Backès-Clément. "Un visionnaire." *La Quinzaine Littéraire*, no. 55, 1-15 août 1968, p. 20.

92 Backès-Clément, Catherine. "Lévi-Strauss ou la philosophie du non-savoir." *La Quinzaine Littéraire*, no. 95, 16-31 mai 1970, pp. 12-13.

93 Bakker, Reinout. "Een antropologisch gezichtspunkt van Claude Lévi-Strauss." *Algemeen Nederlands Tijdschrift voor Wijsbegeerte*, vol. LXIII, 1971, pp. 42-59. [See Jaeger's response, no. 138]

94 Balandier, Georges. "Le hasard et les civilisations." *Cahiers du Sud*, no. 319, 1953.

95 Balandier, Georges. "Le XXe siècle ne se connaît pas." *Le Nouvel Observateur*, no. 119, 22-28 févirer, 1967, pp. 43-45.

96 Balliu, Julien. "L'aliénation et les avatars de l'ontologie." *Revue de l'Université de Bruxelles*, 20e année, no. 5, août-septembre 1968, pp. 403-419.

97 Bastide, Roger. "La nature humaine: le point de vue du sociologue et de l'ethnologue." *'La Nature humaine'*, Actes du XIe Congrès des sociétés de philosophie de langue française, Paris, 1961.

98 Bataille, Georges. *La Part maudite*. Paris: Gallimard, 1967.

GENERAL DISCUSSION

99 Bell, J. H., and Von Sturmer, J. R. "An Introduction to Claude Lévi-Strauss." *Meanjin Quarterly*, vol. XXV, no. 3, 1966, pp. 318-325.

100 Benjamin, Geoffrey. "Lévi-Strauss is an anthropologist." *Cambridge Review*, vol. LXXXIXa, no. 2158, November 18, 1967, pp. 122-123; and *Ibid.*, no. 2159, November 25, 1967, pp. 149-151.

101 Berndt, Ronald M. "Two in one, and more in two. . .", pp. 1040-1068 in no. 35.

102 Blanchot, Maurice. "L'homme au point zéro." *La Nouvelle Revue Française*, avril 1956. Reprinted in *L'Amitié*. Paris: Gallimard, 1971, pp. 87-97.

103 Brain, Robert. "Pattern-Making." *The Sunday Times*, no. 7694, November 15, 1970, p. 32.

104 Brosse, Jacques. "Comment lire Lévi-Strauss." *Arts-Lettres-Spectacles*, no. 977, octobre 1964.

105 Brosse, Jacques. "Les clés de Lévi-Strauss." *Les Nouvelles Littéraires*, 46e année, no. 2135, 22 août 1968, pp. 1-10.

106 Boon, James A. "Lévi-Strauss, Claude." *Encyclopaedia Britannica*, 1971 edition.

107 Bryson, Norman. "Lévi-Strauss and the machine for the suppression of time." *Granta*, vol. LXXV, no. 3, February 1970, pp. 18-19.

108 Cantoni, R. *Illusione e pregiudizio*. Milano: Il Saggiatore, 1967, ch. II, sezione 6.

109 Caronna, G. "Sull'antropologia strutturale di Lévi-Strauss." *Uomo e Cultura*, no. 1, 1969.

110 Caruso, Paolo. "Il caso Lévi-Strauss." *Panorama*, July 1965.

111 Caillois, Roger. "Théorie des jeux." *Revue de Métaphysique et de Morale*, no. 1, tome LXIII, janvier-mars 1958.

112 Caillois, Roger. "Illusions à rebours." *La Nouvelle Revue Française*, no. 24, décembre 1954, pp. 1010-1024; and *Ibid.*, no. 25, janvier 1955, pp. 58-70. [Réponse: C. Lévi-Strauss, "Diogène couché." *Les Temps Modernes*, 1955, and Réponse à Roger Caillois, *Ibid.*]

113 Caruso, Paolo. "Introduzione" a C. Lévi-Strauss, *Razza e storia e altri studi di antropologia*. Torino: Einaudi, 1967, pp. 7-43.

114 Chatel de Brancion, Paul. "Remarques sur une lecture 'idéale'." *(Pré) Publications*, 11, juillet 1974, pp. 11-19.

115 Clastres, Pierre. "Entre silence et dialogue." *L'Arc*, no. 26, 1965, pp. 76-78.

116 Cockburn, Alexander. "In Praise of treachery." *New Statesman*, vol. LXXIV, no. 1909, October 13, 1967, p. 477.

117 Crozier, Michel. "The cultural revolution: Notes on the changes in the intellectual climate of France," in Stephen R. Graubard, ed., *A New Europe?* Boston: Houghton Mifflin, 1964.

118 Deleuze, Gilles, et Félix Guattari. *Capitalisme et schizophrénie. L'Anti-Oedipe*. Paris: Les Editions de Minuit, 1972.

119 De Man, Paul. *Blindness and insight. Essays in the rhetoric of contemporary criticism*. London-New York: Oxford University Press, 1971.

120 Derrida, Jacques. "Force et signification," in *L'Ecriture et la différence*. Paris: Editions du Seuil, 1967, pp. 9-49.

121 Derrida, Jacques. "La structure, le signe et le jeu dans le discours des sciences humaines," in *L'Ecriture et la différence*, pp. 409-428 (see above).

English translation "Structure, sign and play in the discourse of the human sciences," pp. 247-265 in Richard Macksey and Eugenio Donato, eds., *The Language of criticism and the Sciences of man: The structuralist controversy*. Baltimore: Johns Hopkins Press, 1969, pp. 247-265. (Discussion, pp. 265-272).

German translation, pp. 387-463 in Lepenies & Ritter, *Orte des Wilden Denkens*, see no. 55.

28   GENERAL DISCUSSION

122   Derrida, Jacques. "Nature, culture, écriture. La violence
      de la lettre de Lévi-Strauss à Rousseau." *Cahiers pour
      l'Analyse*, no. 4, septembre-octobre 1966, pp. 1-45.
      Reprinted in *De la Grammatologie*. Paris: Editions du
      Seuil, 1967.

      Italian translation, R. Balzarotti. Milano: Yaca
      Book, 1969.

      Donato, Eugenio, see 410.

123   Eco, Umberto. "L'antropologo al Luna Park." *L'Espresso*,
      November 28, 1965.

124   Eco, Umberto. "Lévi-Strauss, Claude." in *Enciclopedia
      Filosofica*, a cura del Centro di studi filosofici di
      Gallarate. Firenze: Sansoni, 1967.

125   Ferry, Jacqueline F. "L'envers et l'endroit," pp. 35-47 in
      Australasian Universities Language and Literature
      Association, 1966. *Proceedings and papers* of the Tenth
      Congress held at the University of Auckland, 2-9 February
      1966. Peter Dane, ed. Auckland, New Zealand: University
      of Auckland Bindery, 1966, pp. 35-47.

126   Frank, J. N. "Il buon selvaggio." *Il Mundo*, July 1959.

127   *Französische Kultur*. Dokumente 1961. Köln: Verlag der
      Dokumente, 1961, 108p.

128   Geertz, Clifford. "The cerebral savage: On the works of
      Claude Lévi-Strauss." *Encounter*, vol. XXVIII, no. 4,
      April 1967, pp. 25-32.

129   Gonzalez, O. "Notas sobre Claude Lévi-Strauss." *Actéon*
      (Bogóta), nos. 1-2, 1968.

130   Gramont, Sanche de. "There are no superior societies,"
      pp. 3-21, see 9.

131   Guerrieri, A. M. "Claude Lévi-Strauss e la sollectizione
      a pensare." *Psicoterapia e Scienze Umane*, June 1967.

132   Guiart, Jean. "Survivre à Lévi-Strauss." *L'Arc*, no. 26,
      1965, pp. 61-64.

133   Hays, H. R. "Claude Lévi-Strauss," in *Explorers of man.
      Five pioneers in anthropology*. New York: Crowell-
      Collier Press, 1971, pp. 141-172.

134 Hodgson, Godfrey. "All the eggheads in one basket." *The Sunday Times Magazine*, April 16, 1967, pp. 41, 43-44, 46.

135 Hughes, Henry Stuart. see 9

136 Huxley, Francis. "Which may never have existed." *The Kenyon Review*, vol. XXIV, no. 1, Winter 1962, pp. 150-156. Reprinted, pp. 61-69 in 9.

137 Huxley, Francis. "An antidote to Lévi-Strauss." *Encounter*, vol. XXXIV, no. 5, May 1970, pp. 71-77.

138 Jager, M. "Manttekeningen bij Professor Bakker's artikel 'Een antropologisch gezichtspunkt van Lévi-Strauss'." *Algemeen Nederlands Tijdschrift voor Wijsbegeerte*, vol. LXIII, 1971, pp. 60-62. (See Bakker above, no. 93)

139 Lacroix, Jean. "Le structuralisme de Claude Lévi-Strauss," in *Panorama de la philosophie française contemporaine*. Paris: Presses Universitaires de France, 1966.

140 Leach, Edmund R. see 674.

141 Leach, Edmund R. "New Hat." *New Statesman*, vol. LXIX, no. 1771, February 19, 1965, pp. 286-287.

142 Leach, Edmund R. "Claude Lévi-Strauss." *Nation*, vol. CXI, December 28, 1970, pp. 692-694.

143 Leach, Edmund R. "Progress through the looking glass." *New Edinburgh Review*, no. 13, June 1971, pp. 14-19.

144 Lefebvre, Henri. *Positions contre les technocrates*. Paris: Editions de Minuit, 1968.

145 Lefebvre, Henri. "Claude Lévi-Strauss et le nouvel éléatisme." *L'Homme et la Société*, no. 1, juillet-septembre 1966, pp. 21-31; and *Ibid.*, no. 2, octobre-décembre 1966, pp. 81-104. Reprinted in *Au-delà du structuralisme*. Paris: Editions Anthropos, 1971, pp. 261-311.

146 Lepenies, Wolf, und Ritter, Hanns H. "Einleitung," in 55.

147 Lyotard, Jean-François. "A propos de Claude Lévi-Strauss: 'Les Indiens ne cueillent pas les fleurs'," *Annales (Economies--Sociétés--Civilisations)*, 20e année, no. 1, janvier-février 1965, pp. 62-83.

GENERAL DISCUSSION

148 Locher, G. W. "Claude Lévi-Strauss," in *Filosofen van de 20e eeuw*. Onder redactie van C. P. Bertels en E. Petersma. Assen, Amsterdam, Van Gorcum; Amsterdam, Brussel: Intermediair, 1972.

149 Molnar, Thomas. *Sartre: Ideologue of our time*. New York: Funk & Wagnalls, 1968, pp. 126-130 and passim. French translation, *Sartre, philosophe de la contestation*. Paris: Le Prieuré, 1970.

150 Moravia, Sergio. "Filosofia e scienze umane nella cultura francese contemporanea." *Belfagor*, vol. XXIII, 1968, pp. 649-681.

151 Macksey, Richard, and Eugenio Donato, eds. *The Language of criticism and the sciences of man: The structuralist controversy*. Baltimore: Johns Hoplins Press, 1970.

152 Melhman, Jeffrey. *A Structural study of autobiography: Proust, Leiris, Sartre, Lévi-Strauss*. Ithaca, N. Y.: Cornell University Press, 1974.

153 Murphy, David. "Claude Lévi-Strauss or the meeting of cultures." *New Writing for Zambia*, vol. VII, no. 1, 1971, pp. 3-6.

154 Murphy, Robert F. "Connaissez-vous Lévi-Strauss?" *Saturday Review*, May 17, 1969, pp. 52-53. Reprinted pp. 164-169 in 9.

155 Parain, Brice. "Les sorciers." *L'Homme Nouveau*, mai 1956.

156 Pividal, Raphael. "Signification et position de l'oeuvre de Lévi-Strauss." *Annales (Economies--Sociétés--Civilisations)*, 19e année, no. 6, novembre-décembre 1964, pp. 1087-1099.

157 Pocock, D. F. "Claude Lévi-Strauss--Anthropologist." *The Oxford Review*, no. 7, (Hilary 1968), pp. 23-29.

158 Pouillon, Jean. "L'oeuvre de Claude Lévi-Strauss." *Les Temps Modernes*, 12e année, no. 126, juillet 1956, pp. 150-172. Reprinted in C. Lévi-Strauss, *Race et Histoire*. Paris: Gonthier, 1967.

159 Revel, Jean-François. *Pourquoi des philosophes?* Paris: Jean-Jacques Pauvert, 1964, c. 1957; edition augmentée, 1965. Italian translation M. V. Predeval, *A che servono i filosofi?* Milano: Lerici, 1958, ch. VII.

160 Roy, Claude. "Claude Lévi-Strauss ou l'homme en question." *La Nef*, no. 28, mai 1959.

161 Sahlins, Marshall D. "On the Delphic writings of Claude Lévi-Strauss." *Scientific American*, vol. CCXIV, no. 6, 1966, pp. 131-136.

162 Said, Edward W. "The totalitarianism of mind." *The Kenyon Review*, vol. XXIX, no. 2, March 1967, pp. 256-268.

163 Servier, J. "Osservazioni su Claude Lévi-Strauss," appendice a C. Lévi-Strauss, *Primitivi e civilizzati*. Milano: Rusconi, 1970. Translated by Cattabiani [*Conversazioni* con G. Charbonnier]

164 Seymour-Smith, Martin. "Cape of Good Hope." *The Spectator*, vol. CCXXI, no. 7329, December 13, 1968, pp. 849-850.

165 Simone, F. "Le radici di Claude Lévi-Strauss nella cultura classica francese." *La Stampa*, July 13, 1969.

166 Sierksma, Fokke. "Met en tegen Lévi-Strauss." *Tirade* (Antwerp), vol. VII, 1963, pp. 306-330.

167 Simonis, Yvan. "Silence du structuralisme, silence de la religion." *Projet*, novembre 1967.

168 Solotaroff, Theodore. "A kind of survival." *The New Republic*, vol. CLVI, no. 19, May 13, 1967, pp. 21-22,24.

169 Sontag, Susan. "The anthropologist as hero," pp. 69-81 in 9.

170 Tarn, Nathaniel. "Pansies for thoughts: Reflections on the work of Claude Lévi-Strauss." *The Listener*, vol. LXXVII, May 11, 1967, pp. 618-619, 635.

171 Valeri, Valerio. "Struttura, trasformazione, 'esaustività'. Un'esposizione di alcuni concetti di Lévi-Strauss." *Annali della Sculoa Normale Superiore di Pisa*. Classe di Lettere, Storia e Filosofia II, 39, 1970, pp. 347-386.

32   GENERAL DISCUSSION

172   Toynbee, Philip. "Semantic Frontiersmen." *The Observer*,
      no. 9205, December 17, 1967, p. 21.

173   Trotignon, Pierre. *Les Philosophes français d'aujourd'hui*.
      Paris: Presses Universitaires de France, 1967.

174   Weightman, John. "The play as fable." *Encounter*, vol.
      XXVIII, no. 2, February 1967, pp. 55-57.

175   Weightman, John. "Visit to Lévi-Strauss." *Encounter*,
      vol. XXXVI, February 1971, pp. 38-42.

176   Yurick, Sol. "The politics of the imagination: The
      problem of consciousness." *Tri-Quarterly*, Winter &
      Spring 1972, "Literature in Revolution," pp. 501-551.

177   Zimmermann, Robert L. "Lévi-Strauss and the primitive,"
      pp. 215-234 in 9.

SECTION 4: STUDIES DEVOTED TO INDIVIDUAL WORKS
OF CLAUDE LEVI STRAUSS

STUDIES DEVOTED TO INDIVIDUAL WORKS OF CLAUDE LEVI-STRAUSS
(Including Book Reviews)

LES STRUCTURES ELEMENTAIRES DE LA PARENTE (1949)

178   Anonymous. "Supreme Rules of the Gift." *Times Literary Supplement*, no. 3500, March 27, 1969, p. 321.

179   Anonymous. "Confronting the classics." *The Times Literary Supplement*, August 14, 1970. Reprinted in *T.L.S. 9, 1970. Essays and Reviews from the Times Literary Supplement*. London, New York, Toronto: Oxford University Press, 1970, pp. 113-120.

180   Bataille, Georges. "L'inceste et le passage de l'animal à l'homme." *Critique*, VII, no. 44, janvier 1951, pp. 43-61. Reprinted, "L'énigme de l'inceste," in *L'Erotisme*. Paris: Editions de Minuit, 1957. English translation *Death and Sensuality. A study of eroticism and the taboo*. New York: Walker Press, 1962. Italian translation A. Dell'Orto. Milano: Sugar, 1962; restampa a cura di Paolo Caruso. Milano: Mondadori, 1969.

181   Beauvoir, Simone de. *"Les Structures élémentaires de la parenté." Les Temps Modernes*, 5e année, no. 49, novembre 1949, pp. 943-949.

182   Berting, J. and H. Philipsen. "Solidarity, stratification, and sentiment: The unilateral cross-cousin marriage according to the theories of Lévi-Strauss, Leach, Homans, and Schneider." *Bijdragen tot de Land-, Taal-, en Volkenkunde*, vol. CXVI, 1960, pp. 55-80.

36 INDIVIDUAL WORKS

183 Buchler, Ira R. and Henry A. Selby. *Kinship and social organization: An Introduction to Method and Theory.* New York: Macmillan, 1968.

184 Buchler, Ira R. and R. Freeze. "Measuring the development of kinship terminologies: Scalogram and transformational accounts." *American Anthropologist,* vol. LXVIII, 1966, pp. 765-788.

185 Buchler, Ira R. "A formal account of the Hawaiian- and Eskimo-type kinship terminologies." *Southwestern Journal of Anthropology,* vol. XX, 1964, pp. 286-318.

186 Bulmer, Ralph. "Which came first, the chicken or the egghead?" in Jean Pouillon and Pierre Maranda, eds., *Echanges et communications.* Mélanges offerts à Claude Lévi-Strauss à l'occasion de son 60e anniversaire. The Hague-Paris: Mouton, 1970, vol. II, pp. 1069-1091.

187 Cordero, Rodrigo. "Mito e totemismo en Sigmund Freud y Claude Lévi-Strauss." *Revista de Filosofía de la Universidad de Costa Rica,* vol. XI, no. 32, January-June 1973, pp. 117-163.

188 Coult, Allan D. "Causality and cross-sex prohibitions." *American Anthropologist,* vol. LXV, 1963, pp. 266-277.

189 Cuisenier, Jean. "Formes de la parenté et formes de la pensée." *Esprit,* no. 322, novembre 1963, pp. 547-563.

190 Davy, Georges. *"Les Structures élémentaires de la parenté."* L'Annee Sociologique, 3e série, 1948-1949, pp. 350-358.

191 Dumont, Louis. "Descent or intermarriage? A relational view of Australian section systems." *Southwestern Journal of Anthropology,* vol. XXII, no. 3, 1966, pp. 231-250.

192 Forge, Anthony. "Other Men's Sisters." *New Society,* vol. XIII, no. 336, March 6, 1969, pp. 373-374.

193 Fortes, Meyer. "Totemism and Taboo." *Proceedings of the Royal Anthropological Institute,* 1967, pp. 7-18.

194 Fortes, Meyer. "Exchange and Mart." *The Spectator,* vol. CCXXII, no. 7343, March 21, 1969, pp. 376-377.

195 Fox, Robin. *Kinship and marriage.* London, 1967.

196 Gallini, Carlo. "La famiglia primitiva vista da Lévi-Strauss." *La Stampa,* June 22, 1969.

197 Goody, J. "The mother's brother and the sister's son in West Africa." *Journal of the Royal Anthropological Institute,* 1959, vol. LXXXIX.

198 Guier, Jorgé Enrique. "Incesto, matrimonio y derecho." *Revista de Filosofía de la Universidad de Costa Rica,* vol. XI, no. 32, January-June 1973, pp. 83-116.

199 Hart, C. W. M. *"Les Structures élémentaires de la parenté." American Anthropologist,* vol.LII, 1950, pp. 392-393.

200 Heusch, Luc de. "A propos d'une mise en question par le R. P. de Souberghe des thèses sociologiques de M. Lévi-Strauss." *Zaire,* no. 8, Octobre 1955, pp. 849-861. Reprinted, with modifications, "Pourquoi épouser celle-ci plutôt que celle-là?" in *Pourquoi l'épouser? et autres essais.* Paris: Gallimard, 1971, pp. 72-85.

201 Heusch, Luc de. *Essais sur le symbolisme de l'inceste royal.* Bruxelles, 1958.

202 Heusch, Luc de. "L'oeuvre de M. Lévi-Strauss et l'évolution de l'ethnologie française." *Zaire,* no. 8, août 1958.

203 Homans, George C. and David M. Schneider. *Marriage, Authority and Final Causes: A Study of Unilateral Cross-Cousin Marriage.* Glencoe, Ill." The Free Press, 1955.

204 Homans, George C. *Sentiments and activities. Essays in social science.* Glencoe, Ill.: The Free Press, 1962, pp. 202-256.

205 Kortmulder, K. "An ethnological theory of the incest taboo and exogamy, with special reference to the views of Claude Lévi-Strauss." *Current Anthropology,* vol. IX, 1968, pp. 437-449.

206 Josseling de Jong, M. P. B. de. *Lévi-Strauss's theory on kinship and marriage.* Mededelingen van het Rijksmuseum voor Volkenkunde, no. 10. Leiden: Brill, 1952.

INDIVIDUAL WORKS

207 Korn, Francis. *Elementary structures reconsidered. Lévi-Strauss on kinship.* Berkeley: University of California Press, 1973, 168p.

208 Korn, Francis, and Rodney Neeham. *Lévi-Strauss on the Elementary structures of kinship: A concordance to pagination.* London: Royal Anthropological Institute, 1969.

209 Leach, Edmund R. "The structural implications of matrilateral cross-cousin marriage." *Journal of the Royal Anthropological Institute,* vol. LXXXI. Reprinted in *Rethinking Anthropology.* London: Athlone Press, 1961, chapter III.

210 Lefort, Claude. "L'échange et la lutte des hommes." *Les Temps Modernes,* 6e année, février 1951, pp. 1400-1417.

211 Lefort, Claude. "Sociétés sans histoire et historicité." *Cahiers Internationaux de Sociologie,* vol. VII, 1952, pp. 91-114.

212 Littlejohn, James. "The rules of the game." *New Statesman,* vol. LXXVII, no. 1985, March 28, 1969, p. 452.

213 Lounsbury, Floyd G. Review of Rodney Needham, *Structure and Sentiment. American Anthropologist,* vol. LXIV, 1962, pp. 1302-1310.

214 Maybury-Lewis, David. "The analysis of dual organizations: A methodological critique." *Bijdragen tot de Tall-, Land-, en Volkenkunde,* vol. CXVI, no. 1, 1960, pp. 17-44.

215 Métais, C. "*Les Structures élémentaires de la parenté.*" *Revue de l'Histoire des Religions,* tome CXLII, 1952, pp. 112-118.

216 Moore, F. C. T. "*The Elementary structures of kinship.*" *Man,* vol.IV, no. 4, 1969, pp. 660-662.

217 Muller, Jean-Claude. "On preferential/prescriptive marriage and the function of kinship systems: The Rukuba case (Benue Plateau State, Nigeria)." *American Anthropologist,* vol. LXXV, no. 5, October 1973, pp. 1563-1576.

Needham, Rodney. see *Structure and Sentiment*--19

218 Needham, Rodney. "Terminology and alliance." *Sociologus,* vols. XVI-XVII, 1967, pp. 39-54.

218a Peristiany, J. "Social anatomy." *Times Literary Supplement*, February 22, 1957.

219 Pouillon, Jean. *Fétiches sans fétichisme.* Coll. 'Bibliothèque d'anthropologie'. Paris: François Maspéro, 1975, 356p.

Pouillon, Jean, & Pierre Maranda. see 35

220 Rossi, Ino. "Structure and history in *'The Elementary structures of kinship',*" in 23.

221 Salisbury, A. A. "Asymetrical marriage systems." *American Anthropologist*, vol. LVIII, 1956, pp. 639-655.

222 Schechner, R. "Incest and culture: A reflection on Claude Lévi-Strauss." *The Psychoanalytic Review*, vol. LVIII, 1971-1972, pp. 563-572.

223 Sartre, Jean-Paul. *Critique de la raison dialectique.* Paris: Gallimard, 1960, pp. 487-505.

224 Scheffler, H. W. "*Elementary Structures of kinship,* by C. Lévi-Strauss." *American Anthropologist*, vol. LXXII, April 1970, pp. 251-268.

225 Scholte, Bob. "Epistemic paradigms: Some Problems in cross-cultural research on social anthropological history and theory." *American Anthropologist*, vol. LXVIII, 1966, pp. 1192-1201. Reprinted in Hayes & Hayes, eds. *Claude Lévi-Strauss: The anthropologist as hero.* Cambridge, Mass.--London: The M.I.T. Press, 1970, pp. 108-122.

226 Schuwer, C. "*Les Structures élémentaires de la parenté.* C. Lévi-Strauss." *Revue Philosophique de la France et de l'Etranger,* tome LXXVII, 1952, pp. 581-585.

227 Slamet-Velsink, Ina E. "Les organizations dualistes existent-elles? Het historisch Perspektief." *Bijdragen tot de Taal-, Land-, en Volkenkunde*, vol. CXIV, 1958, pp. 292-305.

228 Sousberghe, Louis de. *Structures de parenté et d'alliance d'après des formules Pende.* Académie Royale des Sciences Coloniales, Classe des Sciences morales et politiques. Mémoires, IV. Bruxelles, 1956.

229 Vernant, Jean-Pierre. "Oedipe sans complexe." *Raison Présente*, no. 4, août-septembre-octobre, 1967.

40   INDIVIDUAL WORKS

230   Wagner, Roy. "Claude Lévi-Strauss, *The Elementary Structures of kinship.*" *Journal of the Polynesian Society*, vol. LXXIX, 1970, pp. 245-253.

231   Wallace, A. F. C., & S. Atkins. "The meaning of kinship terms." *American Anthropologist*, vol. LXII, 1960, pp. 58-80.

232   Warner, Lloyd W. et al. "Mungin social organization," in Paul Bahannon and John Middleton, eds., *Kinship and social organization*. Garden City, N.Y.: The Natural History Press, 1968, pp. 301-357. (see specially pp. 351-356)

233   White, H. *An Anatomy of kinship. Mathematical models for structures of cumulated roles.* Englewood Cliffs, N.J.: Prentice-Hall, 1963.

RACE ET HISTOIRE (1952; reedited 1967)

234   Abbagnano, Nicolà. "Razza, cultura e storia." *La Stampa*, June 24, 1967. Reprinted in *Per o contro l'uomo*. Milano: Rizzoli, 1968, pp. 257-260.

235   Caruso, Paolo. "Introduzione," a C. Lévi-Strauss, *Razza e storia e altri studi di antropologia*. Torino: Einaudi, 1967, pp. 7-43.

236   Rodinson, M. "Racisme et civilisation." *La Nouvelle Critique*, vol. VII, juin 1955, no. 66, pp. 120-140.

TRISTES TROPIQUES (1955)

237   Abel, Lionel. "Jacques Derrida: His 'difference' with melodrama." *Salmagundi*, no. 25, Winter 1974, pp. 3-21. (see specially pp. 6-9)

238   Anonymous. "*Tristes Tropiques* by Claude Lévi-Strauss." *Times Literary Supplement*, February 22, 1974, p. 188.

INDIVIDUAL WORKS   41

239   Anonymous. "Versions and animadversions of Lévi-Strauss."
      Times Literary Supplement, no. 3755, February 22, 1974,
      p. 188.

240   Aron, Raymond. "L'ethnologue entre les primifs et la
      civilisation." *Le Figaro Littéraire*, 24 décembre 1955.

241   Balandier, Georges. "Grandeur et servitude de l'ethnologue."
      Cahiers du Sud, 43e année, no. 337, 1956, pp. 337-347.

242   Bastide, François R. "Les aventures d'un nouveau Chateau-
      briand." *Demain*, 29 décembre 1955.

243   Bastide, Roger. "Lévi-Strauss ou l'ethnographe à la
      recherche du temps perdu." *Présence Africaine*, no. 7,
      avril-mai 1956, pp. 150-155.

244   Bataille, Georges. "Un livre humain, un grand livre."
      Critique, vol. X, no. 105, 1956, pp. 99-112.

245   Beck, B. "Claude Lévi-Strauss." *La Revue de Paris*,
      avril 1956.

246   Bryson, Norman. "Lévi-Strauss and the machine for the
      suppression of time." *Granta*, vol. LXXV, no. 3, February
      1970, pp. 18-19.

247   Caltofen, Segura R. "Estudio indigena." *Hispanoamericano*,
      vol. LVII, no. 1428, August 31, 1970, pp. 49-50. [Review
      of *Tropicos tristes*]

248   Colette, Jacques. "Le philosophe et la pensée sauvage."
      La Revue Nouvelle, 19e année, tome XXXVII, no. 5,
      15 mai 1963, pp. 520-522.

249   Deas, Malcolm. "Modern Eden." *The Listener*, vol. XC,
      no. 2334, December 20, 1973, pp. 857-858.

250   Donato, Eugenio. "*Tristes Tropiques:* The endless journey."
      Modern Language Notes, vol. LXXXI, no. 3, May 1966,
      pp. 270-287.

251   Duvignaud, Jean. "Le vicaire des tropiques." *Les Lettres
      Nouvelles*, juillet-août, 1958.

252   Etiemble, René. "Des Tarahumaras aux Nambikwaras, ou du
      peyotl à la tendresse humaine." *Evidences*, mars-avril
      1956.

42   INDIVIDUAL WORKS

253   Fouchet, Max-Pol. "L'expérience du regret," *Preuves*,
      octobre 1956. Reprinted in *Les Appels*. Paris: Mercure
      de France, 1967, pp. 157-172.

254   Heusch, Luc de. "Les vacances de la science." *Zaire*,
      no. 7, juillet 1956.

255   Jelenski, K. A. *"Tristes tropiques."* *Kultura*, nr. 2/100,
      January-February 1956, pp. 137-141.

256   Lacroix, Jean. "Tristes tropiques." *Le Monde*, 13-14
      octobre 1957.

257   Leiris, Michel. "A travers *Tristes tropiques*. *Les Cahiers
      de la République*, no. 2, juillet 1956. Reprinted in
      Brisées. Paris: Mercure de France, 1966, pp. 199-209.
      Also in *Cinq Études d'ethnologie*. Paris: Denoël/Gonthier,
      1969, pp. 113-127.

258   Lipsius, Frank. *"Tristes tropiques* by Claude Lévi-Strauss."
      Commentary, vol. LVIII, no. 3, September 1974, pp. 88-91.

259   McNelly, Cleo. "Natives, women and Claude Lévi-Strauss:
      A reading of *Tristes Tropiques*." *The Massachusetts
      Review*, Winter 1975, pp. 7-29.

      Melhman, Jeffrey. see 79 and 152

260   Oppitz, Michael. "Wissenschaftliche Phantasie." *Die Zeit*,
      no. 25, 19 Juni 1970, pp. 18-19.

261   Picon, Gaëtan. *"Tristes tropiques* ou la conscience
      malheureuse," in *L'Usage de la lecture*, vol. II. Paris:
      Gallimard, 1961, pp. 155-162.

262   Vercier, Bruno. "Les livres qui ont marqué notre époque."
      Réalités, no. 307, août 1971, pp. 11-17.

263   Willems, E. *"Tristes tropiques."* *American Anthropologist*,
      vol. LVIII, 1956, pp. 928-929.

                    ANTHROPOLOGIE STRUCTURALE (1958)

264   Arregui, C. *"Antropologia structurale."* *Cuadernos
      Urugyayos de Filosofía*, vol. V, 1968, pp. 167-169.

265 Bharati, A. "Lévi-Strauss, *Strukturale Anthropologie*."
    Zeitschrift für Philosophische Forschung, vol. XXIII,
    October-December 1969, pp. 659-661.

266 Bharati, A. "*Strukturale Anthropologie*." *Deutsche
    Zeitschrift für Philosophie*, vol. XXIII, 1969, pp. 559-
    561.

267 Bouteiller, M. "*Anthropologie structurale*." *L'Anthro-
    pologie*, nos. 3-4, 1958.

268 Cardoletti, P. "*Antropologia strutturale*." *La Scuola
    Cattolica*, tomo 95, 1967, supp. bibliografico, pp. 76-78.

269 Caronna, G. "Sull' *antropologia strutturale* di Lévi-
    Strauss." *Uomo e Cultura*, no. 1, 1969.

270 Cereda, Giuseppe. "Claude Lévi-Strauss: verso un nuevo
    umanesimo." *Vita e Pensiero*, anno 50, no. 5, May 1967.

271 Douglas, Mary. "Language of a new structure." *The Sunday
    Times*, no. 7554, March 10, 1968, p. 52.

272 Furer-Haimendorf, C. von. "Magic logic." *The Spectator*,
    vol. CCXX, no. 7290, March 15, 1968, pp. 331-332.

273 Laing, R. D. "Structure the model." *New Society*, vol.
    III, no. 88, June 4, 1964, p. 24.

274 Lancelotti, Mario A. "Claude Lévi-Strauss: *Antropologia
    estructural*." *Sur*, no. 318, May-June 1969, pp. 99-105.

275 Pepper, G. "Lévi-Strauss, *Structural Anthropology*."
    Cross Currents, vol. XV, 1965, pp. 104-107.

276 Sansom, Basil. "The psychic skeleton." *The Guardian*,
    no. 37, 834, March 1, 1968, p. 7.

277 Schmidbauer, Wolfgang. "Die Zukunft der 'Primitiven',"
    Die Zeit, no. 43, March 29, 1968.

278 Sontag, Susan. "A hero of our time." *The New York Review
    of Books*, vol. I, no. 7, 1963, pp. 6-8.

44 INDIVIDUAL WORKS

279 Sontag, Susan. "The anthropologist as hero," in *Against Interpretation and other essays*. New York: Farrar, Straus & Giroux, 1966, pp. 69-81. Reprinted in Hayes & Hayes, eds., *Claude Lévi-Strauss: The anthropologist as hero*. Cambridge, Mass.--London: The M.I.T. Press, 1970, pp. 184-196.

LEÇON INAUGURALE (1960, THE SCOPE OF ANTHROPOLOGY)

280 Sini, G. "Lévi-Strauss, *Elogio dell'antropologia*, *Aut aut*, no. 88, 1965. Also in *Revue Internationale de Philosophie*, no. 73-74, 1965, pp. 321-323.

ENTRETIENS AVEC CLAUDE LEVI-STRAUSS (G. Charbonnier, 1961)

Annette Loren. see 5

Edmund Leach. see 6

M. Freedman. see 29

LA GESTE D'ASDIWAL (1959)

281 Adams, John W. "Dialectics and contingency in 'The Story of Asdiwal': An ethnographic note," in Ino Rossi, ed., *The Unconscious in culture: The structuralism of Claude Lévi-Strauss in perspective*. New York: E. P. Dutton and Co. Inc., 1974.

282 Douglas, Mary. "The meaning of myth, with special reference to 'La Geste d'Asdiwal," in Edmund R. Leach, ed., *The Structural study of myth and totemism*. London: Tavictock Publications, 1967, pp. 49-70.

LE TOTEMISME AUJOURD'HUI (1962)

283   Anonymous. "Confronting the classics." *The Times Literary Supplement*, August 14, 1970. Reprinted in *T.L.S. 9. Essays and Reviews from the Times Literary Supplement, 1970*. London, New York, Toronto: Oxford University Press, pp. 113-120.

284   Barthes, Roland. "Sociologie et socio-logique: A propos de deux ouvrages récents de Claude Lévi-Strauss." *Information sur les Sciences Sociales/Social Science Information*, vol. II, no. 4, 1962, pp. 114-122.

285   Baudry, Jean-Louis. "Pensée sauvage et pensée commune." *Tel Quel*, no. 11, Autumn 1962, pp. 67-69.

286   Bidney, David. "*Le Totémisme aujourd-hui*. A review." *Journal of American Folklore*, vol. LXXII, April 1964, pp. 184-185.

287   Burgess, Anthony. "If Oedipus had read his Lévi-Strauss." *Washington Post Book World*, no. 12, November 26, 1967, p. 6. Reprinted in *Urgent Copy. Literary Studies*. London: Jonathan Cape, 1968, pp. 258-261.

288   Burgess, Anthony. "Short sharp stimulants." *The Sunday Times*, no. 7532, October 8, 1967, p. 32.

289   Burridge, K. O. L. "Lévi-Strauss and myth," in Edmund Leach, ed., *The Structural study of myth and totemism*. London: Tavistock Publications, 1967, pp. 91-115.

290   Calogeras, R. C. "Lévi-Strauss and Freud: Their structural approach to myth." *American Imago*, vol. XXX, no. 1, Spring 1973, pp. 57-73.

291   Cordero, Rodrigo. "Mito y totemismo en Sigmund Freud y Claude Lévi-Strauss." *Revista de Filosofía de la Universidad de Costa Rica*, vol. XI, no. 32, January-June 1973, pp. 117-163.

292   Fortes, Meyer. "Totemism and taboo." *Proceedings of the Royal Anthropological Institute*, 1967, pp. 7-18.

293   Fox, Robin. *Kinship and Marriage*. London, 1967.

46   INDIVIDUAL WORKS

294 Fox, Robin. "Animal codes for society." *New Society*, vol. IV, no. 105, October 1, 1964, pp. 28-30.

295 Fox, Robin. "*Totem and Taboo* reconsidered," in Edmund R. Leach, ed., *The Structural Study of Myth and Totemism*. London: Tavistock Publications, 1967, pp. 161-177.

296 Makarius, Raoul, & Laura Makarius. "On Soviet views on totemism." *Current Anthropology*, vol. VIII, no. 3, June 1967, pp. 258-260.

297 Poole, Roger C. "Introduction," to Lévi-Strauss, *Totemism*. Translation by Rodney Needham. Harmondsworth, Middlesex: Penguin Books, 1969, pp. 9-63.

298 Stuck, Heiner. "Claude Lévi-Strauss, *Das Ende des Totemismus*." *Das Heft*, no. 8-9, 1967.

299 Worsley, Peter. "Groote Eylandt totemism and *'Le Totémisme aujourd'hui'*," in Edmund R. Leach, ed., *The Structural Study of Myth and Totemism*. London: Tavistock Publications, 1967, pp. 141-160. Reprinted in D. M. Emmet and A. C. MacIntyre, eds., *Sociological Theory and Philosophical Analysis*. New York: Macmillan, 1970, pp. 204-222.

LA PENSEE SAUVAGE (1962)

300 Anderson, Robert. "*The Savage Mind*. By Claude Lévi-Strauss." *The Western Humanities Review*, vol. XXII, no. 2, Spring 1968, pp. 179-180.

301 Barthes, Roland. "Sociologie et socio-logique: A propos de deux ouvrages récents de Claude Lévi-Strauss." *Information sur les Sciences Sociales/Social Science Information*, vol. I, no. 4, pp. 114-122.

302 Bastide, Roger. "La pensée obscure et confuse." *Le Monde non-chrétien*, no. 75-76, 1965.

303 Baudry, Jean-Louis. "Pensée sauvage et pensée commune." *Tel Quel*, no. 11, Autumn 1962, pp. 67-69.

304 Bidney, David. "*La Pensée sauvage*. A review." *Journal of American Folklore*, vol. LXXII, April 1964, pp. 182-183.

INDIVIDUAL WORKS   47

305   Broderick, Alan Houghton. "Law of opposites." *The Sunday Times*, no. 7482, October 16, 1966, p. 53.

306   Boon, James A. "Poetic straw man: Self-aware syntheses of *Pensée sauvage*," pp. 108-138 in James A. Boon, *From Symbolism to Structuralism. Lévi-Strauss in a Literary tradition*. Oxford: Basil Blackwell,--New York: Harper & Row, 1972.

307   Carpenter, Edmund. "Man the pattern maker." *The New York Times Book Review*, December 18, 1966, p. 12.

308   Caruso, Paolo. "Ragione analitica e ragione dialettica nella nuova antropologia." *Aut Aut*, no. 82, 1965, pp. 93-103; and *Ibid.*, no. 84, 1965, pp. 52-60.

309   Chopra, S. "Structuren primitiven Denkens." *Alternative*, no. 54, 1967, pp. 100-106.

310   Colette, Jacques. "Le philosophe et la *'Pensée sauvage'*." *La Revue Nouvelle*, 19e année, tome 37, no. 5, 15 mai 1963, pp. 520-525.

311   Colette, Jacques. "Le moraliste et la pensée sauvage." *La Revue Nouvelle*, 26e année, tome LII, November 1970, pp. 422-429.

312   Conn, W. E. "Primitive consciousness-mythic, symbolic and pre-logical: A cognitional analysis." *Proceedings of the Catholic Philosophical Association*, vol. XLV, 1971, pp. 146-157.

313   Cuisenier, Jean, et al. "La Pensée sauvage et le structuralisme." *Esprit*, vol. XXXI, no. 11, Novembre 1963, pp. 545-563 [Special number devoted to structuralism]

314   *Esprit*, "La Pensée sauvage et le structuralisme." [Numéro spécial, exposés de J. Cuisenier, N. Ruwet, M. Gaboriau, P. Ricoeur, suivis de 'Discussion avec Lévi-Strauss."], vol. XXXI, no. 322, novembre 1963, pp. 543-653.

315   Florenne, Yves. *"La Pensée sauvage."* *Le Monde*, 6-7 mai, 1962 [Revue des revues].

316   Fortini, F. *"Il Pensiero selvaggio."* *Questo e Altro*, no. 2, 1962, pp. 94-96.

INDIVIDUAL WORKS

317 Gasché, Rodolphe. "Das wilde Denken und die Ökonomie der Repräsentation. Zum Verhältnis von Ferdinand de Saussure und Claude Lévi-Strauss," in no. 55.

318 Gaboriau, Marc. "Anthropologie structurale et histoire." pp. 579-595 in 314.

319 Gallagher, Patrick. "The world of Lévi-Strauss." *The New Republic*, vol. CLVI, no. 1, January 7, 1967, pp. 38-40.

320 García, Tobas. *"El pensamiento salvaje."* Estafeta Literaria, no. 467, May 1, 1971, pp. 555-556.

321 Gorer, Geoffrey. "Time and the primitive mind." *The Observer*, no. 9144, October 9, 1966, p. 27.

322 Lacroix, Jean. *"La Pensée sauvage."* Le Monde, 27 novembre, 1962.

323 Leach, Edmund R. "Telstar et les aborigènes ou La pensée sauvage." *Annales* (Economies-Sociétés-Civilisations), 19e année, no. 6, novembre-décembre, 1964, pp. 1100-1116. English translation in D. M. Emmet and A. C. MacIntyre, eds., *Sociological Theory and Philosophical Analysis*. New York: Macmillan, 1970, pp. 183-203.

324 Leach, Edmund R. "Claude Lévi-Strauss-Anthropologist and philosopher." *New Left Review*, no. 34, November-December 1965, pp. 12-27. Reprinted in R. A. Manners and D. Kaplan, eds., *Theory in Anthropology*. Chicago: Aldine, 1972.
French translation, "Claude Lévi-Strauss, anthropologue et philosophe [présentation de P. Vidal-Naquet]," *Raison Présente*, no. 3, mai-juin-juillet 1967, pp. 91-106. German translation in *Orte des Wilden Denkens. Zur Anthropologie von Claude Lévi-Strauss*. Herausgegeben von Wolf Lepenies und Hanns Henning Ritter. Frankfurt am Main: Suhrkamp Verlag, 1970, pp. 49-76.
Spanish translation, *Lévi-Strauss, antropólogo y filósofo* [seguido de Claude Lévi-Strauss: El oso y el barbero]. Trad. del ingles por José R. Llobera (Col. Cuadernos anagrama, 2). Barcelona: Ed. Anagrama, 1970, 73p.

INDIVIDUAL WORKS 49

325 Leach, Edmund R. "Brain-twister." *The New York Review of Books*, vol. IX, no. 6, October 12, 1967, pp. 6, 8, 10. Reprinted in A. N. Hayes and T. Hayes, eds., *Claude Lévi-Strauss: The anthropologist as hero*. Cambridge, Mass.-London: The M.I.T. Press, 1970, pp. 123-132.

326 Matarasso, Michel. "Lecture de Claude Lévi-Strauss: Pensée sauvage et logique première." *Revue Française de Sociologie*, vol. IV, no. 2, avril-juin 1963, pp. 195-205.

327 Morazé, C. "Pensée sauvage et logique géométrique," in Jean Pouillon et Pierre Maranda, eds., *Echanges et communications. I and II*. Mélanges offerts à Claude Lévi-Strauss à l'occasion de son 60e anniversaire. The Hague-Paris: Mouton, 1970.

327a Needham, Rodney. "C. Lévi-Strauss, *The Savage Mind*." *Man*, vol. II, no. 2, 1967.

328 Nettl, Peter. "Lévi-Strauss." *New Statesman*, vol. LXXII, no. 1865, December 9, 1966, pp. 880-881.

329 Philip, Jim, and Riley, Peter. "On Lévi-Strauss '*The Savage Mind*'," *The English Intelligencer*, November 1967, pp. 520-525.

330 Piguet, Jean-Claude. "Les conflits de l'analyse et de la dialectique." *Annales (Economies-Sociétés-Civilisations)*, 20e année, no. 3, mai-juin 1965, pp. 547-557.

331 Pividal, Raphael. "Peut-on acclimater *La Pensée sauvage? Annales (Economies-Sociétés-Civilisations)*, 20e année, no. 3, mai-juin 1965, pp. 558-563.

332 Revel, Jean-François. "*La Pensée sauvage.*" *France-Observateur*, 27 novembre 1962.

333 Revel, Jean-François. "Appendice I. *La Pensée sauvage*, in *Pourquoi des philosophes? 2. La cabale des dévôts*. Edition augmentée. Paris: Jean-Jacques Pauvert, 1965, pp. 266-271.

334 Revel, Jean-François. "*La Pensée sauvage*," in *Contrecensures*. Paris: Jean-Jacques Pauvert, 1966, pp. 206-210.

INDIVIDUAL WORKS

335 Singerman, Ora. "Lévi-Strauss and savage thinking [In Hebrew]," *Iyyun*, vol. XXI, July-October 1970, pp. 183-218.

336 Stack, George. *"The Savage Mind."* The *Thomist*, vol. XXXIII, 1969, pp. 194-197.

337 Turnbull, Colin M. "The nature of reality." *Natural History*, vol. LXXVI, no. 5, May 1967, pp. 58, 60, 62-63. Reprinted in A. N. Hayes and T. Hayes, eds., *Claude Lévi-Strauss: The anthropologist as hero*. Cambridge, Mass.-London: 1970, p. 140-144.

338 Vita, Luis Washington. "El Pensamiento salvaje." *Revista Brasileira de Filosofia*, vol. XV, 1965, pp. 121-123.

339 Warnock, Mary. "Anthropological omnivore." *New Society*, vol. VIII, no. 211, October 13, 1966, pp. 585-586.

340 Worsley, Peter. "Only connections." *The Guardian*, no. 37, 407, October 14, 1966, p. 7.

341 Wunderlich, D. *"Das wilde Denken."* *Philosophische Literaturanzeiger*, vol. XXII, 1969, pp. 1129-1136.

342 Yalman, Nur. *"La Pensée sauvage.* By C. Lévi-Strauss." *American Anthropologist*, vol. LXVI, October 1964, pp. 1179-1182.

343 Zimmerman, Robert L. "Lévi-Strauss and the primitive." *Commentary*, vol. XLV, no. 6, May 1968, pp. 54-61. Reprinted in A. N. Hayes and T. Hayes, eds., *Claude Lévi-Strauss: The anthropologist as hero*. Cambridge, Mass.-London: 1970, pp. 215-234.

LES CHATS (de Charles Baudelaire, in Collaboration with R. Jakobson (1962)

344 Bellour, Raymond. "L'ethnologue, le linguiste et les chats." *Le Magazine Littéraire*, no. 58, novembre 1971, pp. 17-18.

345 Durand, Gilbert. "Les chats, les rats et les structuralistes. Symbole et structuralisme figuratif. Etude critique de la lecture structuraliste du poème de Baudelaire *'Les Chats'* par Roman Jakobson et Claude Lévi-Strauss." *Cahiers Internationaux du Symbolisme*, nos. 17-18, 1969, pp. 13-23.

346 Frandon, I.-M. "Le structuralisme et les caractères de l'oeuvre littéraire: A propos des 'Chats' de Baudelaire." *Revue d'Histoire Littéraire de la France*, 72e année, no. 1, janvier-février 1972, pp. 101-116.

347 Gadoffre, Gilles. "Sur le Colloque Baudelaire de Nice." *Le Monde*, 20 octobre 1970.

348 Mounin, Georges. "Baudelaire devant une critique structuraliste," in *Baudelaire. Actes du Colloque de Nice* (mai 1967) publiés in *Annales de la faculté des lettres et sciences humaines de Nice*, no. 4-5, 1968, pp. 155-160.

349 Riffaterre, Michel. "Describing poetic structures: Two approaches to Baudelaire 'Les Chats'," *Yale French Studies*, no. 36-37, October 1966, pp. 200-242. Reprinted in *Structuralism*. Edited with an Introduction by Jacques Ehrmann. Garden City, N.Y.: Doubleday Anchor original, 1970, pp. 188-229.

350 Scholes, Robert. "Poetic theory: Jakobson and Lévi-Strauss versus Riffaterre's superreader," in *Structuralism in Literature. An Introduction*. New Haven-London: Yale University Press, 1974, pp. 22-40.

MYTHOLOGIQUES
    I: LE CRU ET LE CUIT (1964)
   II: DU MIEL AUX CENDRES (1966)
  III: L'ORIGINE DES MANIERES DE TABLE (1968)
  IV: L'HOMME NU (1971)

351 Abbagnano, Nicolà. "L'uomo e il mito." *La Stampa*, October 14, 1967. Reprinted in *Per o contro l'uomo*. Milano: Rizzoli, 1968, pp. 260-264.

352 Amoros, Celia. *"De la miel a las cenizas."* *Teorema*, vol. III, 1973, pp. 162-165.

INDIVIDUAL WORKS

353 Anderson, E. N. Jr. "Sacred fish." *Man*, vol. IV, 1969, pp. 443-449.

354 Anonymous. Anonymous. "Au jour le jour: Lettres, arts, spectacles." *Le Nouvel Observateur*, no. 26, 13 mai 1965, pp. 26-27.

355 Anonymous. "La semaine." *Arts*, no. 1010, 16-22, juin 1965, p. 4.

356 Anonymous. "Sounding the Sixties --3: Outside English." *The Times Literary Supplement*, no. 3318, September 30, 1965, pp. 839-841.

357 Anonymous. "Structure and society." *The Times Literary Supplement*, no. 3318, September 30, 1965, pp. 863-865.

358 Anonymous. "Comme une églogue." *Le Nouvel Observatuer*, no. 112, 4-10 janvier, 1967, p. 32.

359 Anonymous. "Lévi-Strauss' mind." *Newsweek*, vol. LXIX, January 23, 1967, p. 90.

360 Anonymous. "Matrix and myth." *The Times Literary Supplement*, no. 3407, June 15, 1967, pp. 521-522. [M. II]

361 Anonymous. "Deep waters." *The Times Literary Supplement*, no. 3424, October 12, 1967, p. 960.

362 Anonymous. "Claude Lévi-Strauss and Roland Barthes," in *T.L.S. 6. Essays and Reviews from the Times Literary Supplement, 1967*. London, New York, Toronto: Oxford University Press, 1968, pp. 35-40.

363 Anonymous. "Claude Lévi-Strauss." *The Times Literary Supplement*, May 2, 1968.

364 Anonymous. "Man's new dialogue with man: Time Essay." *Time*, vol. LXXXIX, June 30, 1967, pp. 34-35.

365 Anonymous. "Anthropology's pope." *The Times Literary Supplement*, no. 3453, May 2, 1968, pp. 445-447.

366 Anonymous. "High priest on the couch." *The Times Literary Supplement*, no. 3472, September 12, 1968, p. 970.

367 Anonymous. "Claude Lévi-Strauss." *The Times Literary Supplement*, January 29, 1970.

368 Anonymous. "Myth and meaning: Claude Lévi-Strauss."
     Sunday Times, November 15, 1970, p. 27.

369 Anonymous. "Entretien: Lévi-Strauss et les *Mythologiques*:
     'Réconcilier le sensible et l'intelligible'," *Le Monde*
     [*des Livres*], no. 8339, 5 novembre 1971, pp. 17, 20.
     [M. IV]

370 Anonymous. "The myth of mythology." *The Times Literary
     Supplement*, no. 3658, April 7, 1972, pp. 381-383
     [M. IV]

371 Azancot, Leopoldo. "Lévi-Strauss: *Mitológicas*." *Indice*,
     núm. 263-264, february, 1970, pp. 53-54.

372 Backès-Clément, Catherine. "Réflexions sur Claude Lévi-
     Strauss." *La Nouvelle Critique*, no. 24, mai 1969.

373 Backès-Clément, Catherine. "Un visionnaire." *La Quin-
     zaine Littéraire*, no. 55, 1-15 août, 1968, p. 20.

374 Backès-Clément, Catherine. "Du miel aux cendres: l'envers
     et l'endroit." *L'Arc*, no. 26, 1965, pp. 30-37. [Numéro
     spécial sur Lévi-Strauss]

375 Backès-Clément, Catherine. "Lévi-Strauss ou la philosophie
     du non-savoir." *La Quinzaine Littéraire*, no. 95, 16-31
     mai 1970, pp. 12-13.

376 Backès-Clément, Catherine. "Une encyclopédie anthropolo-
     gique." *Le Monde* [*des Livres*], no. 8339, 5 novembre 1971,
     p. 20.

377 Backès-Clément, Catherine. "Etude: Lévi-Strauss et les
     Mythologiques--Le cru et le nu. *Le Monde* [*des Livres*],
     no. 8339, 5 novembre 1971, p. 20.

378 Bamberger, Joan. "A continuing revolution in the study
     of myth." *New York Times Book Review*, June 3, 1973,
     pp. 23-27. [*From Honey to Ashes*]

379 Barden, G. "*L'Homme nu*." *Human Context-Le Domaine Humain*,
     vol. V, Spring 1973, pp. 229-231.

380 Bellour, Raymond. "Entretien avec Claude Lévi-Strauss."
     Les Lettres Françaises, no. 1165, 12 janvier 1967.
     Reprinted in *Le Livre des autres*. Paris: Edition de
     l'Herne, 1971, pp. 145-161.

54 INDIVIDUAL WORKS

381 Bellour, Raymond. "*Mythologiques III.*" *Les Lettres Françaises*, no. 1252, September 15, 1968, pp. 4-5. Reprinted in *Le Livre des autres*, pp. 115-120.

382 Benoist, Jean-Marie. "*L'Homme nu.*" *Human Context-Le Domaine Humain*, vol. V, Spring 1973, pp. 194-208.

383 Bidney, David. "*Le Cru et le cuit.* A review." *Journal of American Folklore*, vol. LXXIX, October 1966, pp. 612-613.

384 Boon, James A. "Lévi-Strauss and 'narrative'," *Man*, vol. V, no. 4, 1970, pp. 702-703.

385 Bourdillon, Michael. "Lévi-Strauss and myth." *The Month*, CCXXV, no. 1207, March 1968, pp. 149-163.

386 Brosse, Jacques. "Comment lire Lévi-Strauss." *Arts-Lettres-Spectacles*, no. 977, octobre 1964.

387 Brosse, Jacques. "Avec Claude Lévi-Strauss le lecteur mène l'enquête." *Arts-Loisirs*, no. 77, 15-21 mars, 1967, pp. 20-22. [M. II]

388 Brosse, Jacques. "Les clés de Lévi-Strauss." *Les Nouvelles Littéraires*, 46e année, no. 2135, 22 août 1968, pp. 1, 10.

Buchler, Ira R. and H. A. Selby. see 983

389 Burgess, Anthony. "Culture as a hot meal." *The Spectator*, vol. CCXXV, no. 7410-7411, July 4-11, 1970, pp. 13-41. [*The Raw and the Cooked*]

390 Calogeras, R. C. "Lévi-Strauss and Freud: Their structural approach to myth." *American Imago*, vol. XXX, no. 1, Spring 1973, pp. 57-59.

391 Caruso, Paolo. "*Il crudo e il cotto.*" *Aut Aut*, no. 88, July 1965, pp. 62-69.

392 Caruso, Paolo. "*Il crudo e il cotto.*" *Rinascità*, no. 46, November 19, 1966.

393 Caws, Peter. "Man's myths--Beings that think and act for him." *Chicago Tribune Book World*, vol. III, no. 45, November 9, 1969, p. 6. *The Raw and the Cooked*

394 Châtelet, François. "Le Miel et le tabac." *La Quinzaine Littéraire*, no. 21, 1-15 février 1967, pp. 3-4. [M. II]

395 Cixous, Hélène. "Une lecture imprudente." *Le Monde* [*des Livres*], no. 8339, 5 novembre 1971, p. 21.

396 Cohen, Percy S. "Theories of myth." *Man*, vol. IV, no. 3, 1969, pp. 337-353.

397 Colette, Jacques. "*Mythologiques I.*" *La Revue Nouvelle*, vol. 47, 1968, pp. 366-367.

398 Cornwell, John. "An expedition into the jungle of man." *Oxford Mail*, no. 13, 716, February 8, 1973, p. 7. [*From Honey to Ashes*]

Courtès, J. Recherches sémiotiques sur les "*Mythologiques*" de Lévi-Strauss, le vraisemblable de la démonstration. see 76

Courtès, J. *Lévi-Strauss et les contraintes de la pensée mythique. Une lecture sémiotique des 'Mythologiques'.* see 31.

399 Cousteix, P. "Claude Lévi-Strauss: *Mythologiques.*" *L'Ecole Libératrice*, no. 25, 12 mars 1965.

400 Cuisenier, Jean. "Lévi-Strauss ou le structuralisme accompli." *Le Magazine Littéraire*, no. 58, novembre 1971, pp. 8-12.

401 Culler, Jonathan. "*L'homme nu.*" *Human Context-Le Domaine Humain*, vol. V, Spring 1973, pp. 227-229.

402 Cruz, Juan Cruz. "Sentido antropologico del mito." *Anuario Filosófico*, vol. IV, 1971, pp. 33-86.

403 Daix, Pierre. "Entretien avec Lévi-Strauss sur les *Mythologiques. I. -La signification des mythes américains.*" *Les Lettres Françaises*, no. 1406, 13 octobre 1971, pp. 3-4.
German translation "Die Bedeutung der amerikanischen Mythen: Ein Gespräch mit Pierre Daix," in Adelbert Reif, hrsg., *Antworten der Strukturalisten*, Hoffman und Campe, 1973, pp. 89-104.

INDIVIDUAL WORKS

404 Daix, Pierre. "Entretien avec Lévi-Strauss sur Les *Mythologiques II*. -Structuralisme, humanisme, matérialisme." *Les Lettres Françaises*, no. 1407, 20-26 octobre 1971, pp. 6-7.

405 Davy, John. "Of myths and men." *The Observer*, no. 9330, May 10, 1970, p. 31. [*The Raw and the Cooked*]

406 Deliège, Célestin. "Sur quelques motifs de l'ouverture aux *Mythologiques*." *L'Arc*, no. 26, 1965, pp. 69-70, 73-76.

407 Dening, Gregory. "Claude Lévi-Strauss cooked." *Meanjin Quarterly*, vol. XXX, no. 3, September 1971, pp. 331-333.

408 Detienne, M., and J.-P. Vernant. "Eurydice, la femme-abeille." *Le Monde* [*des Livres*], no. 8339, 5 novembre 1971, p. 21.

409 Domenach, Jean-Marie. "Le requiem structuraliste." *Esprit*, no. 422, mars 1973, pp. 692-703. [*L'Homme nu*]

410 Donato, Eugenio. "Lévi-Strauss and the protocols of distance." *Diacritics*, vol. V, no. 3, Fall 1975, pp. 2-12.

411 Douglas, Mary. "Smothering the differences--Mary Douglas in a savage mind about Lévi-Strauss." *The Listener*, vol. 84, no. 2162, September 3, 1970, pp. 313-314. [*The Raw and the Cooked*]

412 *Esprit*. "Le mythe aujourd'hui." No. 4, 1971. [Articles by Barthes, Rabant, Boyer, Lévi-Strauss, Ramnoux, etc.]

413 Estava-Fabregat, Claudio. *"L'Homme nu." Human Context-Le Domaine Humain*, vol. V, Spring 1973, pp. 231-234.

414 Ferraro, Guido. "Simbolo e significato nelle *Mitologiche* di Lévi-Strauss." *Strumenti Critici*, no. 27, 1975, pp. 219-240.

Ferry, Jacqueline F. "L'envers et l'endroit." see 125

415 Freedman, R. L. "Wanted: A journal of culinary anthropology." *Current Anthropology*, vol. IX, 1968, pp. 62-63.

416 Gardner, Howard. *"L'Homme nu." Human Context-Le Domaine Humain*, vol. V, Spring 1973, pp. 222-227.

INDIVIDUAL WORKS 57

417 Gardner, Howard. "The structural analysis of protocols and myths. A comparison of the methods of Jean Piaget and Claude Lévi-Strauss." *Semantics*, vol. V, 1972, pp. 31-57.

418 Gaudet, Pierre. "Que donnait à lire. . ." *Poétique*, no. 13, 1973, pp. 95-110.

419 Gibson, Mickey. *"Mythologiques II."* *Dialogue*, vol. VII, 1968-1969, pp. 161-168.

420 Glusksmann, A. "La déduction de la cuisine et les cuisines de la déduction." *Information sur les Sciences Sociales*, vol. IV, no. 2, juin 1965.

421 Gordón, Sigfredo. "Mitos y creencias." *Hispano Americano*, vol. LIV, núm. 1390, 23 dic. 1968, pp. 57-58. [On *Mitológicas*, translated by Juan Almela]

422 Greimas, A.-J. "Elements pour une théorie de l'interprétation du récit mythique." *Communications*, 1966.

423 Guérin, G. *"Mythologiques I: Le cru et le cuit."* *Etudes*, tome CCCXXII, 1965, pp. 589-590.

424 Henriques, Fernando. "The 'noble savage' myth." *Tribune*, vol. XXX, no. 42, October 21, 1966, p. 10.

425 Hess, John. "The mythical Lévi-Strauss." *The New York Times Book Review*, February 20, 1972, p. 2, 28.

426 Heusch, Luc de. "Vers une mytho-logique?" *Critique*, 16e année, vol. XXI, nos. 219-220, août-septembre 1965, pp. 687-715. Reprinted in *Pourquoi l'épouser? et autre essais*. Paris: Gallimard, 1971, pp. 13-42.

427 Hodgson, Godfrey. "All the eggheads in one basket." *The Sunday Times Magazine*, April 16, 1967, pp. 41, 43-44, 46.

428 Hultkrantz, O. *"Mythologiques."* *American Anthropologist*, vol. LXXI, 1969, pp. 735-737.

429 Izard, Michel. "A l'écoute des mythes." *Le Nouvel Observateur*, no. 366, 15-21 novembre 1971, pp. 46-48.

430 Jesi, Furio. *Mito*. Milano: Isedi, 1973.

INDIVIDUAL WORKS

431 Josselin de Jong, P. E. de. "Voltooide symphonie: De *Mythologiques* van Lévi-Strauss." *Forum der Letteren*, jaarg. 14, no. 2, juni 1973, pp. 95-120.

432 King, A. R. "Claude Lévi-Strauss: *Les Mythologiques*. Review essay." *Ethnomusicology*, vol. XVIII, January 1974, pp. 101-111.

433 Kirk, G. S. "Lévi-Strauss and the structural approach," pp. 42-83 in *Myth: Its Meaning and functions in ancient and other cultures*. see

434 Kockelmans, Joseph J. "On myth and its relationship to hermeneutics." *Cultural Hermeneutics*, vol. I, April 1973, pp. 47-86.

435 Lacroix, Jean. *"Le cru et le cuit."* *Le Monde*, 2 janvier 1965.

436 Lacroix, Jean. "Le miel et le tabac." *Le Monde*, no. 6887, 4 mars 1967, p. 15.

436a Lacroix, Jean. "*Mythologiques III*, de Claude Lévi-Straus Strauss." *Le Monde [des Livres]*, no. 7320, 27 juillet 1968, p. 1.
English translation, "Lévi-Strauss and the 'primitives' --On with his *Mythologiques*." *Atlas*, vol. XVII, no. 1, January 1969, pp. 64-66. [*Mythologiques* III]

437 Lapouge, Gilles. "Claude Lévi-Strauss collectionne infatigablement les mythes." *Le Figaro Littéraire*, 2 février 1967.

438 Lavers, Annette. "Myth sacred." *New Society*, vol. XV, no. 398, May 14, 1970, pp. 832-833. [*The Raw and the Cooked*]

439 Leach, Edmund R. *"Mythologiques I: Le cru et le cuit."* *American Anthropologist*, vol. LXVII, no. 3, 1965, pp. 776-780 [Corrections, in *Ibid.*, decembre 1965, p. 1562-1563]

440 Leach, Edmund R. "New hat." *New Statesman*, vol. LXIX, no. 1771, February 19, 1965, pp. 286-287.

441 Leach, Edmund R. "Claude Lévi-Strauss." *The Nation*, vol. CCXI, December 28, 1970, pp. 692-694.

INDIVIDUAL WORKS 59

442　Leach, Edmund R.   "Progress through the looking glass."
　　　New Edinburgh Review, no. 13, June 1971, pp. 14-19.

443　Lienhardt, Godfrey.   "Debts to the savage."   *The Listener*,
　　　vol. LXXIX, no. 2043, May 23, 1968, pp. 671-672.

444　MacRae, Donald.   "Codes of conduct."   *New Statesman*,
　　　vol. LXXXV, no. 2188, February 23, 1973, pp. 271-272.
　　　[*From Honey to Ashes*]

445　Magaña Esquivel, Antonio.   "Los enigmas antropológicos."
　　　Hispano Americano, vol. LX, núm. 1564, 24 avril 1972,
　　　p. 72.   [*Mitológicas II. De la Miel a las Cenizas*,
　　　translated by Jaun Almela]

446　Malavassi, V. Guillermo.   "Bricolage sobre naturaleza y
　　　estructura."   *Revista de Filosofía de la Universidad de
　　　Costa Rica*, vol. XI, no. 32, January-June 1973, pp. 13-
　　　32.

447　Martinois, B. de.   "A propos de *Le Cru et le cuit*."   *Combat*,
　　　18 novembre 1964.

448　Mepham, John.   "L'homme connu."   *Adam. International Review*,
　　　vol. XXXVII, no. 364-366, 1972, pp. 98-102.   [*L'homme Nu*]

449　Maybury-Lewis, David.   "Science or bricolage?   *Du Miel
　　　aux cendres*."   *American Anthropologist*, vol. LXXI, no. 1,
　　　1969, pp. 114-121.   Reprinted in E. N. Hayes and T.
　　　Hayes, eds., *Claude Lévi-Strauss: The anthropologist as
　　　hero*.   Cambridge, Mass. --London: 1970, pp. 150-613.

450　Maybury-Lewis, David.   "Science by association."   *The
　　　Hudson Review*, vol. XX, no. 4, Winter 1967-1968, pp. 707-
　　　711.   Reprinted pp. 133-139 in Hayes and Hayes, above:
　　　Hayes and Hayes.   see 9

451　Mettra, Claude.   "Conversations avec l'univers."   *L'Express*,
　　　no. 887, 8-14 juillet 1968, p. 35.

452　Miceli, Silvana.   "Struttura e senso del mito."   *Quaderni
　　　del Circolo Semiologico Siciliano*,   no. 1, Palermo, 1973.

453　Morelle, Paul.   "Nous sommes tous des bricoleurs."
　　　Demócratie Nouvelle, no. 7-8, 1965.

454　Morelle, Paul.   "Paradoxes sur un Salon: L'écriture
　　　est-elle un bricolage?"   *Le Monde* [*des Livres*], no. 7098,
　　　8 novembre 1967, p. 8.

INDIVIDUAL WORKS

455 Panoff, Michel. "Lévi-Strauss tel qu'en lui-même."
     Esprit, no. 422, mars 1973, pp. 704-710. [*L'Homme nu*]

456 Pinto, Evelyne. "Du mythe au roman." *Revue d'Esthétique*,
     vol. XXIV, no. 3, juillet-septembre 1971, pp. 257-268.

457 Pochtar, Ricardo. "Claude Lévi-Strauss: *Mitológica I:
     Lo Crudo y lo cocido.*" *Sur*, no. 320, September-October
     1969, pp. 112-116.

458 Pouillon, Jean. "L'analyse des mythes." *L'Homme*, vol.
     VI, no. 1, 1966, pp. 100-105.

459 Pouwer, J. "L'analyse des mythes: a rejoinder."
     Bijdragen tot de Taal-, Land-, en Volkenkunde, vol.
     CXXII, 1966, pp. 151-157.

460 Pouillon, Jean. "Une leçon de maintien." *La Quinzaine
     Littéraire*, no. 55, 1-15 août, 1968, p. 21. [*L'Origine
     des manières de tables*]

461 Pouillon, Jean. "Entretien avec Lévi-Strauss. L'homme
     habillé par le mythe." *Les Nouvelles Littéraires*, 49e
     année, no. 2297, 1er octobre 1971, pp. 14-15.
     German translation, "Der Mensch bekleider durch den
     Mythos. Ein Gespräch mit Jean Pouillon," in Adelbert
     Reif, Hrsg., *Antworten der Strukturalisten*, Hamburg:
     Hoffman and Campe, 1973, pp. 105-110.

462 Régis, Louis-Marie, O. P. "Pour une mythologique."
     Dialogue, vol. VII, March 1969, pp. 616-626. [M. II]

463 Renaud-Vernet, O. "Lévi-Strauss et la pensée mythique."
     La Gazette de Lausanne, juin 1965.

464 Revel, Jean-François. "Appendice 2. *Le Cru et le cuit*,"
     in *Pourquoi des philosophes? 2. La cabale des dévôts*.
     Edition augmentee. Paris: Jean-Jacques Pauvert, 1965,
     pp. 272-278.

465 Revel, Jean-François. "*Le Cru et le cuit*," in *Contre-
     censures*. Paris: Jean-Jacques Pauvert, 1966, pp. 210-
     216.

466 Richard, Philippe. "Analyses des *mythologiques* de Claude
     Lévi-Strauss." *L'Homme et la Société*, no. 4, avril-
     juin 1967, pp. 109-133.

INDIVIDUAL WORKS   61

467   Richard, Philippe. "A propos de *'L'Origine des manières de table'* de Claude Lévi-Strauss." *L'Homme et la Société*, no. 11, 1969, pp. 179-191.

468   Roy, Claude. "Alice au pays de la logique." *Le Nouvel Observateur*, no. 123, 22-29 mars 1967, pp. 34-35.

469   Ruwet, Nicolas. "Qui a hérité?" *Le Monde [des Livres]*, no. 8339, 5 novembre 1971, p. 21.

      Sahlins, Marshall D. "On the Delphic writings of Claude Lévi-Strauss." see 161

470   Saint-Phalle, Thérèse de. "Claude Lévi-Strauss découvreur de mythes." *La Revue de Paris*, 75e année, no. 10, octobre 1968, pp. 85-90.

471   Salman, D. H. "Pensée mythique." *Revue des Sciences Philosophiques et Théologiques*, tome XLIX, no. 4, 1965.

      Scarduelli, Pietro. see 67

472   Scholte, Bob. "Lévi-Strauss's unfinished symphony: The analysis of myth." *Natural History*, vol. LXXIII, no. 2, February 1969, pp. 24-26, 100-101. Reprinted in E. N. Hayes and T. Nayes, eds., *Claude Lévi-Strauss: The anthropologist as hero*. Cambridge, Mass.-London: The M.I.T. Press, 1970, pp. 145-149.

473   Scholte, Bob. "Lévi-Strauss' Penelopian effort. The analysis of myth." *Semiotica*, vol. I, 1969, pp. 99-124. [M. I and II]

474   Schuwer, C. *"Mythologiques II: Du miel aux cendres."* *Revue Philosophique de la France et de l'Etranger*, vol. 98, 1973, pp. 78-80

474a Sebag, Lucien. "Symphonie en trois mouvements." *L'Express*, 21 décembre 1964.

475   Sebag, Lucien. "Le mythe: Code et message." *Les Temps Modernes*, 20e année, 1965, pp. 1607-1623.

476   Seymour-Smith, Martin. "Cape of Good Hope." *The Spectator*, vol. CCXXI, no. 7329, December 13, 1968, pp. 849-850.

INDIVIDUAL WORKS

477   Shalvey, Thomas J. "Lévi-Strauss and mythology."
       Proceedings of American Catholic Philosophical Association, vol. 45, 1971, pp. 114-119.

478   Shankman, N. Paul. "Le rôti et le bouilli: Lévi-Strauss' theory of cannibalism." *American Anthropologist*, vol. LXXI, no. 1, February 1969, pp. 54-69.

479   Smith, Pierre. "The nature of myths." *Diogenes*, no. 82, Summer 1973, pp. 70-87.

480   Steiner, George. "Orpheus with his myths," in *Language and Silence. Essays on language, literature, and the inhuman*. New York: Atheneum, 1967, pp. 239-250.
       [*Le Cru*] Reprinted in E. N. Hayes and T. Hayes, eds., *Claude Lévi-Strauss: The anthropologist as hero*. Cambridge, Mass.-London: The M.I.T. Press, 1970, pp. 170-183.

481   Southwold, Martin. "Talk about culture." *New Society*, vol. XIII, no. 352, June 26, 1969, p. 1005.

482   Turner, T. "*From Honey to Ashes*. A review." *Natural History*, vol. LXXXII, June 1973, pp. 80+.

483   Torrance, John. "Rationality and the structural analysis of myth." *AES*, vol. VIII, no. 2, 1967.

484   Wahl, Jean. "*Le Cru et le cuit.*" *France-Observateur*, no. 758, novembre 1964.

485   Weightman, John. "The play as fable." *Encounter*, vol. XXVIII, no. 2, February 1967, pp. 55-57.

486   Willis, R. G. "The head and the loins: Lévi-Strauss and beyond." *Man*, vol. II, no. 4, 1967, pp. 519-534.

487   Willis, Ray. "The poetry of the tree." *Times Higher Education Supplement*, no. 133, December 14, 1973, p. 16.

488   Weinrich, Harald. "Structures narratives du mythe." *Poétique*, no. 1, 1970, pp. 25-44.

489   Wilson, Carter. "The anatomy of mythology." *The Atlantic Monthly*, vol. CCXXIV, no. 1, July 1969, pp. 95-98.
       [*The Raw and the Cooked*]

490 Young, L. M. "Myths about food." *Books and Bookmen*, vol. XV, no. 9, June 1970, pp. 15-16. [*The Raw and the Cooked*]

491 Yalman, Nur. "The Raw: the Cooked: Nature: Culture--Observations on *Le Cru et le cuit*, in Edmund R. Leach, ed., *The Structural study of myth and totemism.* London: Tavistock Publications, 1967, pp. 71-90.

ANTHROPOLOGIQUE STRUCTURALE DEUX (1973)

492 Anonymous. "Versions and animadversions of Lévi-Strauss." *The Times Literary Supplement*, no. 3755, February 22, 1974, p. 180.

493 Anquetil, Gilles. "L'anthropologie: de la sérénité à l'inquiétude." *Les Nouvelles Littéraires*, 52e année, no. 2410, 3-9 décembre 1973, p. 4.

494 Lafrance, Guy. "A propos d'*Anthropologie structurale deux.*" *Dialogue* (Canada), vol. XIII, no. 3, September 1974, pp. 587-596.

495 Marc-Lipiansky, Mireille. "Le structuralisme en question." *Archives de Philosophie*, tome 38, Cahier 2, avril-juin 1975, pp. 219-238.

496 Rivière, Claude. "Le troisième âge du structuralisme." *La Quinzaine Littéraire*, no. 175, 16-30 novembre 1973, pp. 27-28.

497 Rubio Carracedo, José. "El último Lévi-Strauss (su testamento intelectual)." *Arbor*, Tomo LXXXVI, no. 336, diciembre 1973, pp. 7-22.

SECTION 5: ITEMS ARRANGED BY PROPER NAMES

ITEMS ARRANGED BY PROPER NAMES

ALTHUSSER, Louis

500   Aron, Raymond, "Althusser ou la lecture pseudo-structuraliste de Marx," in *Marxismes imaginaires. D'une sainte famille à l'autre.* Paris: Gallimard, 1970, pp. 193-354.

Glucksmann, A. see no. 8

501   Luporini, Cesare. "Réflexions sur Louis Althusser." *L'Homme et la Société,* no. 4, 1967.

Schmidt, Alfred. see no. 56 and 68

502   Veltmeyer, Henry. "Towards an assessment of the structuralist interrogation of Marx: Claude Lévi-Strauss and Louis Althusser." *Science and Society,* vol. XXXVIII, no. 4, Winter 1974-1975, pp. 385-421.

503   Poster, Mark. "Althusser on history without man." *Political Theory,* vol. II, November 1974, pp. 393-409.

AUDIBERTI, Jacques

504   Audiberti, Jacques. "Lettres à Lévi-Strauss." *L'Ouvre-Boîte, Cahiers Jacques Audiberti,* no. 4, 1975, pp. 11-19.

BACHELARD, Gaston

505   Backès-Clément, Catherine. "Note: Pertinence et impertinence d'un rapprochement." *L'Arc,* no. 2, 1970, p. 90. [consacré à Bachelard]

506   Moravia, Sergio. "Lévi-Strauss e Bachelard," in *La Ragione nascosta. Scienza e filosofia nel pensiero di Claude Lévi-Strauss.* (Saggi, I). Firenze: G. C. Sansoni, 1969.

BARTHES, Roland

507   Barthes, Roland. "Entretien avec Roland Barthes." *Aletheia,* no. 4, mai 1966.

508   Chambers, Ian. "Roland Barthes: Structuralism-Semiotics." *Working Papers in Cultural Studies,* no. 6, Autumn 1974.

BARTHES

509 Ferrata, Giansiro. "Prima della verità.--Lo strutturalismo nel saggio di Roland Barthes." *Rinascità*, no. 32, 7 agosto 1965.

510 Melenk, Harmut. "Die formalen Systeme des französischen Strukturalismus. Claude Lévi-Strauss und Roland Barthes." *Philosophisches Jahrbuch*, vol. LXXIX, 1972, pp. 137-161.

BAUDELAIRE, Charles

see Les Chats, nos. 344 to 350

BORORO

511 Revel, Jean-François. "Lévi-Strauss chez les Bororos." *Le Figaro Littéraire*, 8 octobre 1964.

BRETON, André

512 Steinwachs, Gisela. *Mythologie des Surrealismus oder die Rückverwandlung von Kultur in Natur. Eine strukturale Analyse von Bretons Nadja.* Neuwied-Berlin: Hermann Luchterhand Verlag, 1971.

CASSIRER, Ernst

513 Bartolomei, Giangaetano. "*Ernst Cassirer: Lo strutturalismo nella lingua moderne*, a cura di S. Vega." *Filosofia* (Torino), anno XXI, fasc. 55, octobre 1970, pp. 586-588.

CHOMSKY, Noam

514 Fisher, John B. "The concept of structure in Freud, Lévi-Strauss, and Chomsky." *Philosophy Research Archives*, I, no. 1023, 1975.

515 Nutini, Hugo G. "A comparison of Lévi-Strauss's structuralism and Chomsky's transformational generative grammar," in Hugo G. Nutini and Ira R. Buchler, eds., *Essays in Structural anthropology: in honor of Claude Lévi-Strauss.* New York: Appleton-Century-Crofts, 1970.

516 Rouboud, J. "Structuralisme et linguistique. (Invitation à la lecture de Noam Chomsky)." *Les Lettres Françaises*, no. 1218, janvier 1968.

DERRIDA, Jacques

    Abel, Lionel. "Jacques Derrida: His 'difference' with melodrama." see no. 237

DUFRENNE, Mikel

517 Dumasy, Annegret. *Restloses Erkennen*, pp. 113-144. see no. 53

DURKHEIM, Emile

518 Auzias, Jean-Marie. "De Durkheim à Lévi-Strauss." *Economie et Humanisme* (Paris), no. 179, janvier-février 1968.

519 Gasché, Rodolphe. *Die hybride Wissenschaft. Zur Mutation der Wissenschaftsbegriffs bei Emile Durkheim und im Strukturalismus von Claude Lévi-Strauss.* (Texte Metzler, 26). Stuttgart: Metzler, 1973.

520 Lacapra, Dominick. *Emile Durkheim. Sociologist and Philosopher.* Ithaca, N.Y.: Cornell University Press, 1972, 315p.

FOUCAULT, Michel

521 Cranston, Maurice W. "Michel Foucault." *Encounter*, vol. XXX, no. 6, June 1968, pp. 34-42. Reprinted in *The Masks of Politics and other essays.* New York: Liberal Press, 1973, pp. 137-155.

522 Dufrenne, Mikel. "La philosophie du néo-positivisme." *Esprit*, 35e année, 1967, pp. 781-800.

FRAZER

523 Muntz, Peter. *When the 'Golden Bough' Breaks: Structuralism or Typology?* London and Boston: Routledge and Kegan Paul, 1973, 143p.

FREUD, Sigmund

524 Axelos, Kostas. "Lucien Sebag entre le marxisme, le freudianisme, et le structuralisme." *Aletheia*, 1966, pp. 237-241.

    Calogeras, R. C. "Lévi-Strauss and Freud: Their structural approach to myth." see no. 390

FREUD

Cordero, Rodrigo. see 291

Fisher, John B. see 514

Fortes, Meyer, see 292

525 "*Incidences de la psychanalyse.*" Numéro spécial de la *Nouvelle Revue de Psychanalyse*, no. 1, Spring 1970, 184p.

526 Lee, K. K. "Lévi-Strauss and Freud--Victims of their own myths." *Journal of the British Society for Phenomenology*, vol. I, no. 1, January 1970, pp. 57-67.

527 Mehlmann, Jeffrey. "French Freud," in *French Freud: Structural Studies in Psychoanalysis*. New Haven: Yale French Studies, 1972.

528 Nagel, Herbert. "Claude Lévi-Strauss als Leser Freuds," in *Orte des Wilden Denkens. Zur Anthropologie von Claude Lévi-Struass.* Herausgegeben von Wolf Lepenies und Hanns H. Ritter. Frankfurt am Main: Suhrkamp Verlag, 1970, pp. 225-305.

GOLDMANN, Lucien

529 Zimmerman, Marc Jay. Genetic structuralism: Lucien Goldmann's answer to the advent of structuralism. Ph.D. dissertation, University of California at San Diego, 1975. *Dissertation Abstracts International*, vol. XXXVI, no. 3, September 1975, p. 1489-A.

GRANAI, Georges

530 Dumasy, Annegret. "Was Sprechen sagen will," pp. 101-110 in 53.

GURVITCH, Georges

531 Dumasy, Annegret. "Die Transzendenz des socialen Ganzen: Die Diskussion Gurvitch--Lévi-Strauss," pp. 48-82 in 53.

HAUDRICOURT, André

Dumasy, Annegret, pp. 101-110. see 530

HUSSERL, Edmund

532 Boehm, R. "Les sciences exactes et l'idéal husserlien d'un savoir rigoureux." *Archives de Philosophie*, vol. XXVII, Cahier 3-4, 1964.

JAKOBSON, Roman

Scholes, Robert. see 350

LACAN, Jacques

533 Anonymous. "Doctor Lacan's structuralism." *The Times Literary Supplement*, May 2, 1968. Reprinted in *T.L.S. 7. Essays and Reviews from the Times Literary Supplement*. London, New York, Toronto: Oxford University Press, 1968, pp. 215-218.

534 Mehlman, Jeffrey. "Floating signifier: From Lévi-Strauss to Lacan." *Yale French Studies*, no. 48, 1972, pp. 10-37.

535 Wilden, Anthony. *The Language of the Self*. Baltimore: Johns Hopkins Press, 1968.

LEACH, Edmund R.

Berting, J. and Philipsen, H. see 182

535a Nutini, Hugo G. "Some considerations on the nature of social structure and model building: A critique of Claude Lévi-Strauss and Edmund Leach." *American Anthropologist*, vol. LXVII, 1965, pp. 707-731. Reprinted in E. N. Hayes and T. Hayes, eds., *Claude Lévi-Strauss: The anthropologist as hero*. Cambridge, Mass.-London: The M.I.T. Press, 1970, pp. 70-107.

536 Scholte, Bob, and Simonis, Yvan. "Lévi-Strauss et la pensée leachienne." *Semiotica*, 1974.

537 Sperber, Dan. "Edmund Leach et les anthropologues." *Caheirs Internationaux de Sociologie*, vol. XLIII, 1967, pp. 123-141.

Nathhorst, Bertel. see 934

LEFEBVRE, Henri

537a Dumasy, Annegret, *Restloses Erkennen*, pp. 113-144. in 53

LEFORT, Claude

    Dumasy, Annegret, *Restloses Erkennen*, pp. 113-144, see 53

LEENHARDT, Maurice

538   Gusdorf, Georges. "Situation de Maurice Leenhardt ou l'ethnologie française de Levy-Bruhl à Lévi-Strauss," *Le Monde non-chrétien*, juillet-décembre 1964. Reprinted in *Les Sciences de l'homme sont des sciences humaines*. Paris: Les Belles Lettres, 1967.

LEVY-BRUHL

    Gusdorf, Georges. see 538

539   Saltini, Vittorio. "Levy-Bruhl contro Lévi-Strauss." *Corriere della Sera*, 14 agosto, 1966.

MAKARIUS, Raoul and Laura

540   Dumasy, Annegret. "Ethnologie: Auf der Suche nach dem Sinn oder nach dem Sinnproduktionsgesetz," pp. 83-100 in *Restloses Erkennen*, see 53.

MALLARME

541   Boon, James A. "Interpretations and conclusion: Through Literary correspondences toward a cross-cultural *esprit*," pp. 209-231, and "Poetic straw man: Self aware syntheses of *Pensée sauvage*, pp. 108-138 in no. 1.

542   Boon, James A. "Surface affinities: Contents and interest shared by Lévi-Strauss and Symbolists," pp. 17-37 in no. 2.

MALRAUX, André

    Morauski, Stefan. see 612

MARX, Karl (see also Marxism)

    Schmidt, Alfred. see 56 and 67

    Veltmeyer, Henry. see 502

543   Lepenies, Wolf. "Lévi-Strauss und die strukturalistische Marx-Lecture," pp. 160-224 in 55.

    Topolski, Jerzz. see 814

MAUSS, Marcel

544   Merleau-Ponty, Maurice. "De Mauss à Claude Lévi-Strauss,"
       in *Signes*. Paris: Gallimard, 1960, pp. 143-157.
       English translation in *Signs*. Evanston, Ill.: North-
       western University Press, 1964, pp. 114-125. [Translated
       by Richard C. McCleary]
       Italian translation by G. Alfieri, *Segni*. Milano:
       Il Saggiatore, 1967.

MERLEAU-PONTY, Maurice

545   Lefeuvre, Michel. "Musique et peinture, ou Lévi-Strauss
       et Merleau-Ponty." *Etudes*, tome CCCXL, janvier-juin
       1974, pp. 727-735.

546   Lévi-Strauss, Claude. "De quelques rencontres." *L'Arc*,
       no. 46, 1971, pp. 43-47. [Number devoted to Merleau-
       Ponty]

547   Poole, Roger C. "Indirect communications, 2: Merleau-
       Ponty and Lévi-Strauss." *New Blackfriars*, vol. XLVII,
       no. 555, August 1966, pp. 594-604.

MONTHERLANT, Henri de (see also ACADEMIE)

548   Boussard, Léon. "Lévi-Strauss succède à Henri de Monther-
       lant [à L'Académie]." *La Revue des Deux Mondes*, juillet-
       septembre 1974, pp. 349-352.

549   Ethier-Blais, Jean. "Lévi-Strauss et Montherlant." *Les
       Nouvelles Littéraires*, no. 2247, 19 août 1974, p. 5.

PIAGET, Jean

550   Anonymous. "New uses for anthropology," in *T.L.S. 1970*.
       Essays and Review from the *Times Literary Supplement*.
       Cambridge University Press, 1971, pp. 113-121.

551   Gardner, Howard. "Piaget et Lévi-Strauss: The quest for
       mind." *Social Research*, vol. XXXVII, no. 3, Autumn
       1970, pp. 348-365.

552   Gardner, Howard. *The Quest for Mind: Piaget, Lévi-
       Strauss and the structuralist movement*. New York:
       Knopf, 1973.

553 Gardner, Howard. "Structure and development." *Human Context, Le Domaine Humain*, vol. V, Spring 1973, pp. 50-67.

Gardner, Howard. see 987

PROPP, V.

554 Meijer, P. W. M. de. "Een voudige vertelstructure: Propp en Lévi-Strauss." *Forum*, vol. XI, auf. 3-4, 1970, pp. 145-159.

Nathhorst, Bertel. see 934

555 Scholes, Robert. "The mythographers: Propp and Lévi-Strauss," in *Structuralism in Literature. An Introduction*. New Haven-London: Yale University Press, 1974, pp. 60-73.

RADCLIFFE-BROWN

556 Dyson-Hudson, Neville. "Structure and infrastructure in privitive society: Lévi-Strauss and Radcliffe-Brown," In Richard Macksey and Eugenio Donato, eds., *The Language of criticism and the sciences of man: The structuralist controversy*. Baltimore: Johns Hopkins Press, 1969, pp. 218-246.

557 Marin, L. "Présentation de Radcliffe-Brown et Lévi-Strauss," in A. R. Radcliffe-Brown, *Structure et fonction dnas la société primitive*. Paris: Editions de Minuit, 1968.

RADIN, Paul

558 Vidich, Arthur J. "Paul Radin and contemporary anthropology." *Social Research*, Winter 1965, pp. 375-407 [see pp. 382, 391-398]

RICARDOU, Jean

559 Roudiez, Leon S. "Jean Ricardou and French writing today," in *French fiction today. A new direction*. New Brunswick, N.J.: Rutgers University Press, 1972, pp. 369-388.

RICOEUR, Paul

560   Dumasy, Annegret.   "Paul Ricoeur," in *Restloses Erkennen*,
      pp. 155-158. see 53

RIFFATERRE, Michel

      Scholes, Robert. see 350

RIMBAUD, Arthur

561   Boon, James A. "Introduction: A 'way in'," pp. 1-16
      and 17-37 in no. 1.

ROUSSEAU, Jean-Jacques

562   Derrida, Jacques. "Nature, culture, écriture. La violence
      de la lettre de Lévi-Strauss à Rousseau." *Cahiers pour
      l'Analyse*, no. 4, septembre-octobre 1966, pp. 1-45.
      Reprinted in *De la grammatologie*. Paris: Editions du
      Seuil, 1967.
      Italian translation, R. Balzarotti, Milano: Yaca Book,
      1969.

563   Prado, Bento. "Philosophie, musique et botanique. De
      Rousseau a Lévi-Strauss," in Jean Pouillon et Pierre
      Maranda, eds., *Echanges et communications*. see 35

564   Preti, G. "Rousseau alla Sorbona." *Il Mondo*, vol. XXII,
      no. 916, 5 april 1970.

565   Ritter, Hanns Henning. "Claude Lévi-Strauss als Leser
      Rousseaus. Exkurse zu einer Quelle ethnologischer
      Reflexion," in *Orte des Wilden Denkens. Zur Anthropologie
      von Claude Lévi-Strauss*. Herausgegeben von Wolf Lepenies
      und Hanns H. Ritter. Frankfurt am Main: Suhrkamp Verlag,
      1970, pp. 113-159.

SARTRE, Jean-Paul

566   Abel, Lionel. "Sartre vs. Lévi-Strauss," *Commonweal*,
      vol. LXXXIV, no. 13, June 17, 1966, pp. 364-368.
      Reprinted in *Hayes*, pp. 235-246. see 9

567   Anonymous. "Réconcilier Sartre et Lévi-Strauss." *Le
      Monde*, 30 mars 1967.

SARTRE

568 Caruso, Paolo. "Ragione analitica e ragione dialettica nella nuova antropologia." *Aut Aut*, no. 82, 1965, pp. 93-103; and *Ibid.*, no. 84, 1965, pp. 52-60.

569 Daix, Pierre. "Sartre est-il dépassé?" *Les Lettres Françaises*, no. 1168-1169, février 1967.

570 Dumasy, Annegret. "Jean-Paul Sartre," pp. 169-191 in *Restloses Erkennen*, see 53.

571 Glueksmann, A. "Le structuralisme ventriloque." *Les Temps Modernes*, mars 1967.

572 Goldmann, Lucien. "Jean-Paul Sartre: 'Question de méthode'," in *Marxisme et sciences humaines*. Paris: Gallimard, 1970, pp. 241-258.
English translation, *The Human Sciences and Philosophy*. London: Jonathan Cape, 1969.

573 Hartmann, Klaus. "Lévi-Strauss et Sartre." *Journal of the British Society for Phenomenology*, vol. II, no. 3, October 1971, pp. 37-45.

574 Jeanson, Francis. "On secoue trop tôt le cocotier. . . ." *Le Nouvel Observateur*, no. 103, 2-8 novembre 1966, pp. 33-34.

575 Johansen, Svend. "En fortaelling om aegget og honen." *Vindrosen*, vol. XVI, no. 7, 1969, pp. 26-33. [On continuity and discontinuity in Lévi-Strauss and Sartre]

576 Lanteri-Laura, Georges. "Zwischen Sartre und Lévi-Strauss." *Neues Forum*, Marz-April 1968, vol. XV, no. 171-172, pp. 205-206.

577 Levin, David Michael. "On Lévi-Strauss and existentialism." *The American Scholar*, vol. XXXVIII, no. 1, Winter 1968-1969, pp. 69-82.

Mehlman, Jeffrey. see 79 and 152

578 Piguet, Jean-Claude. "Les conflits de l'analyse et de la dialectique." *Annales (Economies--Sociétés--Civilisations)*, 20e année, no. 3, mai-juin 1965, pp. 547-557.

579 Pingaud, Bernard. "Interview: Sartre répond." *La Quinzaine Littéraire*, no. 14, 15-31 octobre 1966, pp. 4-5.

580 Pingaud, Bernard, ed. *Sartre aujourd'hui*. *L'Arc*, no. 30, 1966.

581 Pouillon, Jean. "Sartre et Lévi-Strauss. Analyse/ dialectique d'une relation dialectique/analytique." *L'Arc*, no. 26, 1965, pp. 60-65.

582 Pouillon, Jean. "Sartre and Lévi-Strauss." *Critical Anthropology*, vol. I, 1970, pp. 34-39.

583 Rosen, Lawrence. "Language, history and the logic of inquiry in the works of Lévi-Strauss and Sartre." *History and Theory*, vol. X, no. 3, 1971, pp. 269-294. Reprinted in Ino Rossi, ed., *The Unconscious in culture: The Structuralism of Claude Lévi-Strauss in perspective*. New York: E. P. Dutton and Co. Inc., 1974.

584 Rubio Carracedo, José. "Estructura o dialectica? Nota sobre el debate entre Lévi-Strauss y Sartre." *Estudio Agustiniano*, vol. IV, 1969, pp. 547-555.

585 Ruyer, R. "Le mythe de la raison dialectique." *Revue de Métaphysique et de Morale*, vol. LXVI, nos. 1-2, janvier-juin 1961, pp. 1-35.

586 Sartre, Jean-Paul. *Critique de la raison dialectique*. Paris: Gallimard, 1960, pp. 487-505.

587 Sartre, Jean-Paul. "Replies to structuralism: An interview with Jean-Paul Sartre." English translation in *Telos*, no. 6, Fall 1971, pp. 110-116.

588 Scholes, Robert. "The illiberal imagination." *New Literary History*, vol. IV, no. 3, Spring 1973, pp. 521-540.

589 Tibaldi, G. "Storia e dialettica. A proposito della polemica tra Lévi-Strauss e Sartre." *Il Mulino*, vol. XIII, no. 9, 1964, pp. 969-973.

590 Védrine, Hélène. *Les Philosophes de l'histoire*. Paris: Petite Bibliothèque Payot, 1974.

591 Ziegler, Jean. "Sartre et Lévi-Strauss." *Le Nouvel Observateur*, no. 25, 6 mai 1965.

SAUSSURE

SAUSSURE, Ferdinand de

592 Gasché, Rodolphe. "Das wilde Denken und die Ökonomie der Repräsentation. Zum Verhältnis von Ferdinand de Saussure und Claude Lévi-Strauss." in *Orte des Wilden Denkens. Zur Anthropologie von Claude Lévi-Strauss.* Herausgegeben von Wolf Lepenies und Hanns H. Ritter. Frankfurt am Main: Suhrmkamp Verlag, 1970, pp. 306-385.

593 Greimas, A.-J. "L'actualité du saussurisme." *Le Francais Moderne*, juillet 1956.

594 Nethold, Ana Maria, ed. *Ferdinand de Saussure*, por E. Benveniste et al. Ed. Selc. y trad. a cargo de A. M. Nethold. Buenos Aires: Siglo Veintiuno Argentina Edit., 1971. [Godel, Greimas, Hjemslev, Starobinski, R. E. Wells]

SEBAG, Lucien

Axelos, Kostas. see 942

SEVE, Lucien

595 Godelier, Maurice. "Logique Dialectique et Analyse des Structures, Réponse à Lucien Sève." *La Pensée*, no. 149, février 1970, pp. 3-28.

VALERY, Paul

596 Boon, James A. pp. 17-37 and 108-138 in no. 1.

VICO, Giambattista

597 Leach, Edmund R. "Vico and Lévi-Strauss on the origins of humanity," in G. Tagliacozza, ed., *Giambattista Vico: An International Symposium.* Baltimore: Johns Hopkins Press, 1969, pp. 309-318.

598 Merquior, J. G. "Vico et Lévi-Strauss." *L'Homme*, tome X, no. 2, avril-juin 1970, pp. 81-93.

WHITEHEAD, Alfred N.

599 Paci, Enzo. *La Filosofia di Whitehead e i problemi del tempo e della struttura.* Milano: La Goliardica, 1965, pp. 150-200.

WITTGENSTEIN, Ludwig

600 Pettit, Philip. "Wittgenstein and the case for structuralism." *Journal of the British Society for Phenomenology*, vol. III, no. 1, January 1972, pp. 46-57.

SECTION 6: ITEMS ARRANGED BY SUBJECTS

ITEMS ARRANGED BY SUBJECTS

ACADEMIE FRANCAISE (see also Montherlant)

601 Anonymous. "On en parlera demain: Un académicien structuré." *Le Nouvel Observateur*, no. 446, 28 mai - 3 juin 1973, pp. 39-40.

602 Anonymous. "Claude Lévi-Strauss académicien." *Combat*, no. 9000, 30 mai 1973, p. 10.

Boussard, Léon. see 548

603 "L'Académie Française a reçu M. Claude Lévi-Strauss. Discours du récipiendaire, Réponse de Roger Caillois." *Le Monde*, 28 juin 1974, pp. 19-22.

Ethier-Blais, Jean. see 549

604 Kaufmann, Herbert. "Die Wohltat eines Stammbaums. Lévi-Strauss und die Initiations--riten der Académie Française." *Frankfurter Allgemeine Zeitung*, no. 157, 11.Juli 1974, p. 17.

605 Laffly, Georges. "La réception de Lévi-Strauss à l'Académie." *Les Ecrits de Paris*, no. 339, septembre 1974, pp. 95-103.

AESTHETICS (and ART) see also PAINTING

606 Bernabei, F. "Lévi-Strauss e la critica delle arti figurative." *La Biennale di Venezia*, no. 64-65, 1969.

607 Bernabei, F. "Strutturalismo e critica d'arte." *Marcattè*, no. quadruplo, 46-49, October 1968-January 1969, pp. 198-211.

608 Dorfles, Gillo. "Pour ou contre une esthétique structuraliste?" *Revue Internationale de Philosophie*, no. 73-74, 1965, pp. 409-441.
English translation by Stephen Bann and Philip Steadman, "For or against a structuralist aesthetic?" *Form* (Cambridge), no. 2, September 1, 1966, pp. 15-19.

609 Duvignaud, Jean. "The myths of aesthetic expression," in *The Sociology of art*. Translated from the French by Timothy Wilson. London: Paladin, 1972, pp. 23-34.

AESTHETIC

Lefeuvre, Michel. see 545

610 Marchan, Simon. "La obra de arte y el estructuralismo." *Revista de Ideas Estéticas*, vol. XXVIII, no. 100, april-junio 1970, pp. 92-119.

611 Michelson, A. "Art and the structuralist perspective," pp. 37-59 in *On the future of art*. Essays by Arnold J. Toynbee and others. Introduction by Edward F. Fry. Sponsored by The Solomon R. Guggenheim Museum. New York: Viking Press, 1970

612 Morawski, Stefan. *L'absolu et la forme. L'esthétique d'André Malraux*. (Translated from the Polish by Yolande Lamy-Grun). Paris: Klincksieck, 1972.

613 Morisani, Ottavio. "Intorno al linguaggio dei pittori impressionisti e ad alcune osservazione di Claude Lévi-Strauss." *Rivista di Studi Crociani*, vol. VII, April-June 1970, pp. 164-181.

614 Nodelman, Sheldon. "Structural analysis in art and anthropology." *Yale French Studies*, no. 36-37, 1966, pp. 89-103. Reprinted in Jacques Ehrmann, *Structuralism*. Garden City, N.Y.: Doubleday, Anchor Books, 1970, pp. 79-93.

615 Parain-Vial, Jeanne. "Expérience concrète et analyse structurale en esthétique." *Annales d'Esthétique*, vol. VIII, 1969, pp. 43-68.

616 Piselli, Francesco. "Lévi-Strauss e l'estetica." *Il Ponte*, no. 10, octobre 1965, pp. 1365-1366.

617 Rosner, K. "L'oeuvre de Lévi-Strauss en tant que source de l'inspiration dans les recherches esthétiques," in Slaw Krzemien-Ojak, ed., *Studia Estetyczne* (Etudes esthétiques). Warsaw: Panstwowe Wydawnictwo Naukowe, 1972, 419p.

618 Tagliaferri, Aldo. *L'Estetica dell'oggettivo*. Milano: Feltrinelli, 1967.

619 Urmeneta, Fermín de. "Sobre estética estructuralista." *Revista de Ideas Estéticas*, vol. XXVII, no. 105, January-March 1969, pp. 55-58.

620 Anonymous. "Anthropology's pope." *The Times Literary Supplement*, no. 3453, May 2, 1968, pp. 445-447.

621 Anonymous. "High priest on the couch." *The Times Literary Supplement*, no. 3472, September 12, 1968, p. 970.

622 Anonymous. "Confronting the classic." *The Times Literary Supplement*, August 14, 1970. Reprinted in *T.L.S. 9. Essays and Reviews from The Times Literary Supplement*, Cambridge University Press, 1971, pp. 113-121.

Ardener, Edwin. see 872

Anquetil, Gilles. see 493

623 Anonymous. "L'esprit et la lettre." *Le Nouvel Observateur*, no. 432, 19-25 février, 1973, p. 70.

624 Anonymous. "L'esprit et la lettre." *Le Nouvel Observateur*, no. 416, 30 octobre-5 novembre 1972, p. 67.

Ardener, Edwin. see 872

625 Backès-Clément, Catherine. "Le voyageur, Balzac et Wagner." *Le Magazine Littéraire*, no. 58, novembre 1971, pp. 13-16.

Bakker, Reinout. "Een antropologisch gezichtspunkt van Claude Lévi-Strauss." see 93

626 Balandier, Georges. *Anthropologie politique*. Paris, Presses Universitaires de France, 1967.

Balandier, Georges. "Le hasard et les civilisations." see 94

Balandier, Georges. "Le XXe siècle ne se connait pas." see 95

Banton, Michael, ed. *The Relevance of models for social anthropology*. see 976

627 Banaji, Jacrus. "The crisis of British anthropology." *New Left Review*, no. 64, November-December 1970, pp. 71-86.

628 Barnes, J. A. *Three Styles in the study of kinship*. London: Tavistock Publications, 1961.

629   Barnes, J. A. "Time flies like an arrow." *Man*, vol. VI, 1971, pp. 537-552.

630   Barthes, Roland. "Les sciences humaines et l'oeuvre de Lévi-Strauss." *Annales (Economies--Sociétés--Civilisations)*, 19e année, no. 6, novembre-décembre 1964, pp. 1085-1086.

631   Beattie, J. H. M. "Rituals of Nyoro kinship." *Africa*, vol. XXIX, 1959, pp. 134-145. [relies on Lévi-Strauss]

632   Bell, J. H. "Claude Lévi-Strauss: Social anthropology and history." *Australian Journal of Politics and History*, vol. XVI, August 1970, pp. 218-226.

Bell, J. H. and von Sturmer, J. R. "An introduction to Claude Lévi-Strauss." see 99

633   Bender, Donald. "The development of French anthropology." *Journal of the History of the Behavioral Sciences*, vol. I, 1965, pp. 139-151.

634   Bendow, Burton. "The instinct for order." *The Nation*, vol. CCXI, no. 22, December 28, 1970, pp. 692-694. [Review of Leach, *Lévi-Strauss*]

Benjamin, Geoffrey. "Lévi-Strauss, anthropologist." see 100

Berting, J. and H. Philipsen. see 182

635   Berndt, Ronald M. "Two in one, and more in two. . ." see 35

636   Bharati, Agiehananda. "Anthropological approach to the study of religion: Ritual and belief systems," in *Biennal Review of Anthropology, 1971*. Stanford: Stanford University Press, 1972, specially pp. 248-255.

637   Bonomi, A. "Implicazioni filosofiche nell antropologia di Claude Lévi-Strauss." *Aut Aut*, nos. 96-97, 1967, pp. 47-73.
Portuguese translation, "Implicações filosoficas na antropologia de Claude Lévi-Strauss," in Luis Costa Lima, ed., *O Estruturalismo de Lévi-Strauss*. Petropolis: Vozes, 1969, pp. 114-139.

ANTHROPOLOGY   87

638   Brogger, J.   "Linguistics and social anthropology."   *Ethnos*, 1966, pp. 151-160.

Buchler, Ira R. and H. A. Selby.   see 983

Buchler, Ira R. and Henry A. Selby.   see 868

639   Bulmer, Ralph.   "Which came first, the chicken or the egg-head?" in Jean Pouillon et Pierre Maranda, eds., *Echanges et Communications*, vol. II, no. 5, pp. 1069-1091, see 35

640   Burling, Robbins.   "Cognition and componential analysis: God's truth or hocus-pocus?"   *American Anthropologist*, vol. LXVI, no. 1, February 1964, pp. 20-28.

Burridge, K. O. L.   pp. 91-115.   see 984

641   *Cahiers de Philosophie*, janvier 1966, no. 1.   [numéro spécial consacré a *l'Anthropologie*]

Caillois, Roger.   "Théorie des jeux."   see 111

Caillois, Roger.   "Illusions à rebours."   see 112

Caruso, Paolo.   "Ragione analitica e ragione dialettica nella nuova antropologia," see 568.

642   Clastres, Pierre.   "Echange et pouvoir: Philosophie de la chefferie indienne."   *L'Homme*, vol. II, no. 1, 1962.

Clastres, Pierre.   "Entre silence et dialogue."   see 115

643   Colby, Benjamin N.   "The analysis of culture content and patterning of native concern in texts."   *American Anthropologist*, vol. LXVIII, 1966, pp. 374-388.

644   Colby, Benjamin N.   "Comment on Fischer: The sociopsychological analysis of folktales."   *Current Anthropology*, vol. IV, 1963, p. 275.

645   "Confrontations over myth."   *New Left Review*, no. 62, June-August 1970, pp. 57-74.   [Translated from *Esprit*, P. Ricoeur, J. Cuisenier, M. Gaboriau, J. J. Faye, etc.]

646   Cohen, Percy.   "Theories of myth."   *Man*, vol. IV, no. 3, 1969, pp. 337-353.

Coult, Allan D.   "Causality and cross-sex prohibitions."
          see 188

647   Coult, Allan D.   "The structuring of structure."   *American Anthropologist*, vol. LXVIII, 1966, pp. 438-443.

648   Courchay, C.   "Gros rouge et Bororos."   *Les Temps Modernes*, 26e année, no. 285, avril 1970, pp. 1702-1710.

      Crumrine, N. Rose, and Barbara Jane Macklin, see 23.

649   Cuisenier, Jean.   "Formes de la parenté et formes de la pens e."   *Esprit*, 31e année, no. 322, novembre 1963, pp. 547-563.

      Courtes, Jean.   see 31

650   Delfendahl, Bernard.   "Critique de l'anthropologie savante: Claude Lévi-Strauss, homeliste et scolastique."   *L'Homme et la Société*, no. 22, octobre-novembre-décembre 1971.

      Delfendahl, Bernard.   see 34

      Davenport, William.   "Social organization."   see 1090

      Daix, Pierre.   "L'anthropologie pour quoi faire? Lévi-Strauss invité du dimanche."   see 843

651   Devereux, George.   *From Anxiety to method in the behavioral sciences*.   Preface by Weston La Barre.   The Hague: Mouton, 1967, 376p.

652   Diamond, Stanley.   "Anthropology in question," in D. H. Hymes, ed., *Rewriting Anthropology*.   New York: Pantheon Books, 1973, pp. 401-429.

653   Diamond, Stanley.   "Introduction: The uses of the primitive," in Stanley Diamond, ed., *Primitive views of the world*.   New York: Columbia University Press, 1964.

654   Diamond, Stanley.   "Man and superman: Anthropology in question."   *Partisan Review*, no. 2, 1971, pp. 167-182.

      Douglas, Mary.   Pp. 49-70 in 282.

      Dumont, Louis.   "Descent or intermarriage? A relational view of Australian section systems."   see 191

655 Dundes, A. *The Morphology of North-American Indian Folktales.* Helsinki: Tiedeakatemie, 1964.

Dyson-Hudson, Neville. see 556

Echanges et communications, I and II. see 5

656 Edmond, Michel-Pierre. "L'anthropologie structuraliste et l'histoire." *La Pensée,* no. 123, octobre 1965, pp. 43-50.

657 Esteva-Fabrigat, Claudio. "Sobre il metodo y los problemas de la antropología estructural." *Convivium,* no. 34, 1969, pp. 3-54.

Fages, J.-B. see 38

658 Fanizza, Franco. "Lo scientifico nell'umano." *Giornale Critico della Filosofia Italiana,* April-June 1970, pp. 271-297.

659 Fischer, John L. "The sociopsychological analysis of folktales." *Current Anthropology,* vol. IV, 1963, pp. 235-295.

Fortes, Meyer. see 193 and 194

Fox, Robin. see 195

Gaboriau, Marc. see 796

Geertz, Clifford. "The cerebral savage: On the works of Claude Lévi-Strauss." see 128

650a Geertz, Hildred. "Comment." *Journal of Asian Studies,* vol. XXIV, 1965, pp. 294-297.

651a Gellner, Ernest. "Time and theory in social anthropology." *Mind,* vol. LXVII, no. 266, 1958, pp. 182-202.

652a Giannotti, G. *La Scienza della cultura.* Bologna: Il Mulino, 1967, pp. 123-135.

653a Gibson, Mickey. "Lévi-Strauss: Notes toward a phenomenological social anthropology." *Human Inquiries; Review of Existential Psychology and Psychiatry,* vol. X, nos. 1-3, 1970, pp. 161-168.

ANTHROPOLOGY

654a Gilsenan, M. "Myth and the history of African religion," in T. O. Ranger and I. N. Kimambo, eds., *The Historical study of African Religion*. Berkeley: University of California Press, 1972.

655a Goddard, D. "Lévi-Strauss and the anthropologists." *Social Research*, vol. XXXVII, no. 3, Autumn 1970, pp. 366-378.

656a Goddard, D. "Conceptions of structure in Lévi-Strauss and British anthropologists." *Social Research*, vol. XXXII, Winter 1965, pp. 408-427.

Goody, J. see 197

657a Goodenough, Ward H. "Frontiers of cultural anthropology: Social organization." *Proceedings of the American Philosophical Society*, vol. CXIII, no. 5, 1969, pp. 329-335.

Guier, Jorgé Enrique. "Incesto, matrimonio y derecho." see 198

658a Harris, Marvin. *The Rise of anthropological theory. A history of theories of culture*. New York: Thomas Y. Crowell, 1968, pp. 482-513.

Hayes, E. N. and T. Hayes, eds. see 9

Hays, H. R. "Claude Lévi-Strauss." see 133

659a Hauck, Gerhard. "Die 'Strukturale Anthropologie' von C. Lévi-Strauss." *Sociologus*, Neue Folge, vol. XVIII, Heft 1, 1968, pp. 63-83.

660 Haudricourt, A. G. "Sur le degré d'immanence des infrastructures," pp. 606-608 in no. 5.

Heusch, Luc de. see 200, 201, 202

Heusch, Luc de. "Les vacances de la science." see 254

Heusch, Luc de. "Anthropologie structurale et symbolisme." see 1246

661 Heusch, Luc de. "Situations et positions de l'anthropologie structurale." *L'Arc*, no. 26, 1965, pp. 6-18.

ANTHROPOLOGY 91

662 Hoffmann, Hans. "Mathematical anthropology." in Bernard J. Seigel, ed., *Biennial Review of Anthropology 1969*. Stanford: Stanford University Press, 1970, pp. 41-79.

Homans, George C. and David M. Schneider. see 203

Homans, George C. see 204

Hymes, Dell H., ed. *Language in Culture and society. A reader in linguistics and Anthropology*. New York: Harper & Row, 1964. see 906

663 Hymes, Dell H., and Frake, C. O. "Comments on Burlings' article, and Burling's rejoinder." *American Anthropologist*, vol. LXVI, 1964, no. 1, pp. 116-122. see 640

664 Jacques, François. "Profil: L'homme-laboratoire." *Le Nouvel Observateur*, no. 345, 21-27 juin 1971, pp. 39-40.

Jager, M. "Manttekeningen bij Professor Bakker's artikel 'Een antropologisch gezichtspunt van Lévi-Strauss'," see 138

Josseling de Jong, J. P. B. de. see 10

Josseling de Jong, J. P. B. de. see 431

665 Kang, Shin-pyo. "The structural principle of Chinese world view," in 23.

666 Kasakoff, Alice. "Lévi-Strauss' idea of social unconscious: The problem of elementary and complex structures in Gitksan marriage choice," in 23.

667 Kongas, Elli-Kajia, and Maranda, Pierre. "Structural models in folklore." *Midwest Folklore*, vol. XXII, 1962, pp. 133-192.

668 Korn, Francis. "The logic of some concepts in Lévi-Strauss." *American Anthropologist*, vol. LXXI, January 1969, pp. 70-71.

Krader, Lawrence. see 1075

669 Kuper, Adam. "Lévi-Strauss and British neo-structuralism," pp. 214-226, chapter VII, in *Anthropologists and Anthropology. The British School, 1922-1972*. New York: Pica Press- Toronto: Longman, 1973.

Kortmulder, K. "An ethnological theory of the incest taboo and exogamy, with special reference to the views of Claude Lévi-Strauss." see 205

670 Lassudrie-Dechene, B. "La consommation ostentatoire et l'usage des richesses." *Butlletin S. E. D. E. I. S., Etudes,* no. 933, 1965.

671 Leach, Edmund R. Genesis as myth and other essays. London: Jonathan Cape, 1962, 1969.

Leach, Edmund R. see 209

672 Leach, Edmund R. "The comparative method in anthropology," in *International Encyclopaedia of the Social Sciences,* vol. I, 1968, pp. 339-354. Macmillan and The Free Press, 1968.

673 Leach, Edmund R. "Lévi-Strauss in the Garden of Eden: An examination of some recent developments in the analysis of myth." *Transactions of the New York Academy of Sciences,* series 2, vol. XXIII, no. 4, 1961, pp. 386-396. Reprinted, William A. Lessa and Evon Z. Vogt, eds., *Reader in Comparative Religion.* New York: Harper & Row, 1965, pp. 575-581. Also in HAYES.

674 Leach, Edmund R. "Claude Lévi-Strauss, anthropologist and philosopher." *New Left Review,* November-December 1965.
French translation, "Claude Lévi-Strauss, anthropologue et philosophe." [présentation de P. Vidal-Naquet]. *Raison Présente,* no. 3, mai-juin-juillet 1967, pp. 91-106.
German translation in *Orte des Wilden Denkens.* see 55
Spanish translation, *Lévi-Strauss, antropólogo y filósofo.* see 70

Leach, Edmund R. see 323

675 Leach, Edmund R. "'Kachin' and 'Haka Chin': A rejoinder to Lévi-Strauss." *Man,* vol. IV, June 1969, pp. 277-285.

Leach, Edmund R. see 882 and 883

Lefebvre, Henri. "Claude Lévi-Strauss et le nouvel éléatisme." see 165

676 Lefort, Claude. "Sociétés sans histoire et historicité." *Cahiers Internationaux de Sociologie*, 7e année, 1952, pp. 91-114. [See Lévi-Strauss's response in *Anthropologie structurale*, chapter XVI]

Lefort, Claude. see 210

Lepenies, Wolf, und Ritter, Hanns H. see 55

Lévi-Strauss. *L'Arc*, no. 26, 1965. Special issue devoted to Lévi-Strauss See no. 73 for contents.

677 Licciardello, Pasquale. "Lévi-Strauss e il famismo." *Biologia Culturale*, vol. VIII, no. 1, marzo 1973, pp. 7-28.

678 Lienhardt, Godfrey. *Social Anthropology*. London: Oxford University Press, 1964.

679 Lienhardt, Godfrey. "Debts to the savage." *The Listener*, vol. LXXIX, no. 2043, May 23, 1968, pp. 671-672.

Lyotard, Jean-François. "A propos de Claude Lévi-Strauss: 'Les Indiens ne cueillent pas les fleurs'," see 147.

680 Makarius, Raoul, and Laura Makarius. "Des jaguars et des hommes." *L'Homme et la Société*, no. 7, janvier-mars 1968. Reprinted in 44.

681 Makarius, Raoul, and Laura Makarius. "Le symbolisme de la main gauche." *L'Homme et la Société*, no. 9, juillet-septembre 1969. Reprinted in 44.

682 Makarius, Raoul, and Laura Makarius. "Lévi-Strauss et les structures inconscientes de l'esprit." *L'Homme et la Société*, no. 18, octobre-décembre 1970. Reprinted in 44.

683 Makarius, Raoul, and Laura Makarius. "L'apothéose de Cinna." *L'Homme et la Société*, no. 22, octobre-décembre 1971. Reprinted in 44.

684 Makarius, Raoul. "Parenté et infrastructure." *La Pensée*, no. 149, 1970, pp. 51-55.

685 Makarius, Raoul. "Dialectique de la parenté." *La Pensée*, no. 168, mars-avril 1973, pp. 21-36.

686 Makarius, Raoul, et Laura Makarius. *L'Origine de l'exogamie et du totémisme.* Paris: Gallimard, 1961.

687 Makarius, Laura. "La chasse aux aigles chez les Hidatsa." *L'Homme et la Société*, no. 9, juillet-septembre 1969, pp. 231-254. Reprinted in 44.

688 Makarius, Raoul et Laura Makarius. "On Soviet views on totemism." *Current Anthropology*, vol. VIII, no. 3, June 1967, pp. 258-260.

689 Makarius, Laura. "Dalla morte del 'primitivo' alla morte dell'uomo." *Critica Marxista*, anno 5, no. 6, November-December 1967, pp. 133-140.

690 Maranda, Pierre. "Formal analysis and inter-cultural studies." *Social Science Information*, vol. VI, 1967, pp. 7-36.

691 Maranda, Pierre. *Calcul et formalisation dans les sciences de l'homme.* Paris: Editions du Centre de la recherche scientifique, 1968.

692 Maranda, Pierre. "An anthropologist in Paris," in Pouillon et Maranda, see 35.

693 Maranda, Pierre. "Anthropological analytics: Lévi-Strauss' concept of social structure," in Hugo Nutini and Ira Buchler, eds., *The Anthropology of Claude Lévi-Strauss.* New York: Appleton-Century-Crofts, 1970

Maybury-Lewis, David. "Science by association." see 450

Maybury-Lewis, David. "Science or bricolage?" see 451

Mendelson, E. Michael. see 1249

694 Mercier, P. *Histoire de l'anthropologie.* Paris: Presses Universitaires de France, 1966, pp. 144-151, and passim.

Maquet, Jacques. see 23

Matarasso, Michel. see 326

Maybury-Lewis, David. "The analysis of dual organization: A methodological critique." see 214

695 Miotto, A. "Antropologia strutturale e antropologia culturale." *Rivista Internazionale di Scienze Sociali,* vol. XXIX, fasc. 6, 1958.

696 Montes, Santiago. *Los Derechos humanos a la luz de la antropología.* San Salvador: Publicaciones de la Universidad José Simeon Canas, 1970.

697 Muller, Jean-Claude. "On preferential/prescriptive marriage and the function of kinship systems: The Rukuba case (Benue Plateau State, Nigeria)." *American Anthropologist,* vol. LXXV, no. 5, October 1973, pp. 1563-1576.

698 Muntz, Peter. *When the Golden Bough Breaks: Structuralism or typology?* see 523

699 Murdock, George P. "Changing emphases in social structure." *Southwestern Journal of Anthropology,* vol. XI, 1955, pp. 361-370.

Murphy, David. "Claude Lévi-Strauss or the meeting of cultures." see 153

Nodelman, Sheldon. see 614

700 Needham, Rodney. "Terminology and alliance." *Sociologus,* 16-17, 1967, pp. 39-54.

701 Nutini, Hugo G. "Science and ideology." *Bijdragen tot de Taal-, Land-, en Volkenkunde,* vol. CXXVII, no. 1, 1971, pp. 1-14.

Nutini, Hugo G. see 535a

702 Nutini, Hugo G. "On the concepts of epistemological order and coordinative definitions." *Bijdragen. Tot de Taal-, Land-, en Volkenkunde,* vol. CXXIV, no. 1, 1968, pp. 1-21.

703 Nutini, Hugo G. "Structural history: A programatic synthesis of the nomothetic and idiographic elements of anthropological studies." *L'Homme,* Revue française d'anthropologie, 1971.

704 Nutini, Hugo G. see 822

705 Orans, Martin. "Social organization," in Bernard J. Siegel, ed., *Biennial/Review of Anthropology, 1969.* Stanford: Stanford University Press, 1970, pp. 132-190.

706 Ortigues, Edmond. "Nature et culture dans l'oeuvre de
Claude Lévi-Strauss." *Critique*, vol. XIX, no. 189,
février 1963, pp. 142-157.

707 Paci, Enzo. "Strutturalismo, fonologia e antropologia."
Aut Aut, no. 77, 1963, pp. 9-17.

708 Paci, Enzo. *Fenomenologia e antropologia*. Milano: La
Goliardica, 1962, pp. 159-190.

709 Paci, Enzo. "Antropologia strutturale e fenomenologia."
Aut Aut, no. 88 July 1965, pp. 42-54.
Portuguese translation in Luiz Costa Lima, *O Estruturalismo de Lévi-Strauss*. Petropolis: Vozes, 1969,
pp. 94-106.

710 Parain, Brice. "Les sorciers." *L'Homme Nouveau*, mai
1956.

711 Pirson, Pierre. "Le laboratoire de Claude Lévi-Strauss."
La Revue Nouvelle, 22e année, tome 44, no. 9, 15
septembre 1966, pp. 159-174.

712 Paci, Enzo. "Antropologia ed entropologia--Pensiero
concreto--Naturalismo e crisi della presenze." *Aut Aut*,
no. 88, July 1965, pp. 70-75.

Pochtar, Ricardo. see 781

Pocock, D. F. "Claude Lévi-Strauss--Anthropologist."
see 157

Poole, Roger. see 891

713 Posner, Charles. "Sociological theory, II: Lévi-Strauss'
eidetic utopia." *The Cambridge Review*, vol. LXXXIX,
no. 2152, June 10, 1967, pp. 400-404.

Pouillon, Jean. "L'oeuvre de Claude Lévi-Strauss." see 158

714 Pouillon, Jean. "Présentation: Un essai de definition."
Les Temps Modernes, 22e année, no. 246, novembre 1966,
pp. 769-790.

Pouillon, Jean, et Pierre Maranda, eds. *Echanges et
Communications* I and II. see 35

715 Pouillon, Jean. "Traditions in French anthropology," *Social Research*, vol. XXXVIII, 1971, pp. 73-92. Translated from the French by Marie J. Corngold, from chapter in *Anthropological traditions*, edited by Stanley Diamond. Philadelphia: University of Pennsylvania Press, 1971.

716 Pouillon, Jean. *Fétiches sans fétichisme*. Paris: François Maspero, 1975.

717 Pouwer, Jan. "The structural and functional approach in cultural anthropology." *Bijdragen. Tot de Taal-, Land-, en Volkenkunde*, vol. CXXII, 1966, pp. 129-144.

718 Pouwer, Jan. "Referential and inferential reality: A rejoinder." *Bijdragen. Tot de Taal-, Land-, en Volkenkunde*, vol. CXXII, 1966, pp. 151-157.

719 Pouwer, Jan. The structural-configurational approach: A methodological outline," in 23.

720 Rayfield, J. R. "Dualism of Lévi-Strauss." *International Journal of Comparative Sociology*, vol. XIII, December 1971, pp. 267-280.

721 Robinson, Marguerite S. "'The house of the mighty hero', or 'The house of enough paddy'. Some implications of a Sinhalese myth," in Edmund R. Leach, ed., *Dialectic in practical religion*. Cambridge University Press, 1968, pp. 122-152.

Rossi, Ino, ed. see 23

722 Ruyer, R. "Perception, croyance, monde symbolique." *Revue de Métaphysique et de Morale*, vol. LXVII, no. 1, janvier-mars 1962.

Salisbury, A. see 221

Scholte, Bob. see 82 and 225

723 Scholte, Bob. "Claude Lévi-Strauss," in John Honigman, ed., *Handbook of social and Cultural anthropology*. Chicago: Rand McNally, 1974, pp. 676-716.

724 Scholte, Bob. "Toward a self-reflexive anthropology: An introduction with some examples." *Critical Anthropology*, vol. I, no. 2, 1970, pp. 3-33.

725 Scholte, Bob. "Toward a reflexive and critical anthropology," in Dell H. Hymes, eds., *Reinventing Anthropology*. New York: Pantheon, 1971.

726 Scholte, Bob. "Discontents in anthropology." *Social Research*, vol. XXXVIII, 1971, pp. 777-807.

727 Schneider, D. M. "Some muddles in the models; or, how the system really works," in Michael Banton, ed., *The Relevance of models for social anthropology*. London: Tavistock Publications -New York: Frederick A. Praeger, 1965, pp. 25-85.

728 Scholte, Bob. "Epistemic paradigms: Some problems in cross-cultural research in social anthropological history and theory." *American Anthropologist*, vol. LXVIII, October 1966, pp. 1192-1201. Reprinted, pp. 108-122 in 9.

729 Selby, Henry A. "Social organization," in *Biennial Review of Anthropology 1971*. Stanford: Stanford University Press, 1972, [spec. pp. 311-314]

Shankmann, Paul. see 478

730 Sharpe, Eric J. "Structural anthropology," in *The Twentieth Century Mind III: History, ideas and literature*, ed. by C. B. Cox and A. E. Dyson. London: Oxford University Press, 1972, pp. 185-200.

731 Solimini, Maria Ponzio. "Antropologia, storia, etnolinguistica." *Filosofia* (Torino), vol. XXIV, July 1973, pp. 281-314.

732 Simonis, Yvan. "Echange, 'praxis', code et message." *Cahiers Internationaux de Sociologie*, 1968, pp. 117-129.

733 Slamet-Velsink, Ina E. "Les organizations dualistes existent-elles? Het historisch perspektief." *Bijdragen. Tot de Taal-, Land-, en Volkenkunde*, vol. CXIV, 1958, pp. 292-305.

734 Southwold, Martin. "Talk about culture." *New Society*, vol. XIII, no. 352, June 26, 1969, pp. 1005-1006.

735 Sperber, Dan. "Le structuralisme en anthropologie," in O. Ducrot, T. Todorov, D. Sperber, M. Safouan, F. Wahl, *Qu'est-ce que le structuralisme?* Paris: Editions du Seuil, 1968, pp. 167-237.

736 Sturtevant, William C. "Studies in ethno-science," in
Transcultural Studies in Cognition, ed. by A. K. Romney
and R. G. D'Andrade, pp. 99-131. *American Anthropologist*, vol. LXVI, 1964, no. 3, part 2 [special issue].

737 Swanson, Guy E. "Frameworks for comparative research;
structural anthropology and the theory of action," in
Ivan Vallier, ed., *Comparative methods in sociology.
Essays on Trends and Applications*. Berkeley: University
of California Press, 1971, pp. 141-202.

738 Tax, Sol. ed. *An Appraisal of anthropology today*. Chicago:
University of Chicago Press, 1953.

739 Tennekes, J. *Anthropology, Relativism and Method*. An
inquiry into the methodological principles of a science
of culture. Assen, Van Gorcum, 1971, p. 228.

Turnbull, Colin M. see 337

740 Tullio-Altan, C. "Lo strutturalismo di Lévi-Strauss e la
ricerca antropologica." *Studi di Sociologia*, vol. IV,
1966, pp. 229-253.

741 Tullio-Altan, C. "Linguistica e antropologia culturale."
Rivista di Sociologia, vol. V, 1967, pp. 25-108.

Tullio-Altan, C. see 1214

742 Tullio-Altan, C. *Antropologia funzionale*. Milano:
Bompiani, 1968, pp. 21-36 and passim.

Vidich, Arthur J. see 558

743 Vogt, Evon C. and Vogt, Catherine. "Lévi-Strauss among
the Maya." *Man*, vol. V, September 1970, pp. 379-392.

744 Ward, B. E. "Varieties of the conscious model: The
fisherman of South China," in Michael Banton, ed., *The
Relevance of models for social anthropology*. London:
Tavistock Publications- New York: Frederick A. Praeger,
1965.

Wallace, A. F. C. and S. Atkins. see 231

Warner, Lloyd W. et al. see 232

Willis, R. G. "The head and the loins: Lévi-Strauss and
beyond." see 486

100 ANTHROPOLOGY

Willis Ray. "The poetry of the tree." see 487

Worsley, Peter. see 299

ARCHAISM

745 Queiroz, M. I. Pereira de. "A noção de arcaismo em etnologia e a organização social dos Xerente." *Revista de Antropologia*, vol. I, no. 2, Sao Paulo, 1953.
[Réponse de Lévi-Strauss, in *Anthropologie structurale*, chapter VI]

ATHEISM

746 Chabanis, Christian, et al. *Dieu existe-t-il? Non, répondent . . . Claude Lévi-Strauss.* Paris: Fayard, 1973, 412p.

747 Rubio Carracedo, José. "El ateismo de Lévi-Strauss." *Arbor*, vol. LXXXIX, no. 345-346, September-October 1974, pp. 43-58.

BOTANIQUE

Prado, Bento. see 563

CANNIBALISM

Shankmann, Paul. see 478

CHINESE WORLD VIEW

749 Kang, Shin-pyo. see 23

CINEMA

750 Bettitini, Gianfranco. *Cinema: lingua e scrittura.* Milano: Bompiani, 1968.

COLLECTIVE

Shalvey, Thomas J. see 83

COMMUNICATIONS

Poole, Roger. see 547

CONSCIOUSNESS

751 Conn, W. "Primitive consciousness-mythic, symbolic, and pre-logical: A cognitive analysis." *Proceedings* of the Catholic Philosophical Association, vol. XLV, 1971, pp. 146-157.

CRITIQUE

752 Brandi, Cesare. *Teoria generale della critica.* Torino: G. Einaudi, 1974.

753 Corti, Maria, e Cesare Segre, eds. *I Metodi attuali della critica in Italia.* Torino: Ediz. Radiotelevisione Italiana, 1970.

CULTURE (and Nature)

754 Derrida, Jacques. see 562

Ortigues, Edmond. "Nature et culture dans l'oeuvre de Claude Lévi-Strauss." see 706

Steinwachs, Gisela. see 512

"DAS KAPITAL"

Godelier, Maurice. see 945

DIALECTIC

Abdel-Malek, A. see 941

Caruso, Paolo. see 568

Godelier, Maurice. "Logique dialectique et analyse des structures. Réponse à Lucien Sève." see 600

Lagadec, Claude. see 801

Rubio Carracedo, José. "Estructura o dialectica?" see 584

755 Ruyer, R. "Le mythe de la raison dialectique." *Revue de Métaphysique et de Morale,* tome LXVI, nos. 1-2, janvier-juin 1961, pp. 1-35.

Tibaldi, G. see 813

Sebag, Lucien. see 959

DUALISM

Rayfield, J. R. "Dualism of Lévi-Strauss." see 720

ECOLOGY

McGinn, Thomas. see 765

EPISTEMOLOGY

De Ipola, Emilio Rafael. see 768

756 Morot-Sir, Edouard. "Essai d'épistémologie structuraliste. 3. L'anthropologie structuraliste de Lévi-Strauss," in *La Pensée française d'aujourd'hui*. Paris: Presses Universitaires de France, 1971, pp. 89-96.

757 Mosconi, J. "Analyse et genèse: Regards sur la théorie du devenir de l'entendement au XVIIIe siècle." *Cahiers pour l'Analyse*, no. 4, septembre-octobre 1966.

758 Mouloud, Noël. "La logique des structures et l'épistemologie." *Revue Internationale de Philosophie*, no. 73-74, 1965, pp. 314-334.

759 Mouloud, Noël. "L'esprit des sciences structurales et la philosophie de la raison." *Revue de Métaphysique et de Morale*, vol. LXXI, 1966, pp. 339-358.

760 Nutini, Hugo G. "On the concepts of epistemological order and coordinative definitions." *Bijdragen. Tot de Taal-, Land-, en Volkenkunde*, vol. CXXIV, no. 1, 1968, pp. 1-21.

Scholte, Bob. see 225

761 Simonis, Yvan. "Comments to Anthony Wilden, 'Structuralism as epistemology of closed systems," in 23

762 Van Loon, J. F. Glastra. "Language and the epistemological foundations of the social sciences," in *Report of the Fifteenth annual (First International) Round Table Meeting on Linguistics and Language Studies*, ed. C. I. J. M. Stuart, pp. 171-185. Washington, D.C.: Georgetown University Press, 1964.

763 Wilden, Anthony. "Structuralism as epistemology of closed system," in 23.

ETHICS

Colette, Jacques. see 311

764 Hund, William B. "Structuralism and ethics." *Proceedings of the Catholic Philosophical Association*, vol. XLVII, 1973, pp. 177-187.

765 McGinn, Thomas. "Ecology and ethics." *International Philosophical Quarterly*, vol. XIV, June 1974, pp. 149-160.

ETHNOLOGY

766 Balandier, Georges. "Sociologie, ethnologie et ethnographie," in Georges Gurvitch, ed., *Traité de Sociologie*. Paris: Presses Universitaires de France, 1958, tome I. Italian translation by L. Solaroli. Milano: Il Saggiatore, 1967.

767 Bastide, Roger. "L'ethnologie et le nouvel humanisme." *Revue Philosophique de la France et de l'Etranger*, tome 154, 1964.

768 De Ipola, Emilio Rafael. "Ethnologie et histoire dans l'epistémologie structuraliste." *Cahiers Internationaux de Sociologie*, vol. XLVIII, 1970, pp. 37-56.

769 Damisch, H. "L'horizon ethnologique." *Les Lettres Nouvelles*, no. 32, février 1963, pp. 81-106.

770 Granai, G. "La définition et la méthode de l'ethnologie." *Revue Philosophique*, vol. CXLII, 1952.

771 Guiart, J. "L'ethnologie, qu'est-elle?" *Cahiers Internationaux de Sociologie*, vol. XLII, 1968.

772 Guiart, J. "Réflexions sur la méthode en ethnologie." *Cahiers Internationaux de Sociologie*, vol. XLV, 1968.

773 Gusdorf, Georges. "Situation de Maurice Leenhardt ou l'ethnologie française de Levy-Bruhl à Lévi-Strauss." *Le Monde non-Chrétien*, juillet-décembré 1964. Reprinted in *Les Sciences de l'homme sont des sciences humaines*. Paris: Les Belles Lettres, 1967. Publications de la Faculté des lettres de l'Université de Strasbourg, Collection Petit Format, no. 1, 1967.

ETHNOLOGY

Heusch, Luc de. "L'oeuvre de M. Lévi-Strauss et l'évolution de l'ethnologie française." see 202

Makarius, Raoul and Laura Makarius. see 44

774 Makarius, Raoul, et Laura Makarius. "Ethnologie et structuralisme," in 44.

775 Miguelez, Roberto. "L'explication en ethnologie." *Social Science Information*, vol. VIII, no. 3, 1969, pp. 27-58.

776 Poirier, J. ed., *Ethnologie générale*. Encyclopédie de la Pleiade. Paris: Gallimard, 1968.

777 Remotti, Francesco. "L'etnografia di Claude Lévi-Strauss." *Libri Nuovi*, no. 8, 1970.

778 *Revue de l'Enseignement Supérieur*, "Les sciences ethnologiques." vol. III, 1965.

779 Rodinson, M. "Ethnographie et relativisme." *La Nouvelle Critique*, 1955, pp. 46-63.

EXISTENCE

Stern, Alfred. see 1029

EXISTENTIALISM

Goldmann, Lucien. see 947

780 Levin, David Michael. "On Lévi-Strauss and existentialism." *The American Scholar*, vol. XXXVIII, no. 1, Winter 1968-1969, pp. 69-82.

EXPERIENCE

781 Pochtar, Ricardo. "Acerca del concepto de experiencia en la antropologia estructural," in Emilio Sosa Lopez, ed., *Temas de filosofia contemporanea*. Buenos Aires: Editorial Sudamerica, 1971, pp. 185-205.

EVOLUTION

782 Saltini, Vittorio. "Lévi-Strauss contro l'evoluzione." *L'Espresso*, no. 45, November 8, 1970.

GOD

783 Kamstra, J. H. "Structuralisme en Godsdienstwetenschap." *Tijdschrift voor Filosofie*, vol. XXXI, December 1969, pp. 706-731.

GROUP

784 Régnier, André. "De la théorie des groupes à la pensée sauvage." *L'Homme et la Société*, no. 7, janvier-mars 1968, pp. 201-214.

785 Simonis, Yvan. "Two ways of approaching concrete reality: 'Group dynamics' and Lévi-Strauss's structuralism," in 23.

HERMENEUTICS

786 Esbroeck, Michel van. *Herméneutique, structuralisme et exégèse*. Paris: Desclée de Brouwer, 1968.

787 Fessard, G. "Le fondement de l'herméneutique." *Archivio di Filosofia*, nos. 1-2, 1963.

788 Fialkowski, Aldine. "Structuralisme et herméneutique." *Esprit*, 34e année, 1966, pp. 16-30.

789 Kockelmans, Joseph J. "On myth and its relationship to hermeneutics." *Cultural Hermeneutics*, vol. I, April 1973, pp. 47-86.

790 Ricoeur, Paul. "Structure et herméneutique." *Esprit*, 31e année, no. 322, novembre 1963, pp. 596-627. Portuguese translation, "Strutura e hermeneutica," in Luis Costa Lima, *O Estruturalismo de Lévi-Strauss*. Petropolis: Vozes, 1969, pp. 157-191.

791 Ricoeur, Paul. "Symbole et temporalité." *Archivio di Filosofia*, no. 1-2, 1963. Reprinted above.

HISTORY

Bell, J. H. see 632

792 Besançon, A. "Vers une histoire psychanalytique." *Annales (Econimies-Sociétés-Civilisations)*, no. 3, mai-juin 1969.

106 HISTORY

793   Braudel, F. "Histoire et sciences sociales. La longue
      durée." *Annales (Economies--Sociétés--Civilisations)*,
      no. 4, 1958.

      Cotroneo, Girolamo. see 944

794   D'Amico, Robert. Consciousness and history. Phenomeno-
      logical and structuralist philosophies of the human
      sciences. Ph.D. dissertation, SUNY at Buffalo, 1974.
      Dissertation Abstracts International, vol. XXXVI, no. 3,
      September 1975, p. 1575-A.

      De Ipola, Emilio Rafael. see 77

      De Ipola, Emilio Rafael. see 768

      Edmond, Michel-Pierre. "L'anthropologie structuraliste et
      l'histoire." see 656

795   Finley, M. I. *The Use and abuse of history. From the
      myths of the Greeks to Lévi-Strauss*. New York: Viking,
      1975.

796   Gaboriau, Marc. "Anthropologie structurale et histoire."
      Esprit, 31e année, no. 322, novembre 1963, pp. 579-595.
      English translation, "Structural anthropology and history,"
      in Michael Lane, ed., *Structuralism: A reader*. London:
      Cape, 1970, New York: Basis Books, 1970, pp. 156-159.
      Portuguese translation, "Antropologia estrutural e
      historia," in Luiz Costa Lima, *O Estruturalismo de Lévi-
      Strauss*. Petropolis: Vozes, 1969, pp. 140-156.

797   Godelier, Maurice. "Mythe et histoire." *Annales,
      (Economies--Sociétés--Civilisations)*, 26e année, mai-
      août, 1971, pp. 541-552.
      English translation, "Myth and history." *New Left Review*,
      no. 69, September-October 1971, pp. 93-112.

798   Green, André. "La psychanalyse devant l'opposition de
      l'histoire et de la structure." *Critique*, vol. XIX,
      no. 194, juillet 1963, pp. 648-662.

799   Heusch, Luc de. "Histoire et technique." *Les Temps
      Modernes*, no. 211, 1963, pp. 1022-1037. Reprinted in
      Pourquoi l'épouser? et autres essais. Paris: Gallimard,
      1971, pp. 141-154.

800 Jacob, André. "Nature et histoire à la lumière de la linguistique." *Revue de Métaphysique et de Morale*, vol. LXVI, 1961, no. 3.

801 Lagadec, Claude. "Histoire, structure et dialectique." *Dialogue*, vol. IV, no. 1, June 1965, pp. 26-47.

802 Lanteri-Laura, G. "Histoire et structure dans la connaissnace de l'homme." *Annales (Economies--Sociétés--Civilisations)*, no. 3, mai-juin 1967.

802a Lanteri-Laura, G. "History and structure in anthropological knowledge." *Social Research*, vol. XXXIV, 1967, pp. 115-161.

803 Lefebvre, Henri. "Réflexions sur le structuralisme et l'histoire." *Cahiers Internationaux de Sociologie*, vol. XXXV, juillet-décembre 1963, pp. 3-24.

Lefort, Claude. "Sociétés sans histoire et historicité." see 211

804 Locher, G. W. "De Antropoloog Lévi-Strauss en het probleem van de geschiedenis." *Forum der Letteren*, November 1961.

805 Medina, Angel. "Demythologizing history." *Proceedings of the Catholic Philosophical Association*, vol. XLV, 1971, pp. 139-146.

806 Morazé, Charles. "L'histoire et l'unité des sciences de l'homme." *Annales (Economies--Sociétés--Civilisations)*, no. 2, mars-avril 1968.

Greimas, A.-J. see STRUCTURE

Nutini, Hugo G. "Structural history: A programmatic synthesis of the nomothetic and idiographic elements of anthropological studies." see 703

807 Parain-Vial, Jeanne. "Structuralisme et histoire." *La Pensée* (numéro spécial consacré au structuralisme), no. 135, octobre 1967, pp. 38-52.

Poster, Mark. "Althusser on history without man." see 503

Pouillon, Jean. see 581

108 HISTORY

808 *Raison Présente,* "Structure sociale et histoire." No. 7, 1968. [Labrousse, Goldman, Martinet, Soboul, Vidal-Naquet, Reberloux]

809 Ravis, G. "L'anthropologie et l'histoire (Réflexions sur Claude Lévi-Strauss)." *La Nouvelle Critique,* no. 25, juin 1969.

Remotti, Francesco. see 64

Rossi, Ino. "Structure and history in *'The Elementary Structures of kinship'.*" see 200

Rosen, Lawrence. see 583

Schintholzer, Birgit. see 81

Schmidt, Alfred. see 56 and 68

810 Sebag, Lucien. "Histoire et structure." *Les Temps Modernes,* no. 195, août 1962.

Scholte, Bob. see 728

Solimini, Maria Ponzio. see 731

811 Vidal-Naquet, P. "Application et limites du structuralisme à l'histoire. Un cas, un exemple: la Sparte archaïque et classique." *Raison Présente,* no. 7, 1968, pp. 59-62.

812 Védrine, Hélène. *Les Philosophes et l'histoire.* Paris: Petite Bibliothèque Payot, 1974.

813 Tibaldi, G. "Storia e dialettica." *Il Mulino,* vol. XIII, no. 9, 1964, pp. 969-973.

814 Topolski, Jerzy. "Lévi-Strauss and Marx on history." *History and Theory,* vol. XII, 1973, pp. 192-207.

815 White, Hayden. "Interpretation in history." *New Literary History,* vol. IV, no. 2, Winter 1973, pp. 281-314.

HUMAN NATURE

Bastide, Roger. see 97

HUMANISM

Akoun, A. A. et al. see 830

816 Pautasso, S. "Il nuovo umanesimo di Claude Lévi-Strauss," in Georges Charbonnier- Claude Lévi-Strauss, *Colloqui*, trad, it. di B. Garufi. Milano: Silva, 1966.

IDEOLOGY (see also STRUCTURALISM)

817 Cacciari, M. e F. Dal Co. "Lévi-Strauss: strutturalismo e ideologia." *Angelus Novus*, vol. I, 1966, pp. 53-101.

818 Castel, R. "Méthode structurale et idéologies structuralistes." *Critique*, vol. XX, no. 210, novembre 1964, pp. 963-978.

819 Gritti, J. et P. Toinet. *Le Structuralisme, science ou idéologie?* Paris: Beauchesne, 1968.

820 Lepenies, Wolf. "Der französische Strukturalismus: Methode und Ideologie." *Soziale Welt*, nos. 3-4, 1968, pp. 301-327.

821 Makarius, Raoul. "Structuralism--Science or ideology?" *The Socialist Register*, 1974, Merlin Press, London, pp. 189-225.

822 Nutini, Hugo G. "The ideological bases of Lévi-Strauss's structuralism." *American Anthropologist*, vol. LXXIII, no. 3, 1971, pp. 537-544. [see Rossi's reply]

823 Nutini, Hugo G. "Science and ideology." *Bijdragen. Tot de Taal-, Land-, en Volkenkunde*, vol. CXXVII, no. 1, 1971, pp. 1-14.

824 Parain-Vial, Jeanne. *Analyses structurales et idéologies structuralistes.* Toulouse: Privat, 1969.

825 Rossi, Ino. "Reply to Nutini's 'The ideological basis of Lévi-Strauss's structuralism." *American Anthropologist*, vol. LXXIV, 1972, pp. 784-787.

826 Rubio Carracedo, José. "Lévi-Strauss--ciencia o ideologia?" *Arbor*, no. 301, January 1971, pp. 17-25.

INCEST (see *Les Structures élémentaires de la parenté*)

Bataille, Georges. see 180

110 INCEST

827 Guier, Jorgé Enrique. "Incesto, matrimonio y derecho."
     see 198

828 Heusch, Luc de. *Essais sur le symbolisme de l'inceste
     royal.* Bruxelles, 1958.

829 Schechner, R. "Incest and culture: A reflection on Claude
     Lévi-Strauss." *The Psychoanalytic Review*, vol. LVIII,
     1971-1972, pp. 563-572.

     Simonis, Yvan. see 84

     Simonis, Yvan. see 48

INFRASTRUCTURE

     Dyson-Hudson, Neville. see 556

     Haudricourt, A. G. "Sur le degré d'immanence des infra-
     structures," pp. 606-608 in vol. I, Pouillon et Maranda.
     see 660.

     Makarius, Raoul. "Parenté et infrastructure." see 684

INTERVIEW

830 Akoun, A. A., and Morin, F., and Mousseau, J. "A conver-
     sation with Claude Lévi-Strauss: The father of struc-
     tural anthropology takes a misanthropic view of lawless
     humanism." *Psychology Today*, vol. V, no. 12, 1972,
     pp. 37-39, 74-82.

831 Anonymous. "*L'Express* va plus loin avec Claude Lévi-
     Strauss." *L'Express*, no. 1027, 15-21 mars, 1971, pp. 60-
     66.

832 Anonymous. "Myth and meaning." *The Sunday Times*,
     no. 7694, November 15, 1970, p. 27.

833 Bellour, Raymond. "Entretien avec Claude Lévi-Strauss."
     Les Lettres Françaises, no. 1165, 12 janvier 1967.
     Reprinted in *Le Livre des autres*. Paris: Edition de
     l'Herne, 1971, pp. 145-161.

834 Bellour, Raymond. "Entretien avec Claude Lévi-Strauss."
     Les Lettres Françaises, no. 1187, 15 juin 1967. Reprinted
     in *Le livre des autres.*

835 Bellour, Raymond. "Entretien avec Claude Lévi-Strauss." *Les Lettres Françaises*, no. 1125, 31 mars 1966.

Bellour, Raymond. see 381

836 Bellour, Raymond. "Lévi-Strauss: 'Wie arbeite der menschliche Geist? Eine Gespräch with Raymond Bellour," in Adelbert Reif, ed., *Antworten der Strukturalisten*. Hamburg: Hoffman and Campe, 1973, pp. 75-88.

837 Caruso, Paolo. "Interview de Claude Lévi-Strauss avec Paolo Caruso." *Aut Aut*, no. 77, September 1963, pp. 27-45. Reprinted in P. Caruso, *Conversazioni con C. Lévi-Strauss, M. Foucault, J. Lacan*. Milano: Mursia, 1969.

Cahiers de Philosophie, Numéro spécial: Anthropologie, janvier, no. 1, 1966. see 641

838 Caruso, Paolo. "L'umanità si avvicina a se stessa." *Rinascità*, supplemento culturale, no. 5, Roma, May 29, 1965.

839 Caruso, Paolo. "Exploring Lévi-Strauss: Interview." *Atlas*, vol. XI, April 1966, pp. 245-246.

840 Caruso, Paolo. "Interview with Lévi-Strauss." *Paese Sera-Libri*, January 20, 1967. Reprinted in P. Caruso, *Conversazioni con C. Lévi-Strauss*. see 58

841 Chapsal, Madeleine. "Claude Lévi Strauss," in *Les Ecrivains en personne*. Paris: René Julliard-Union Générale d'Editions, 1973, pp. 153-167.

Charbonnier, Georges. see 28

842 "Confrontations over myth," in *New Left Review*, no. 62, June-August 1970, pp. 57-74. Translated from *Esprit* (Ricoeur, Cuisenier, Gaboriau, Faye, Conilh, Hadot)

843 Daix, Pierre. "L'anthropologie pour quoi faire? Lévi-Strauss invité du dimanche." *Les Lettres Françaises*, no. 1392, 30 juin-6 juillet 1971, p. 18.

Daix, Pierre. "Entretien avec Lévi-Strauss sur les *Mythologiques I*." see 403

Daix, Pierre. "Entretien avec Lévi-Strauss sur les *Mythologiques II*." see 404

INTERVIEW

844 Delahaye, M. et J. Rivette. "Entretien avec Claude
    Lévi-Strauss." *Les Cahiers du Cinéma*, tome 26, no. 156,
    1964.

845 *Diacritics*. "Interview with Claude Lévi-Strauss."
    Diacritics, vol. I, no. 1, Fall 1971, pp. 44-50.

846 Dreyfus, Catherine. "'We no longer know how to bring our
    children into the world we have built'. Interview with
    Lévi-Strauss, edited by C. Dreyfus." *Mademoiselle*,
    vol. LXXI, August 1970, pp. 236-237, 324.

847 Dumur, Guy. "A contre-courant." *Le Nouvel Observateur*,
    no. 115, 25-31 janvier, 1967, pp. 30-32.

848 *Fiera Letteraria*. "Intervista con Lévi-Strauss." March 14,
    1968.

849 Gwell, Eugène. "Les clefs du mystère humain. Un entretien
    avec Claude Lévi-Strauss." *Le Patriote Illustré*
    (Bruxelles), no. 35, 27 août 1967, p. 3045, col. 3.

850 Gasbarro, Micola, e Francesco Maiello: "Intervista con
    Lévi-Strauss." *Il Ponte*, vol. XXX, 1974, pp. 65-77.

851 Hiatt, R. "Exchange between Lévi-Strauss and Hiatt,"
    in R. Lee and I. DeVore, eds., *Man the Hunter*. Chicago:
    Aldine Publishing Co., 1968, pp. 210-212.

852 Jacob, François, and Claude Lévi-Strauss. "François Jacob
    et Claude Lévi-Strauss face á face," *Le Figaro
    Littéraire*, no. 1338, 7 janvier, 1972, pp. 13, 16.

853 Kukukdjian, George. "'Le problème ultime des sciences de
    l'homme consistera un jour à ramener la pensée à la
    vie." [Propos recueillis par G. Kukukdjian]. *Le
    Magazine Littéraire*, no. 58, november 1971, pp. 22-29.

854 Lapouge, Gilles. "Claude Lévi-Strauss collectionne
    infatigablement les mythes." *Le Figaro Littéraire*,
    2 février, 1967.

855 Mallet, Francine. "Entretien avec Claude Lévi-Strauss."
    Le Magazine Littéraire, no. 4, février 1967, pp. 42-44.

856 Moonan, Wendy, et al. "An interview with Claude Lévi-
    Strauss." *University Review*, vol. X, 1971, pp. 21-23.

857 Newman, Edwin. "Interview with Claude Lévi-Strauss."
   W.N.B.C. Television. *Speaking Freely.* September 17,
   1971, pp. 1-23.

858 Pouillon, Jean. "L'homme habillé par le mythe: Entretien
   avec C. Lévi-Strauss." *Les Nouvelles Littéraires*, 49e
   année, no. 2297, 1er octobre 1971, pp. 14-15.
   German translation, "Der Mensch, bekleider durch den
   Mythos. Ein Gespräch mit Jean-Pouillon," in Adelbert
   Reif, ed., *Antworten der Strukturalisten.* Hamburg:
   Hoffman and Campe, 1973, pp. 105-110.

859 Rambures, J.-L. "Comment travaillent les écrivains:
   Claude Lévi-Strauss." *Le Monde*, 21 juin 1974.

860 Steiner, George. "A conversation with Claude Lévi-Strauss."
   Encounter, vol. XXVI, no. 4, April 1966, pp. 32-38.

861 Tanneguy de Quenétain. "Claude Lévi-Strauss: Interview."
   Réalités, (Paris), janvier 1965.
   Italian translation in *A.B.C.* (Milano), February 1965.

862 Tréguier, Michel. "Entrevue radiodiffusée avec Michel
   Tréguer, dans la série 'Un Certain Regard', hiver 1968.
   Reprinted in Catherine Backès-Clément, *Claude Lévi-
   Strauss ou la structure et le malheur.* Paris: Seghers,
   1970, pp. 172-188.

863 Tréguier, Michel. "Vivre et parler. Un débat entre
   François Jacob, Roman Jokobson, Claude Lévi-Strauss et
   Philippe l'Héritier, sous la direction de Michel
   Tréguier." *Les Lettres Françaises*, no. 1221, 14-21
   février 1968.
   German translation, "Leben und Sprechen. Eine Diskussion
   unter Leitung von Michel Tréguier," in Adelbert Reif,
   ed., *Antworten der Strukturalisten.* Hamburg: Hoffman
   and Campe, 1973, pp. 45-70.

864 Verón, Eliseo. "La antropologia, hoy: entrevista a
   Claude Lévi-Strauss." *Cuestiones de Filosofía*, vol. I,
   nos. 2-3, Buenos Aires, 1962.

865 Weightman, John. "Visit to Lévi-Strauss." *Encounter*,
   vol. XXXVI, Fall 1971, pp. 38-42.

866 Zehraoui, Absene. "'Le structuralisme n'est pas une
   philosophie': Entretien avec C. Lévi-Strauss.
   Témoignage Chrétien, no. 1241, jeudi, 18 avril 1968,
   pp. 17-18.

KINSHIP

867 Abell, Peter. "The structural balance of the kinship systems of some primitive peoples," in Michael Lane, ed., *Structuralism: A reader*, London: Cape, 1970, pp. 359-366. *Introduction to Structuralism*. New York: Basic Books, 1970, pp. 359-366.

Barnes, J. A. *Three Styles in the study of kinship.* see 628

868 Buchler, Ira R., and Henry A. Selby. *Kinship and social organization: An introduction to Method and theory.* New York: Macmillan, 1968.

869 Buchler, Ira R., and R. Freeze. "Measuring the development of kinship terminologies: Scalogram and transformational accounts." *American Anthropologist*, vol. LXVI, 1966, ppl 765-788.

870 Buchler, Ira R. "A formal account of the Hawaiian- and Eskimo-type kinship terminologies." *Southwestern Journal of Anthropology*, vol. XX, 1964, pp. 286-318.

Fox, Robin. see 195

Muller, Jean-Claude. "On preferential/prescriptive marriage and the function of kinship systems: The rukuba case (Benue Plateau State, Nigeria)." see 697

White H. *An Anatomy of kinship: Mathematical models for structures of cumulated roles.* see 233

KNOWLEDGE (see also EPISTEMOLOGY)

871 Bourdieu, Pierre. "Structuralism and theory of sociological knowledge." *Social Research*, vol. XXXV, 1968, pp. 681-705.

LANGUAGE

872 Ardener, Edwin. "Introductory essay. Social anthropology and language," in *Social Anthropology and Language*, edited by Edwin Ardener. London, New York: Tavistock Publications, 1971.

873 Aubenque, Pierre. "Language, structures, société. Remarques sur le structuralisme." *Archives de Philosophie*, tome 34, juillet-septembre 1971, pp. 353-371.

874 *Bulletin de la Société française de Philosophie.* "Le langage et l'immanence." no. 1, janvier-mars, 1965.

875 Chomsky, Noam. *Language and Mind.* New York: Harcourt, Brace and World, 1968.

876 Culler, Jonathan D. "The linguistic basis of structuralism," in David Robey, ed., *Structuralism: an introduction.* Oxford Clarendon Press, 1973, pp. 20-36.

877 Denat, Antoine. "Critique littéraire et langage philosophique," in *Vu des antipodes. Synthèses critiques.* Paris: Didier, 1969, pp. 28-47.

Derrida, Jacques. see 562

Derrida, Jacques. see 121

878 Donato, Eugenio. "The two languages of criticism," in Richard Macksey and Eugenio Donato, eds., *The Language of criticism and the sciences of man: The structuralist controversy.* Baltimore: Johns Hopkins Press, 1969, pp. 89-97; discussion pp. 110-124.

879 Duvignaud, Jean. *Le langage perdu.* Paris: Presses Universitaires de France, 1973.

880 Edeline, Francis. "Poésie et language (XIX)." *Le Journal des Poètes,* 37e année, no. 3, avril 1967, p. 18.

881 Fontaine de Visscher, Luce. "Des privilèges d'une grammatologie." *Revue Philosophique de Louvain,* vol. LXVII, août 1969, pp. 461-474.

882 Leach, Edmund R. "Anthropological aspects of language: Animal categories and verbal abuse," in Eric H. Lenneberg, editor, *New Directions in the study of language.* Cambridge, Mass.: M.I.T. Press, 1964, pp. 23-63.

883 Leach, Edmund R. "Language and anthropology," in M. Minnis, ed., *Linguistics at Large.* London: Gollancz, 1971, pp. 137-158.

884 Lefebvre, Henri. *Le Langage et la société.* Paris: Gallimard, 1966.

LANGUAGE

885 Macksey, Richard, and Eugenio Donato, eds. *The Language of criticism and the sciences of Man: The Structuralist controversy.* Baltimore: Johns Hopkins Press, 1970.

886 Maci, Guillermo A. "Analisis estructural y filosofia del lenguaje." *Cuadernos de Filosofia,* vol. XII, January-June 1972, pp. 41-61, Buenos Aires.

887 Moore, O. K. and David L. Olmstead. "Language and Professor Lévi-Strauss." *American Anthropologist,* vol. LIV, 1952, pp. 116-119.

888 Mouloud, Noël. *Langage et structures.* Paris: Payot, 1969.

889 Pochtar, Ricardo. "Experiencia del lenguaje y pasividad." *Cuadernos de Filosofia* (Buenos Aires), vol. IX, July-December 1969, pp. 245-262.

890 Poole, Roger C. "Lévi-Strauss: Myth's magician. The language of anthropology." *New Blackfriars,* vol. L, no. 588, May 1969, pp. 432-440.

891 Poole, Roger C. "The language of anthropology," in Anthony Rudolf, ed., *Languages.* Cambridge Opinion Circuit Publication." London: Circuit Magazine, 1969, pp. 21-26.

892 *Raison Présente,* "Sciences du langage et sciences humaines," (articles de Zazzo, Bresson, Culioli, Lefebvre, Martinet).

Rosen, Lawrence. see 583

893 Uscatescu, Jorgé. "El discurso expresionista." *Estafeta Literaria,* no. 525, October 1, 1973, pp. 4-9.

Van Loon, J. F. Glastra. "Language and the epistemological foundations of the social sciences." see 762

LAW

894 Arnaud, A. J. "Structuralisme et droit." *Archives de Philosophie du Droit,* vol. XIII, 1968, pp. 282-301.

895 Mora, Fernando. "Estructuralismo y derecho." *Revista de Filosofía de la Universidad de Costa Rica,* vol. XI, no. 32, January-June 1973, pp. 163-184.

LEFT

896 Furet, François. "Les intellectuels français et le structuralisme." *Preuves*, no. 192, février 1967, pp. 3-12.
English translation, "The French Left." *Survey*, no. 62, 1967, pp. 72-83.

897 Furet, François. "La gauche meurt-elle d'avoir gagné? . . . Un entretien avec Raymond Aron." *Le Nouvel Observateur*, no. 120, 1-8 mars, 1967, pp. 40-44.

898 Améry, Jean. "Französische Sozialphilosophie im Zeichen der 'Linken Frustration'." *Merkur*, no. 215, 1966, pp. 161-177.

899 Puccetti, Roland. "Man, political man, and the luminaries of the 'New Left'," *Mosaic*, vol. IV, no. 4, Summer 1971, pp. 119-127. [Camus, Fanon, Lévi-Strauss]

LINGUISTIC(S)

900 Bermejo, José Maria. "Linguística." *Estafeta Literaria*, no. 512, March 15, 1973, p. 128.

Brogger, J. "Linguistics and social anthropology." see 638

Culler, Jonathan D. see 876

901 Dinnen, Francis P. *An Introduction to General Linguistics*. New York: Holt, Rinehart, and Winston, 1967.

902 Durbin, Marshall. "'Comments' to Georges Mounin, "Lévi-Strauss' use of linguistics," (see 908) in 23.

903 Dubois, Jean. "Structuralisme et linguistique." *La Pensée*, no. 135, 1967, pp. 19-28.

904 Haudricourt, A., and G. Granai. "Linguistique et sociologie." *Cahiers Internationaux de Sociologie*, vol. XIX, 1955, pp. 114-129. [Response of Lévi-Strauss in *Anthropologie Structurale*, chapter V]

LINGUISTIC(S)

905 Hymes, Dell H. "Directions in ethnolinguistic theory," in Transcultural studies in cognition, ed. A. K. Rommey and R. G. D'Andrade. *American Anthropologist*, vol. LXVI, no. 3, part 2, 1964, pp. 6-56. [special issue]

906 Hymes, Dell H. "Linguistic method in ethnography," in Paul L. Garvin, ed., *Method and Theory in Linguistics*. The Hague: Mouton, 1967, pp. 249-325.

907 Hymes, Dell H. *Language in culture and society. A reader in linguistics and Anthropology*. New York: Harper & Row, 1964.

Jacob, André. see 800

908 Mounin, Georges. "Lévi-Strauss' use of linguistics," in 23.

909 Mounin, Georges. "Lévi-Strauss et la linguistique," in *Introduction à la Sémiologie*. Paris: Editions de Minuit, 1970, pp. 199-214.

910 *Revista de Filologia Española*, "Problemas y principios del estructuralismo linguistico," vol. XVI, 1967.

911 Rouboud, J. "Structuralisme et linguistique (Invitation à la lecture de Noam Chomsky)." *Les Lettres Françaises*, no. 1218, janvier 1968.

912 Ruwet, Nicolas. "Linguistique et sciences de l'homme." *Esprit*, 31e année, no. 322, novembre 1963, pp. 564-578. Portuguese translation, "Linguistica e ciencias do homen," in Luiz Costa Lima, *O Estruturalismo de Lévi-Strauss*. Petropolis: Vozes, 1969, pp. 78-93.

913 Pawowski, Tadeusz. "Linguistics and the semiotic theory." *Scientia*, vol. CIX, 1974, pp. 483-487.

914 Ruwet, Nicolas. "Musicology and linguistics." *International Social Science Journal*, vol. XIX, 1967, pp. 79-87.

Solimini, Maria Ponzio. see 731

915 Sommerfelt, Alfred. "Linguistic structures and the structures of social groups." *Diogenes*, vol. LI, 1965, pp. 186-192.

916 Tullio-Altan, C. "Linguistica e antropologia culturale."
     see 741

LITERATURE

917 Bersani, Jacques, et al. *La Littérature en France depuis 1945.* Paris, Montr al, Bruxelles, Lausanne, London: Bordas, Asedi, Spes, Harrap, 1970.

918 Bersani, Jacques. "Is there a science of literature?" *Partisan Review*, vol. XXXIX, no. 4, Fall 1972, pp. 535-553.

919 Boisdeffre, Pierre de. *Une Anthologie vivante de la littérature d'aujourd'hui. 1945-1965.* Roman. Théâtre. Idées. Paris: Librairie Académique Perrin, 1965, 835p.

     Culler, Jonathan. see 1030

920 Detweiler, Robert. "The moment of death in modern fiction." *Contemporary Literature*, vol. XIII, no. 3, Summer 1972, pp. 269-294.

921 Donato, Eugenio. "Of structuralism and literature," in Richard Macksey, ed., *Velocities of Change. Critical Essays from MLN.* Baltimore-London: Johns Hopkins Press, 1974, pp. 153-178.

922 Girard, René. "Des formes aux structures, en littérature et ailleurs." *Modern Language Notes*, vol. LXXVIII, December 1963, pp. 504-519.

923 Girard, René. "Lévi-Strauss, Frye, Derrida, and Shakespeare criticism." *Diacritics*, vol. III, no. 3, Fall 1973, pp. 34-38.

924 Guillén, Claudio. *Literature as System. Essays toward the theory of literary history.* Princeton, N.J.: Princeton University Press, 1971.

925 Hayman, David. "Structuralist thoughts." *Novel*, vol. VI, no. 3, Spring 1973, pp. 288-290.

926 Kalisky, René. "Le théâtre climatisé." *Cahiers Renaud-Barrault*, no. 77, 3e trimestre 1971, pp. 112-123.

927 Kermode, Frank. "The structures of fiction," pp. 179-206. see 921

LITERATURE

928 'Littérature et idéologies. Colloque de Cluny, 2-4 avril, 1970. Paris: La Nouvelle Critique, 1971.

929 Literature in Revolution. Introduction by Charles Newman and George A. White. Tri-Quarterly, no. 23-24, Winter and Spring 1972.

930 Olsen, Michel. "Den strukturelle litteraurforskning," in Niels Egebak, ed., Aspekter af nyere fransk litteraturkritik. Copenhagen: Munksgaard, 1972, pp. 84-112.

931 Pinto, Evelyne. "Du mythe au roman." Revue d'Esthétique, vol. XXIV, no. 3, juillet-septembre 1971, pp. 257-268.

932 Pollmann, Leo. Literaturwissenschaft und Methode, 2 vols. Frankfurt am Main: Athenäum, 1971.

933 Rossi, A. "Structuralismo e analisi letteraria." Paragone, 1964, pp. 180-188.

934 Scholes, Robert. "The illiberal imagination." New Literary History, vol. IV, no. 3, Spring 1973, pp. 521-540.

935 Schober, Rita. Von der wirklichen Welt in der Dichtung. Aufsätze zur Theorie und Praxis des Realismus in der französischen Literatur. Berlin: Aufbau Verlag, 1970, 464p.

936 Weinrich, Harald. Literatur für Leser. Essays und Aufsätze zur Literaturwissenschaft. Stuttgart, Berlin, Koln, Main: Verlag W. Kohlhammer, 1971.

937 Zéraffa, Michel. Roman et société. Paris: Presses Universitaires de France, 1971.

938 Yurick, Sol. "The politics of the imagination: The problem of consciousness," pp. 501-551 in 929.

LOGIC

Culler, Nonathan D. "Mythologic logic." see 1030

Godelier, Maurice. see 600

939 Kobben, A. J. F. "La logique de l'analyse interstructurale." Annales, no. 3, mai-juin 1967.

940 Korn, Francis. "The logic of some concepts in Lévi-Strauss." see 668

MARRIAGE

Guier, Jorge. see 198

Kasakoff, Alice   see 666

Josseling de Jong, J. P. B. de.   see 10

MARXISM

941 Abdel-Malek, A. *La Dialectique sociale.* Paris: Editions du Seuil, 1972.

942 Axelos, Kostas. "Lucien Sebag entre le marxisme, le freudianisme, et le structuralsime." *Aletheia*, 1966, pp. 237-241.

Aron, Raymond. see 500

943 Caruso, Paolo. "Marxismo e strutturalismo, intervento sotto forma di lettera in una discussione con Galvano della Volpe." *Rinascitâ*, no. 45, November 20, 1965, p. 31.

944 Cotroneo, Girolamo. "Il marxismo fra storia e struttura." *Rivista di Studi Crociani*, vol. X, April-June 1973, pp. 184-191.

945 Godelier, Maurice. "Système, structure et contradiction dans *'Le Capital.*" *Les Temps Modernes*, no. 246, 1966. English translation by Phillip Brew, "System, structure and contradiction in *Das Kapital*," in Michael Lane, ed., *Introduction to Structuralism.*   New York: Basic Books, 1970 -London: Cape, 1970, pp. 340-358.

946 Godelier, Maurice. "Logique dialectique et analyse des structures. Réponse à Lucien Sève." *La Pensée*, no. 149, février 1970, pp. 3-28.

947 Goldmann, Lucien. "Structuralisme, marxisme, existentialisme." *L'Homme et la Société*, no. 2, 1966, pp. 105-124.

948 Goldmann, Lucien. *Marxisme et sciences humaines.* Paris: Gallimard, 1970.
English, *The Human Sciences and philosophy.* London: Jonathan Cape, 1969.

MARXISM

949 Gruppi, Luciano. "Structuralisme et marxisme." (Revue
     du numéro spécial de *La Pensée*) *Rinascità*, no. 49,
     December 15, 1967, pp. 23-24.

950 Heusch, Luc de. "Signes, réciprocité et marxisme,"
     in *Pourquoi l'épouser et autres essais*. Paris:
     Gallimard, 1971, pp. 86-140.

     Lepenies, Wolf. see 543

951 Murphy, R. F. "On Zen Marxism." *Man*, vol. LXIII, no. 21,
     February 1963, pp. 17-19.

952 *(La) Pensée*, "Structuralisme et marxisme, numéro spécial,
     no. 135, octobre 1967.

953 Pompeo Faracovi, Ornella. *Il Marxismo francese contem-
     poraneo fra dialettica e struttura (1945-1968)*. Milano:
     Feltrinelli, 1970.

954 Pieri, Sergio. Review of Ornella Pompeo Faracovi (see
     above). *Giornale Critico della Filosofia Italiana*,
     vol. LII, January-March 1973, pp. 145-149.

955 Pouillon, Jean. "Vers une théorie marxiste." *Les Temps
     Modernes*, mai 1966, pp. 1952-1982.

956 Pouillon, Jean. "Du côté de chez Marx." *Les Temps
     Modernes*, mai 1966, pp. 2002-2012.

     Schmidt, Alfred. see 56 and 68

957 Sebag, Lucien. *Marxisme et structuralisme*. Paris: Payot,
     1964.
     Italian translation, *Marxismo e strutturalismo*.

     Review:
958   Alessandro Di Caro, *Gironale di Metafisica*, vol.
        XXIX, March-June 1974, pp. 261-267.

959 Sebag, Lucien. "Méthode structurale et méthode dialec-
     tique." *La Pensée*, no. 135, Octobre 1967, pp. 63-93.

960 Sève, Lucien. "Réponse à Maurice Godelier." *La Pensée*,
     no. 149, février 1970, pp. 29-50. see 946

961 Simonis, Yvan. "Marxisme et structuralisme." *Frères du
     Monde*, no. 45, 1967, pp. 7-35.

962 Suret-Canale, J. "Marxisme et structuralsism." *Clarté*, no. 10, 1967.

Tibaldi, G. see 813

Topolski, Jerzy. see 814

Veltmeyer, Henry. see 502

Zimmermann, Marc Jay. see 529

MASK

963 Jallat, Jeannine. "Le masque ou l'art du déplacement. D'après un article de Jean Starobinski." *Poétique. Revue de Théorie et d'Analyse Littéraire*, no. 8, 1971, pp. 479-488.

MATHEMATICS

964 Barbut, Marc. "Sur le sens du mot structure en mathématique." *Les Temps Modernes*, 22e année, 1966, pp. 791-814.

965 De Vita, R. "Discorso matematico e scienze sociali," in *Strutturalismo filosofico*, a cura del Centro di Studi Filosofici de Gallarate. Padova: Ed. Gregoriana, 1970.

Hoffmann, Hans. "Mathematical anthropology." see 662

METHOD

Krader, Lawrence. see 1095

966 Rossi, Ino. "Structuralism as scientific method," in 23.

Tennekes, J. see 739

MIND

Chomsky, Noam. see 875

967 Fleischmann, Eugene. "L'esprit humain selon Claude Lévi-Strauss." *Archives Européennes de Sociologie*, tome VII, no. 1, 1966, pp. 27-57.
German translation, "Claude Lévi-Strauss über den menschlichen Geist," pp. 77-109 in Wolf Lepenies und Hanns H. Ritter, eds., *Orte des Wilden Denkens*. see BOOK

Makarius, Raoul et Laura Makarius. see 682

968 Tally-Crampe, Michèle. "La notion de structure mentale dans les travaux de Claude Lévi-Strauss." *La Pensée*, no. 135, 1967, pp. 53-62.

MODEL

969 Auger, Pierre. "Les modèles dans les sciences." *Diogène*, no. 52, 1966.

970 Badiou, Alain. *Le Concept de modèle*. Paris: François Maspero, 1968.

971 Eco, Umberto. "Modelli e strutture." *Il Verri*, no. 20, pp. 11-28. [Metaphysical character of structuralism]

972 Granger, Georges. *Modèles abstracts et science appliquée*. Paris: Fondation Nationale des Sciences Politiques, Groupe d'étude methodologiques, 1960.

973 Korn, Frances. "An analysis of the use of the term 'model' in some of Lévi-Strauss's work." *Bijdgragen. Tot de Taal-, Land-, en Volkenkunde*, vol. LXXV, 1969, pp. 1-11.

974 Kongas, Elli-Kaija, and Pierre Maranda. "Structural model in folklore." *Midwest Folklore*, vol. XII, no. 3, 1962, pp. 133-192.

975 Remotti, Francesco. "Modelli e strutture nell'antropologia di Claude Lévi-Strauss." *Rivista di Filosofia*, vol. LIX, October-December 1968, pp. 401-437.

Schneider, David M. "Some muddles in the model: or, how the system really works." see 727

Nutini, Hugo G. see 535a

976 Banton, Michael, ed. *The Relevance of models for social anthropology*. London: Tavistock Publications -New York: Frederick A. Prager, 1965.

Schrag, Calvin O. see 1059

Ward, B. E. "Varieties of the conscious model: The Fisherman of South China." see 744

MUSIC (and MUSICOLOGY)

977 Deliège, Célestin. "La musicologie devant le structuralsime." *L'Arc*, no. 26, 1965, pp. 50-59.

     Lefeuvre, Michel. see 545

     Prado, Bento. see 563

     Ruwet, Nicolas. "Musicology and linguistics." see 914

978 Schiwy, Günther. "Neue Ergebnisse des Strukturalismus: Mythos und Musik und Fragen der literarischen Rezeption." *Wissenschaft und Weltbild*, 25. Jahrg., Heft 2, April-Juni 1972, pp. 113-122.

MYTH (see also MYTHOLOGIQUES)

979 Anonymous. "Structural study of myth." *Journal of American Folklore*, vol. LXVIII, October 1955, pp. 428-444.

980 Anonymous. "Myth and meaning: Claude Lévi-Strauss." *Sunday Times*, November 15, 1970, p. 27.

981 Bourdillon, Michael. "Lévi-Strauss and myth." *The Month*, vol. CCXXV, no. 1207, March 1968, pp. 149-163.

982 Boon, James A. "Poetic everyman: By way of the modern poem (and language) to regain a sense of myth," pp. 62-107 in no. 1.

983 Buchler, Ira R., and Henry A. Selby. *A Formal study of myth*. Center for International Studies of Folklore and Oral History, Monograph Series, no. 1. Austin: University of Texas, 1968.

984 Burridge, K. O. L. "Lévi-Strauss and myth," in Edmund R. Leach, ed., *The Structural Study of Myth and Totemism*. London: Tavistock Publications, 1967, pp. 91-115.

     Calogeras, R. C. see 390

     "Confrontations over myth." see 842

985 Conley, Tom. "The sunset of myth: Lévi-Strauss in the arenas," in *20th Century French Fiction*. Essays for Germaine Brée, edited and with an introduction by George Stanbolean. New Brunswick, N.J.: Rutgers University Press, 1975, pp. 223-240.

Cohen, Percy S. "Theories of myth." see 646

Cordero, Rodrigo. "Mito y totemismo en Sigmund Freud y Claude Lévi-Strauss." see 291

Cruz, Juan Cruz. "Sentido antropologico del mito." see 402

Douglas, Mary. see 282

Dundes, A. *The Morphology of North-American folktales*. see 655

986 *Esprit*, "Le mythe aujourd'hui." no. 4, 1971. [Articles by Barthes, Calvino, Rabant Ramnoux, Lévi-Strauss, Boyer, etc.]

Fischer, John L. "The psychosocial analysis of folktales." see 659

987 Gardner, Howard. "The structural analysis of protocols and myths. A comparison of the methods of Jean-Piaget and Claude Lévi-Strauss." *Semantics*, vol. V, 1972, pp. 31-57.

Gilsenan, M. see 654

Godelier, Maurice. "Mythe et histoire." see 797

988 Izard, Michel. "A l'écoute des mythes." *Le Nouvel Observateur*, no. 366, 15-21 novembre 1971, pp. 46-48.

Kirk, G. S. "Lévi-Strauss and the structural approach." see 433

Kockelmans, Joseph J. "On myth and its relationship to hermeneutics." see 789

989 Leach, Edmund R. "Genesis as myth," in *Genesis as Myth and other essays*. London: Jonathan Cape, 1962, pp. 7-24.

990 Leach, Edmund R., ed. "Introduction," VII-XIX, *The Structural study of myth and totemism*. London: Tavistock Publications, 1967.

991 Leach, Edmund R. "Lévi-Strauss in the Garden of Eden: An examination of some recent developments in the analysis of myth." *Transactions of the New York Academy of Sciences*, series 2, vol. XXIII, no. 4, 1961, pp. 386-396. Reprinted in E. N. Hayes and T. Hayes, eds., *Claude Lévi-Strauss: The anthrolopogist as hero*. Cambridge, Mass. -London: The M.I.T. Press, 1970, pp. 47-60.

992 Leach, Edmund R. "The legitimacy of Solomon," in *Genesis of Myth and other Essays*. London: Jonathan Cape, 1962.

993 Maquet, Jacques. "Isomorphism and symbolism as 'explanations' of myths," in 23.

994 Nathorst, Bertel. *Formal or structural studies of traditional tales:* The usefulness of some methodological proposals advanced by Vladimir Propp, Alan Dundes, Claude Lévi-Strauss, and Edmund Leach. Stockholm Studies in Comparative Religion, no. 9. Stockholm: Almqvist and Wiksell, 1969.

Pinto, Evelyne. see 931

995 Pouillon, Jean. "L'analyse des mythes." *L'Homme*, vol. VI, no. 1, 1966, pp. 100-106.

996 Pouwer, Jan. "L'analyse des mythes: A rejoinder." *Bijdragen. Tot de Taal-, Land-, en Volkenkunde*, vol. CXXII, 1966, pp. 151-157.

997 Renaud-Vernet, O. "Lévi-Strauss et la pensée mythique." *La Gazette de Lausanne*, juin 1965.

Robinson, Marguerite S. see 721

Scarduelli, Pietro. see 67

998 Salman, D. H. "Pensée mythique." *Revue des Sciences Philosophiques et Théologiques*, tome XLIX, no. 4, 1965.

Scholte, Bob. see 472 and 473

999 Sebag, Lucien. "Le mythe: Code et message." *Les Temps Modernes*, 20 année, 1965, pp. 1607-1623.

MYTH

1000 Shalvey, Thomas J. "Lévi-Strauss and mythology." *Proceedings of American Catholic Philosophical Association*, vol. XLV, 1971, pp. 114-119.

1001 Smith, Pierre. "The nature of myths." *Diogenes*, no. 82, Summer 1973, pp. 70-837

1002 Torrance, John. "Rationality and the structural analysis of myth." *AES*, vol. VIII, no. 2, 1967.

1003 Weinrich, Harald. "Structures narratives du mythe." *Poétique*, no. 1, 1970, pp. 25-44.

1004 Schwimmer, Erik. "Objects of mediation: Myth and praxis," in 23.

NARRATIVE

1005 Boon, James A. "Lévi-Strauss and 'narrative'," *Man*, vol. V, no. 4, 1970, pp. 702-703.

NATIVES

   McNelly, Cleo. see 259

NATURE

   Derrida, Jacques. see 562

   Ortigues, Edmond. see 706

   Steinwachs, Gisela. see 512

"NOUVELLE CRITIQUE" (la)

1006 Corti, Maria, e Cesare Segre, eds. *I Metodi attuali della critica in Italia*. Torino: Ediz. Radiotelevisione Italiana, 1970.

1007 "Lévi-Strauss et la 'nouvelle critique'." *Le Monde*, no. 6510, 18 décembre 1965, p. 13. Reprinted from *Paragone*, April 1965.

1008 *Quatre Conférences sur la nouvelle critique*. Torino: Societa Editrice Internazionale 1968, 73p. Supplemento al no. 34 di *Studi Francesi*, January-April 1968.

PAINTING (see also aesthetic)

    Lefeuvre, Michel. see 545

    Morisani, Ottavio. see 613

PEHNOMENOLOGY

1009 Boehm, R. "Les sciences exactes et l'idéal husserlien d'un savoir rigoureux." *Archives de Philosophie,* tome XXVII, Cahiers 3-4, 1964.

    D'Amico, Robert. see 794

    Gibson, Mickey. see 653

1010 Kockelmans, Joseph J. "L'objectivité des sciences positives d'après le point de vue phénoménologique." *Archives de Philosophie,* tome XXVII, cahiers 3-4, 1964.

1011 Magliola, Robert. "Parisian structuralism confronts phenomenology: The ongoing debate." *Language and Style,* vol. VI, no. 4, Fall 1973, pp. 237-248.

1012 Paci, Enzo. *Fenomenologia e antropologia.* Milano: La Goliardica, 1962, pp. 159-190.

1013 Paci, Enzo. "Fenomenologia e antropologia culturale." *Aut Aut,* no. 77, 1963, pp. 9-11.

1014 Paci, Enzo. "Antropologia estruttural e fenomenologia." *Aut Aut,* no. 88, July 1965, pp. 42-54. Portuguese translation in Luiz Costa Lima, *O Estruturalismo de Lévi-Strauss.* see 75

1015 Psathas, George. "Ethnomethods and phenomenology." *Social Research,* vol. XXXV, 1968, pp. 500-520.

1016 Waelhens, Alphonse de. "Savoir scientifique et savoir phénoménologique." *Archives de Philosophie,* tome XXVII, cahiers 3-4, 1964.

PHILOSOPHY (and philosophical)

1017 Améry, Jean. "Französische Sozialphilosophie im Zeichen der 'Linken Frustration'." *Merkur,* no. 215, 1966, pp. 161-175.

1018 Backès-Clément, Catherine. "Lévi-Strauss ou la philosophie du non-savoir." *La Quinzaine Littéraire*, no. 95, 16-31 mai 1970, pp. 12-13.

Bakker, Reinout. see 93

1019 Bonomi, Andrea. "Implicazioni filosofiche nell'antropologia di Claude Lévi-Strauss." *Aut Aut*, nos. 96-97, 1967, pp. 47-73.
Portuguese translation, "Implicacoes filosoficas na antropologia de Claude Lévi-Strauss," in Luiz Costa Lima, *O Estruturalismo de Lévi-Strauss*. Petropolis: Vozes, 1969, pp. 114-139.

1020 Bourdieu, Pierre, and Jean-Claude Passeron. "Sociology and philosophy in France since 1945: Death and resurrection of a philosophy without subject." *Social Research*, vol. XXXIV, 1967, pp. 162-212.

Colette, Jacques. see 248

D'Amico, Robert. see 794

1021 Deligiorgis, Stravos. "Lévi Strauss and the science of self: An essay in philosophical anthropology." *Journal of European Studies*, vol. I, no. 1, March 1971, pp. 32-36.

1022 Flam, Leopold. *La Philosophie au tournant de notre temps*. Bruxelles: Presses Universitaires de Bruxelles, 1970, 216p.

1023 Geras, N. M. "Lévi-Strauss and philosophy." *Journal of the British Society for Phenomenology*, vol. I, no. 3, October 1970, pp. 50-60.

1024 Giacon, C., ed. *Strutturalismo filosofico*. Centro di Studi Filosofici di Gallarte. Padova: Gregoriana, 1970.

1025 Gioanola, Elio. "Struttura e metafisica in Lévi-Strauss." *Rivista di Studi Crociani*, vol. VI, no. 4, October-December 1969, pp. 408-425; and *Ibid.*, vol. VII, no. 1, January-March 1970, pp. 56-74.

Jager, M. see 138

1026   Langlois, Jean. "Structuralisme et métaphysique."
       Science et Esprit (Montréal), vol. XX, fasc., 2,
       mai-septembre 1968.

       Leach, Edmund R.   "Claude Lévi-Strauss anthropologist and
       philosopher." see 674

       Lefebvre, Henri.   "Claude Lévi-Strauss et le nouvel
       éléatisme." see 165

       Mepham, John. see 1078

       Morovia, Sergio.   see 1079

1027   Rivelaygue, Jacques.   "Vers une nouvelle philosophie?"
       *Bulletin de la Société des Professeurs Français en
       Amérique*, 1966, pp. 35-46.

       Valeri, Valerio. "Struttura, trasformazione, 'esaus-
       tività'. Un'esposizione di alcuni concetti di Lévi-
       Strauss." see 171

1028   Waelhens, Alphonse de.   "Philosophie et non-philosophie."
       Revue Philosophique de Louvain, tome LVII, 1959.

       Ronfani, U. see 1084

1029   Stern, Alfred. "Existencia y estructura. El pensamiento
       frances actual, en la perspectiva de Morot-Sir." *Folia
       Humanistica*, vol. XI, no. 121, January 1973, pp. 9-17.

POETIC

1030   Culler, Jonathan. "Mythologic logic," in *Structuralist
       Poetics. Structuralism, linguistics, and the Study of
       literature*. Ithaca, N.Y.: Cornell University Press,
       1975, pp. 40-54 and passim.

       Scholes, Robert. see 350

POETRY

       Edeline, Francis. see 880

PORTRAIT (and Personal)

1031   Beauvoir, Simone de. *Mémoires d'une jeune fille rangée*.
       Paris: Gallimard, 1958, p. 294.
       English translation by James Kirkup: *Memoirs of a
       Dutiful Daughter*. Cleveland: World, 1959.

1032   Beauvoir, Simone de. *La Force des choses*. Paris:
       Gallimard, 1963, p. 185.
       English translation by Peter Green, *Forces of
       Circumstances*. Cleveland: World, 1964.

1033   Caruso, Paolo. "Il caso Lévi-Strauss." *Panorama*,
       July 1965.

1034   Deluy, Henry. "Brief uit Parijs." *Litterair Paspoort*,
       vol. XXI, no. 196, May 1966, pp. 107-108.

1035   Cartier-Bresson, Henri. "Claude Lévi-Strauss: A por-
       trait." *Vogue*, vol. CLII, August 1, 1968, pp. 100-101.

1036   Forge, Anthony. "Gurus of our time--6: Lévi-Strauss."
       New Society, vol. X, no. 266, November 2, 1967, pp. 622-
       623, 625.

1037   Genet (Janet Flanner). "Letter from Paris: un certain
       regard." *New Yorker*, vol. XLIII, February 3, 1968,
       pp. 81-82.

1038   Guerrieri, A. M. "Claude Lévi-Strauss e la sollecita-
       zione a pensare." *Psicoterapia e Scienze Umane*,
       June 1967.

1039   Guiart, Jean. "Survivre à Lévi-Strauss." *L'Arc*,
       no. 26, 1965, pp. 61-64.

1040   Jacques, François. "Profil: l'homme-laboratoire."
       Le Nouvel Observateur, no. 345, 21-27 juin 1971,
       pp. 39-40.

1041   Maranda, Pierre. "An anthropologist in Paris," in
       Echanges et Communications.   see 35

1042   Nannini, Sandro. "Ritratti critici de contemporanei:
       Claude Lévi-Strauss." *Belfagor*, vol. XXVI, no. 5,
       sett. 1971, pp. 554-576.

1043 Simone, F. "Le radice di Claude Lévi-Strauss nella cultura classica francese." *La Stampa*, July 13, 1969.

1044 Tournier, Michel. "Claude Lévi-Strauss, mon maître." *Le Figaro Littéraire*, no. 1410, 26 mai 1973, pp. 15, 18.

1045 Waldberg, Patrick. "Au fil du souvenir," pp. 581-586 in Pouillon et Maranda. see 35

1046 "Au jour le jour: Lettres, arts, spectacles." *Le Nouvel Observateur*, no. 26, 13 mai 1965, pp. 26-27.

1047 "La Semaine." *Arts*, no. 1010, 16-22 juin 1965, p. 4.

1048 "Six selected as candidates for 1965 Viking medal." *American Anthropologist*, vol. LXVII, February 1965, p. 73.

1049 "Sounding the Sixties--3: Outside English." *Times Literary Supplement*, no. 3318, September 30, 1965, pp. 839-841.

1050 "Comme une églogue." *Le Nouvel Observateur*, no. 112, 4-10 janvier 1967, p. 32.

1051 "Man's new dialogue with man: Time Essay." *Time*, vol. LXXXIX, June 30, 1967, pp. 34-35.

1052 "Filtering through." *Times Literary Supplement*, no. 3424, October 12, 1967, p. 961.

1053 "La médaille d'or du C.R.N.S. à Claude Lévi-Strauss." *Les Lettres Françaises*, no. 1217, 17 janvier, 1968, p. 23.

1054 "L'esprit et la lettre." *Le Nouvel Observateur*, no. 432, 19-25 février 1973, p. 70.

1055 Kermode, Frank. "In parvo." *The Listener*, vol. LXXVIII, no. 2011, October 12, 1967, p. 474.

1056 Mettra, Claude. "Conversations avec l'univers." *L'Express*, no. 887, 8-14 juillet 1968, p. 35.

1057 Morelle, Paul. "Nous sommes tous des bricoleurs." *Démocratie Nouvelle*, nos. 7-8, 1965.

134   PORTRAIT

1058   Morelle, Paul. "Paradoxes sur un Salon: L'écriture
        est-elle un bricolage?" *Le Monde [des Livres]*,
        no. 7098, 8 novembre 1967, vol. VIII.

PRAXIS

        Schwimmer, Erik. "Objects of mediation: Myth and
        praxis." see 1004

1059   Schrag, Calvin O. "Praxis and structure: Conflicting
        models in the science of man." *Journal of the British
        Society for Phenomenology*, vol. VI, no. 1, January
        1975, pp. 23-31.

1060   Simonis, Yvan. "Echange, 'praxis', code et message."
        Cahiers Internationaux de Sociologie, vol. XLV,
        1968, pp. 117-129.

PROPHETS AND POPES

1061   Anonymous. "Camus and some others, Fanon, Marcuse,
        Guevera, Lévi-Strauss. 'Masters? One wonders'."
        The Times Literary Supplement, no. 3544, January 29,
        1970, pp. 97-98.

1062   Châtelet, François. "Les nouveaux prophètes." *Le
        Nouvel Observateur*, no. 94, 31 août-6 septembre
        1966, p. 28.

1063a   Fiedler, Leslie A. "Intellectual uncles." *The Guardian*,
        no. 37, 716, October 13, 1967, p. 6.

        Puccetti, Roland. see 899

1063   Weightman, John. "Prophets of our age." *The Observer*,
        no. 9313, January 11, 1970, p. 29. [Camus, Fanon and
        Lévi-Strauss]

1064   Wood, Michael. "The Four Gospels." [Laing, Lévi-
        Strauss, Lorenze and McLuhan]. *New Society*, vol. XIV,
        no. 177, December 18, 1969, pp. 972-975.

PRIMITIVE

        Diamond, Stanley. "Introduction: The uses of the
        primitive." see 653

PSYCHOANALYSIS (see also Freud, Unconscious)

    Axelos, Kostas. see 942

    Green, André. see 798

1064a *Incidences de la psychanalyse.* Numéro spécial de la *Nouvelle Revue de Psychanalyse.* No. 1, printemps 1970, 184p.

RACISM

1065 L., J. "M. Lévi-Strauss ouvre le cycle de conférences sur 'la question raciale et le monde moderne'," *Le Monde,* no. 8148, 25 mars 1971, p. 16.

1066 Rodinson, M. "Racisme et civilisation." *La Nouvelle Critique,* vol. VII, no. 66, juin 1955, pp. 120-140.

REALISM

    Schober, Rita. see 935

RELATIVISM

1067 Rodinson, M. "Ethnographie et relativisme." see 779

    Tennekes, J. see 739

RELIGION

    Bharati, Agiehannanda. "Antrhopological approach to the study of religion: Ritual and belief systems." see 636

    Gilsenan, M. "Myth and the history of African religion." see 654

RIGHTS

    Montes, Santiago. *Los Derechos humanos a la luz de la antropologia.* see 696

RITUAL

1068 Beattie, J. H. M. "Rituals of Nyoro kinship." *Africa,* vol. XXIX, 1959, pp. 134-145. [relies on Lévi-Strauss]

136   RITUAL

1069   Crumrine, N. Rose, and Barbara Jane Macklin. "Sacred ritual vs. unconscious: The efficiency of symbols and structure in North Mexican Folk Saint's cults and general ceremonialism," in 23.

SCIENCE

1070   Aguilar de Alfaro, Adelita. "Los metodos estructuralistas en algunas ciencias sociales." *Revista de Filosofía de la Universidad de Costa Rica*, vol. XI, no. 32, January-June 1973, pp. 33-52.

   Barthes, Roalnd. "Les sciences humaines et l'oeuvre de Lévi-Strauss." see 630

   Charrier, Jean-Paul. see 1119

   D'Amico, Robert. see 794

1071   Dieguez, Manuel de. *Science et nescience*. Paris: Gallimard, 1970.

1072   Fanizza, Franco. "Lo scientifico nell'umano." *Giornale Critico della Filosofia Italiana*, April-June 1970, pp. 271-297.

   Gasché, Rodolphe. see 519

   Goldmann, Lucien. see 948

   Granger, Georges. see 972

1073   Granger, Georges. *Pensée formelle et science de l'homme*. Paris: Aubier, 1960.

1074   Granger, Georges. "Evènement et structure dans les sciences de l'homme." *Cahiers de L'Institut de Science économique appliquée*, serie M., no. 1, 1957. *INSEA*.

   Gruppi, Luciano. see 949

1075   Gusdorf, Georges. *Les sciences humaines et la pensée occidentale*. Paris: Payot, 1967.

1075a   Krader, Lawrence. "Beyond structrualism: The dialectics of the diachronic and synchronic methods in the human sciences," in 23.

   Kockelmans, Joseph J. see 1010

1076　Ladrière, Jean. "Le structuralisme entre la science et la philosophie." *Tijdschrift voor Filosofie*, vol. XXXIII, March 1971, pp. 66-111.

1077　LeBlond, Jean-Marie. "Structuralisme et sciences humaines." *Etudes*, tome CCCXXVII, juillet-août 1967, pp. 147-162.

　　　Maybury-Lewis, David. "Science by association." see 450

　　　Maybury-Lewis, David. "Science or bricolage?" see 449

　　　Maranda, Pierre. "Calcul et formalisation." see 691

1078　Mepahm, John. "The structuralist sciences and philosophy," in David Robey, ed., *Structuralism: An Introduction*. Oxford at Clarendon Press, 1973, pp. 104-137.

1079　Moravia, Sergio. "Filosofia e scienze umane nella cultura francese contemporanea." *Belfagor*, vol. XXIII, 1968, pp. 649-681.

　　　Morazé, Charles. "L'histoire et l'unité des sciences de l'homme." see 806

1080　Mouloud, Noël. "L'esprit des sciences structurales et la philosophie de la raison." *Revue de Métaphysique et de Morale*, tome LXXI, 1966, pp. 339-358.

1081　Nutini, Hugo G. "Lévi-Strauss's conception of science," in Jean Pouillon et Pierre Maranda, eds., *Echanges et communications*, vol. I, pp. 543-570.

1082　Puddu, M. R. "La nozione di scienza nello strutturalismo," in *Strutturalismo filosofico*, ed. by G. Giacon, a cura del Centro di Stidu Filosofici di Gallarate, Padova: Ed. Gregoriana, 1970.

1083　Preti, Giulo. "L'unica scienza è la nostra scienza." *La Fiera Letteraria*, vol. XVII, no. 28, July 13, 1967, p. 24.

　　　Raison Présente, "Sciences du langage et sciences humaines." see 892

1084　Ronfani, U. "Filosofia e scienza in Claude Lévi-Strauss." *Gazetta del Popolo*, December 27, 1967.

138   SCIENCE

  Rossi, Ino. see 966

  Ruwet, Nicolas. see 912

1085 "Les sciences humaines et l'oeuvre de Lévi-Strauss," in
  Annales (Economies--Sociétés--Civilisations), 19e année,
  1964, pp. 1085-1115. [Essays by Roland Barthes,
  Raphael Pividal, Edmund Leach. An excellent set of
  articles]

  Schrag, Calvin O. see 1059

1086 Soto Verges, Rafael. "Ciencias sociales." *Estafeta
  Literaria*, no. 522, August 15, 1973, pp. 1438-1439.

  Van Loon, J. F. Glastra. see 762

  Waelhens, Alphonse de. see 1016

SEMIOTICS

  Chambers, Ian. see 508

  Panowski, Tadeusz. see 913

1087 Wells, Rulon E. "Distinctively human semiotic." *Social
  Science Information*, vol. VI, 1967, pp. 103-124.

SOCIAL GROUP

  Sommerfelt, Alfred. see 915

SOCIAL THOUGHT

1088 Hughes, H. Stuart. "Structure and society," in *The
  Obstructed path: French Social Thought in the Years
  of Desperation, 1930-1960*. New York: Harper and Row,
  1968, pp. 264-290. Reprinted pp. 22-46 in no. 9.

  Review:
    Anonymous. "Isolated intellectuals." *The Economist*,
    vol. CCXXVIII, no. 6522, August 24, 1968, p. 37.

SOCIAL ORGANIZATION AND STRUCTURE

1089 Basehart, Harry. "Social organization," in Bernard J.
  Siegel, ed., *Biennial Review of Anthropology, 1959*.
  Stanford: Stanford University Press, 1960, pp. 132-124.

Buchler, Ira.   see 868

1090 Davenport, William. "Social Organization," Bernard J. Siegel, *Biennial Review of Anthropology, 1963.* Stanford: Stanford University Press, 1963, pp. 192, 194, 196, 208, 215-218.

Goodenough, Ward H. "Frontiers of cultural anthropology: Social organization."   see 657

1091 Gurwitch, Georges. "Le concept de structure sociale." *Cahiers Internationaux de Sociologie,* vol. XIX, 1955. Reprinted in *La Vocation actuelle de la sociologie.* Paris: Presses Universitaires de France, 1963, pp. 403-446.
Italian translation by S. Cernuschi, Bologna: Il Mulino, 1965, pp. 490-545. [Réponse de Lévi-Strauss dans *Anthropologie structurale,* chapter XVI]

1092 Maranda, Pierre. "Anthropological analytics: Lévi-Strauss's concept of social structure," in Hugo G. Nutini and I. Buchler, eds., *The Anthropology of Claude Lévi-Strauss.* New York: Appleton, Century-Crofts, 1970.

1093 Murdock, Georges P. "Changing emphases in social structure." *Southwestern Journal of Anthropology,* vol. XI, 1955, pp. 361-370.

Nutini, Hugo G. "Some considerations on the nature of social structure and model building: A critique of Claude Lévi-Strauss and Edmund Leach."   see 535a

1094 Nadel, Siegfried, F. *The Theory of social structure.* Chicago: The Free Press of Glencoe, 1957.

Orans, Martin. "Social organization."   see 705

Queiroz, M. I. Pereira de.   see 745

1095 *Raison Présente,* "Structure sociale et histoire." No. 7, 1968 [Labrousse, Goldmann, Martinet, Soboul, Vidal-Naquet, Reberioux]

Selby, Henry A. "Social organization."   see 728

Warner, Lloyd W., et al. "Mungin social organization." see 232

140   SOCIALIZATION

SOCIALIZATION

1096   Jahoda, G. "A psychologist's perspective," in Philip
       Mayer, ed., *Socialization*. The Approach from social
       anthropology. London: Tavistock Publications, 1970.

SOCIOLOGY

       Balandier, Georges. see ETHNOLOGY

       Bourdieu, Pierre, and Jean-Claude Passeron. see 1020

       Bourdieu, Pierre. see 871

1097   Lapierre, J. William. "Vers une sociologie concrète."
       Esprit, 19e année, no. 184, novembre 1951, pp. 720-
       730.

1098   Reynolds, Larry T., and Janice M. Raynolds. "The givens
       of Claude Lévi-Strauss. A Value analysis in the
       sociology of knowledge." *The Journal of Value Inquiry*,
       vol. II, Spring 1968, pp. 22-30.

STRUCTURALISM

1099   Albérès-Marill, René. "Cette nouvelle école littéraire
       dont on parle tant: le structuralisme." *A la Page*,
       no. 44, février 1968, pp. 213-221.

       Aletheia. see 1261

       Alternative. see 1262

       Alternative. see 1263

1100   Amodio, L. "Nota su un dibattito in *'Annales'*." *Il
       Corpo*, no. 1, 1965.

1101   Amar, André. "Pour comprendre le structuralisme."
       Planète, no. 37, novembre-décembre 1967, pp. 38-53.

       Anonymous. see 533

1102   Anonymous. "Structuralism in the steets," *The Times
       Literary Supplement*, no. 3469, August 22, 1968,
       p. 897.

       Arnaud, A. J. see 894

Aubenque, Pierre. see 873

L'Arc, see 1265.

Aut Aut, see 1266.

1103 Auzias, Jean-Maris. "Le structuralisme en personne," in
Clefs pour le structuralisme. Paris: Seghers, 2e ed.,
1967, pp. 86-108.
Spanish translation by Santiago Gonzalez Noriega,
El Estructuralismo. Madrid: Alianza Editoria, 1969.
Italian translation di L. Banfi. Milano: Mursia,
1969.

Aron, Raymond. see 500

1104 Bakker, Reinout. "Structuralisme," in Remy C. Kwant,
ed., *Mensbeelden, Filosofie in een pluriforme samen-
leving*. Alphen-ad. -Rijn: Samson, 1973.

1105 Balashov, N. "K kritike novejshykh tendencii v litera-
turovedcheskom strukturalizme." *Kontekst 1973*
(M., 1974), 138-175. (Kontekst 1973, ed. A. S.
Knasnikov et al)

1106 Barthes, Roland. "L'activité structuraliste," in *Les
Lettres Nouvelles*, février 1963, pp. 73-86. Reprinted
in *Essais critiques*. Paris: Editions du Seuil, 1964.
English translation "Structuralist activity," *Partisan
Review*, vol. XXXIV, no. 1, 1967, pp. 83-88.
Italian translation by L. Lonzi, Torino: G. Einaudi,
1966, pp. 245-250.

1107 Barthes, Roland. "La littérature aujourd'hui." see 1106

Bartolomei, Giangaetano. see 513

1108 Benoist, Jean-Marie. *La Révolution structurale*. Paris:
Grasset, 1975.

Bernabei, F. see 607

1109 Bierwisch, M. "Strukturalismus. Geschichte, Probleme
und Methoden." *Kursbuch*, 5, 1966, pp. 77-152.

1110 Blanquart, P. "Le structuralisme, de la terreur au
dialogue." *Signes du Temps*, février 1967, pp. 24-26.

1111 Blanquart, P. "Der Strukturalismus." *Dokumente*, October 1967, pp. 353-354.

1112 Bonomi, Andrea. "Introduzione" a Jean Piaget, *Lo Strutturalismo*. Milano: Il Saggiatore, 1967.

Boon, James A. see 1

1113 Broekman. *Strukturalismus*. Freiburg: K. Alber Verlag, 1972. ["Strukturale Anthropologie und Erkenntnistheorie," pp. 129-129 and passim]

Bourdieu, Pierre. see 871

Cacciari, M. e F. Dal Co. see 817

Cahiers Internationaux de Symbolisme. see 1269

Castel, R. see 818

Caruso, Paolo. see 943

1114 Castello, Vidal Abril. "Que es el estructuralismo?" *Arbor*, tomo LXXXVI, no. 327, marzo 1973, pp. 15-22.

1115 Cebik, L. B. Review of *Structuralism*, ed. by Jacques Ehrmann. *Georgia Review*, vol. XXXVI, no. 2, Summer 1972, pp. 233-237.

Chambers, Ian. see 508

1116 Caws, Peter. "What is structuralism?" *Partisan Review*, vol. XXXV, no. 1, Winter 1968, pp. 79-91. Reprinted in E. N. Hayes and T. Hayes, pp. 197-214.

1117 Caruso, Paolo. "Nota sullo strutturalismo," in introduzione a *Conversazioni*.

1118 Caws, Peter, "The recent literature of structuralism." *Philosophische Rundschau*, vol. XVIII, 1971, pp. 63-77.

1119 Charrier, Jean-Paul. "Lévi-Strauss, le structuralisme et les sciences humaines." *Revue de l'Enseignement Philosophique*, vol. XXII, no. 1, 1971-1972, pp. 14-30.

1120 Châtelet, François. "Où en est le structuralisme?" *La Quinzaine Littéraire*, no. 31, 1-15 juillet 1967, pp. 18-19.

1121 Corvez, Maurice. "Les nouveaux structuralistes." *Revue Philosophique de Louvain*, no. 96, 1969.

1122 Corvez, Maurice. "Le structuralisme ethnologique de Claude Lévi-Strauss." *Nouvelle Revue Théologique*, tome XC, avril 1968, pp. 388-410.

1123 Corvez, Maurice. "Le structuralisme ethnologique de Claude Lévi-Strauss," in *Les Structuralistes. Les linguistes--Michel Foucault--Claude Lévi-Strauss--Jacques Lacan--Louis Althusser--Les critiques littéraires*. Paris: Aubier-Montaigne, 1969, pp. 79-112.

Culler, Jonathan D. see 876

Culler, Jonathan D. see 1030

1124 Crémant, Roger. *Les Matinées structuralistes*, suivies d'un Discours sur l'écriture et précédées d'une Introduction critique par Albert K. Paris: Robert Laffont, 1969.

Cuisenier, Jean. "Lévi-Strauss ou le structuralisme accompli." see 400

1125 Cuisenier, Jean. "Le structuralisme du mot, de l'idée et des outils." *Esprit*, 35e année, no. 360, mai 1967, pp. 825-842.

1126 Daix, Pierre. "Du structuralisme." *Les Lettres Françaises*, no. 1226, mars 1968.

1127 Daix, Pierre. "Structure du structuralisme." *Les Lettres Françaises*, no. 1238, juin-juillet 1968.

1128 Daix, Pierre. "Sartre est-il dépassé?" *Les Lettres Françaises*, nos. 1168-1169, février 1967.

1129 D'Amico, Robert. "The contours and the 'coupures' of structuralist theory." *Telos*, Fall 1973, pp. 70-93.

1130 DeGeorge, Richard, and Fernande DeGeorge, eds. *The Structuralists*. Garden City, N.Y.: Doubleday, 1972.

De Ipola, Emilio Rafael. see 77

De Ipola, Emilio Rafael. see 768

144   STRUCTURALISM

       Daix, Pierre. see 404

       Deliège, Célestin. see 977

       Derrida, Jacques. see 562

       Derrida, Jacques. see 121

1131 Diamond, Stanley. "The myth of structuralism," in Rossi.

1132 Domenach, Jean-Marie. "Le système et la personne." *Esprit*, 35e année, no. 360, mai 1967, pp. 771-780.

       Donato, Eugenio. see 921

       Domenach, Jean-Marie. see 409

       Dorfles, Gillo. see 608

       Dubois, Jean. see 903

1133 Dufrenne, Mikel. "Le règne de la structure," in *Pour l'Homme*. Paris: Editions du Seuil, 1968, pp. 79-90.

1134 Dufrenne, Mikel. "La philosophie du néo-positivisme." *Esprit*, 35e année, no. 360, mai 1967, pp. 781-800.

       Dumasy, Annegret. see 53

       Durand, Gilbert. see 345

       Eco, Umberto. see 971

1135 Eco, Umberto. *La Struttura assente*. Milano: Bompiani, 1968, sezione D.

1136 Eco, Umberto. "Pensiero strutturale e pensiero seriale." *Rivista di Estetica*, anno XIII, fasc. 1, January-April 1968, pp. 25-45.

       Esbroeck, Michel van. see 786

       Esprit, "La Pensée sauvage et le structuralisme." see 1272

       Esprit, "Structuralisme, idéologies et méthode." see 1273

1137 Fages, J.-B. *Comprendre le structuralisme*. Toulouse: Privat, 1967.

1138 Fages, J.-B. *Le Structuralisme en procès*. Toulouse: Privat, 1968.

Ferrata, Giansiro. see 509

1139 Fessard, G. "Politique et structuralisme." *Recherches et Débats*, 1966.

Fialkowski, A. see 788

1140 Francovich, Guillermo. *El Estructuralismo*. Buenos Aires: Ed. Plus Ultra, 1974.

1141 Friedrich, H. "Strukturalismus und Struktur," in *Literaturwissenschaftlicher Hinsicht*. München: Europaische Aufklarung, 1967, pp. 77-86.

1142 Funt, David. "The structuralist debate." *The Hudson Review*, vol. XXII, no. 4, Winter 1969-1970, pp. 623-646.

Frandon, I.-M. see 346

Furet, Francois. see 896

1143 Gatti, Luis. "*C. Lévi-Strauss: Problemas del estructuralismo* por Verstraeten, et al." *Sur*, no. 313, July-August 1968, pp. 77-80.

1144 Genette, Gerard. "Structuralisme et critique littéraire." *L'Arc*, no. 26, 1965, pp. 30-34, and 37-44. Reprinted in *Figures*. Paris: Editions du Seuil, 1966. Italian translation, F. Madonia, Torino: Einaudi, 1969, pp. 133-155.

Gardner, Howard. see 7

1145 Giacon, C. ed., *Strutturalismo filosofico*. Centro di Studi Filosofici di Gallarte. Padova: Ed. Gregoriana, 1970.

1146 Gerber, Rudolph J. "Structuralism in France." *The Modern Schoolman*, vol. XLVI, May 1969, pp. 301-314.

Glucksmann, Miriam. see 8

1147 Glucksmann, A. "Le structuralisme ventriloque." *Les Temps Modernes*, mars 1967.

Goddard, D. see 656a

146   STRUCTURALISM

　　　　　Godelier, Maurice. see 600

1148　Goldmann, Lucien. "Entretien sur le structuralisme."
　　　　L'Homme et la Société, janvier 1967.

　　　　Goldmann, Lucien. "Structuralisme, marxisme,
　　　　existentialisme." see 947.

1149　Gonzalez, O. "Notas sobre Claude Lévi-Strauss." *Acteón*,
　　　　(Bogóta), nos. 1-2, 1968.

1150　Grenet, P. "Prise de contact avec les structuralistes."
　　　　L'Ami du Clergé (Paris), 77e année, 8e serie, no. 44,
　　　　2 novembre 1967, pp. 620ff.

　　　　Gruppi, Luciano. see 949

　　　　Gritti, J. et P. Toinet. see 819

　　　　Heusch, Luc de. see 661

1151　G. P.-M. "De nouvelles pieces au dossier du structur-
　　　　alisme." *Le Monde*, no. 6677, 2 juillet 1966, p. 11.

1152　Hartman, Geoffrey H. "Structuralism: the Anglo-
　　　　American adventure," in *Beyond Formalism: Literary
　　　　Essays 1958-1970*. New Haven: Yale University Press,
　　　　1970, pp. 3-23.

　　　　Hayman, David. see 925

　　　　Hund, William B. see 764

1153　Hund, Wulf D. "Das Ende des Strukturalismus." *Literatur
　　　　und Kritik*, no. 40, November 1969, pp. 586-628.

1154　Hyde, Gordon. "Structuralism: Tool or totem?" *The
　　　　Humanist*, vol. LXXXVI, no. 9, September 1971, pp. 265-
　　　　266.

1155　Jaeggi, Urs. *Ordnung und Chaos: Strukturalismus als
　　　　Methode und Mode*. Frankfurt am Main: Suhrkamp Verlag,
　　　　1969.

1156　Jameson, Fredric. *The Prison House of Language: A
　　　　critical account of structuralism and Russian Formalism*.
　　　　Princeton, N.J.: Princeton University Press, 1972,
　　　　pp. 101-106, 111-120, 130-133.

1157   Kahn, Jean-François. "La minitieuse conquête du structur-
       alisme." *L'Express*, no. 844, 21-27 août, 1967, pp. 39-
       41.

       Kamstra, J. H. see GOD

1158   Kampits, Peter. "Das Ende des Philosophie im franzö-
       sischen Strukturalismus." *Wissenschaft und Weltbild*,
       vol. XXIII, no. 2, Juni 1970, pp. 126-138.

1159   Köbben, A. J. F. "Structuralism vs. comparative
       functionalism: Some comments." *Bijdragen. Tot de
       Taal-, Land-, en Volkenkunde*, vol. CXXII, 1966, pp. 145-
       150.

1160   Kobben, A. J. F. "La logique de l'analyse interstruc-
       turale." *Annales (Economies--Sociétés--Civilisations)*,
       23e année, no. 3, mai-juin 1967.

       Krader, Lawrence. see 1075a

1161   Krause-Jensen, Esbern. *Der Franske Strukturalisme: Pa
       sporet af en teori for de humane videnskaber*. Copen-
       hagen: Berlingske Forlag, 1973.

       Kuper, Adam. see 669

       Kursbuch. see 1275

1162   Lacroix, Jean. "Le structuralisme de Claude Lévi-Strauss,"
       in *Panorama de la philosophie française contemporaine*.
       Paris: Presses Universitaires de France, 1966.

       Ladrière, Jean. see 1076

1163   Ladrière, Jean. "Sens et système." *Esprit*, 35e année,
       no. 360, mai 1967, pp. 822-834.

       Lampo, Mireille. see 78

1164   Lane, Michael, ed. *Introduction to Structuralism*.
       Edited and introduced by Michael Lane. New York: Basic
       Books, 1970. London: Jonathan Cape, 1970.

       Review:
1165   N. E. Wetherich, in *Journal of the British Society for
       Phenomenology*, vol. IV, January 1973, pp. 93-94.

       Langlois, Jean. see 1026

148   STRUCTURALISM

1166   Leach, Edmund R. "Structuralism in social anthropology," in David Robey, ed., *Structuralism: An introduction.* Oxford, Clarendon Press, 1973, pp. 37-56.

   LeBlond, Jean-Marie. see 1077

   Lefebvre, Henri. see 803

   Lefebvre, Henri. see 145

1167   Lefebvre, Henri. *Positions contre les technocrates.* Paris: Editions de Minuit, 1968.

1168   Lemaire, A. H. F. "Het strucutralisme van Claude Lévi-Strauss." *Tijdschrift voor Filosofie,* vol. XXXI, December 1969, pp. 688-705.

1169   Lepenies, Wolf. "Der französische Strukturalismus: Methode und Ideologie." see 820

   Lima, Luiz Costa. see 75

1170   Lopez Martín, Alfonso. "El estructuralismo linguistico." *Revista de Filosofía de la Universidad de Costa Rica,* vol. XI, no. 32, January-June 1973, pp. 3-12.

   Macksey, Richard, and Eugenio Donato, eds. see 151

   Magliola, Robert. see 1011

1171   Mainburger, Gonsalv K. "Die französische Philosophie nach dem Strukturalismus." *Neue Rundschau,* Jahrg. 84, 1973, pp. 437-458.

   Makarius, Raoul, and Laura Makarius. see 44

1172   Makarius, Raoul, and Laura Makarius. "Ethnologie et structuralisme--Questions et réponses." *L'Homme et la Société,* no. 3, janvier-mars, 1967, pp. 187-200.

   Makarius, Raoul. see 821

   Marchan, Simon. see 610

   Marc-Lipiansky, Mireille. see 41

1173 Melenk, Martmut. "Die formalen Systeme des französischen Strukturalismus. Claude Lévi-Strauss und Roland Barthes." *Philosophisches Jahrbuch*, vol. LXXIX, no. 510, 1972, pp. 137-161.

Mepham, John. see 1078

1174 Mariani, Eliodoro. "Introduzione allo strutturalismo filosofico." *Antonianum*, annus XLVI, fasc. 1, January-March 1971, pp. 113-147.

Meddelelser fra Danskloererforeningen. see 1276

1175 Merquior, José-Guiherme. "Sobre alguns problemas da critica estrutural." *Coloquio/Letras*, no. 1, March 1971, pp. 7-13.

Michelson, A. see 611

1176 Milet, André. "Pour ou contre le structuralisme. Claude Lévi-Strauss et son oeuvre." *Confrontations* (Tournai), tome I, no. 3, juillet 1968, pp. 201-246; and *Ibid.*, no. 4, septembre 1968, pp. 281-316.

Milet, André. see 45

1177 Millet, Louise et Madeleine Varin d'Ainville. *Le Structuralisme.* Paris: Editions Universitaires, 1970.

Mora, Fernando. see 895

Morot-Sir, Edouard. see 756

Muntz, Peter. see 523

Nutini, Hugo G. see 822

Nutini, Hugo G. see 823

Olsen, Michel. see 930

1178 Paci, Enzo. "Il senso delle parole: strutturalismo, fonologia e antropologia." *Aut Aut*, no. 77, 1963, pp. 9-11.

Parain-Vail, Jeanne. see 807 and 824

150 STRUCTURALISM

      Parain-Vial, Jeanne. "Analyses structurales et ideologies." see 824

      La Pensee. see 952

1179 Piaget, Jean. "Le structuralisme." *Cahiers Internationaux de Symbolisme*, no. 17-18, 1969, pp. 73-85.

1180 Piaget, Jean. *Le Structuralisme*. Paris: Presses Universitaires de France, 1968.
English translation, *Structuralism*. New York: Basic Books, 1970.
Italian translation, A. Bonomi, Milano: Il Saggiatore, 1968.

1181 Piaget, Jean. "The anthropological structuralism of Claude Lévi-Strauss," and "Structuralism and philosophy," pp. 106-119, and 120-135 in *Structuralism*. New York: Basic Books, Inc., 1970, pp. 106-119 and 120-135.

      La Pensée. see 1278

      Pettit, Philip. see 599

1182 Pingaud, Bernard. "Comment on devient structuraliste." *L'Arc*, no. 26, 1965, pp. 1-5.

1183 Pingaud, Bernard. "Interview: Sartre Repond." *La Quinzaine Litteraire*, no. 14, 15-31, octobre 1966, pp. 4-5.

1184 Pingaud, Bernard, ed. "Sartre aujourd'hui." *L'Arc*, no. 30, 1966.

1185 Poole, Roger C. "Structuralism side-tracked." *New Blackfriars*, vol. L, no. 590, July 1969, pp. 533-544.

      "Problèmes du structuralisme." *Les Temps Modernes*. see 1283

      Pouwer, Jan. "The structural and functional approach." see 1224

      Pouwer, Jan. see 719

1186   Prastaro, A. M. "Lo strutturalismo: dalla linguistica
        all'etnologia," in *Strutturalismo filosofico*, a cura
        del Centro di Studi Filosofici di Gallarate. Padova:
        Ed. Gregoriana, 1970.

        Puddu, M. R. see 1082

1187   Pouillon, Jean. "Présentation: un essai de définition."
        see 774

1188   Reif, Adelbert, ed. *Antworten der Strukturalisten*.
        [R. Barthes, M. Foucault, F. Jacob, C. Lévi-Strauss,
        R. Jakobson]. Hamburg: Hoffman and Campe, 1973.

        Revista de Filosogia Espanola. see 1279

        Rossi, A. see 933

        Rouboud, J. see 911

        Rinascità. see 1282a

1189   Rideau, Emile. "Le Structuralisme." *Nouvelle Revue
        Théologique*, tome XC, no. 9, 1968, pp. 918-935.

1190   Ricoeur, Paul. "La structure, le mot, l'évènement."
        Esprit, 35e année, no. 360, mai 1967, pp. 801-821.
        English translation, "Structure, Word, and event."
        Philosophy Today, vol. XII, 1968, pp. 114-129.

        Ricoeur, Paul. "Structure et hermeneutique." see 790

1191   Robey, David. *Structuralism: An Introduction*. Wolfson
        College Lectures, 1972. Edited with a preface by David
        Robey. Oxford: Clarendon Press, 1973.

        Rossi, A. see 933

        Rossi, Ino. see 80

        Rossi, Ino. see 23

        Rossi, Ino. "Structuralism as scientific method." see 966

        Rossi, Ino. see 825

        Rouboud, J. see 516 and 911

STRUCTURALISM

Rubio Carracedo, José. "Lévi-Strauss--ciencia o ideologia." see 826

1192 Rubio Carracedo, José. "La evolucion del estructuralismo en Lévi-Strauss." *Pensamiento*, vol. XXVII, April-June 1971, pp. 131-160.

Rubio Carracedo, José. "El ultimo Lévi-Strauss." see 497

1193 Runciman, W. G. "What is structuralism?" *British Journal of Sociology*, vol. XX, 1969, pp. 253-265.

1194 Rucinski, Brunon J. "Pewien strukturalizm: Glowne koncepcje Claude Lévi-Strauss." *Studia Philosophiae Christiane*, vol. VII, 1971, pp. 213-241.

1195 *Rinascità*, no. 50, December 18, 1965, p. 35, "Polemiche sullo strutturalismo."

1196 Said, Edward W. "*Abecedarium culturae:* Structuralism, absence, writing." *Tri-Quarterly*, no. 21, Winter 1971, pp. 33-71. Reprinted in John K. Simon, ed., *Modern French Criticism: from Proust and Váléry to Structuralism*. Chicago and London: University of Chicago Press, 1972, pp. 341-391.

1197 Schaff, Adam. "Der Strukturalismus als Geistesströmung." *Wissenschaft und Weltbild*, 25 Jahrg. Nr. 4, Okt.-Dez. 1972, pp. 261-285.

1198 Scheffler, Harold W. "Structuralism in anthropology." *Yale French Studies*, nos. 36-37, 1966, pp. 66-88. Reprinted in Jacques Ehrmann, ed., *Structuralism*. Garden Dity, N.Y.: Doubleday, Anchor Book, 1970, pp. 56-78.

Schintholzer, Birgit. see 81

1199 Schiwy, Günther. *Neue Aspekte des Strukturalismus*. München: Kösel-Verlag, 1971.

1200 Schiwy, Gunther. *Strukturalismus und Christentum*. Freiburg: Herder KG, 1969. English translation by Henry J. Koren, *Structuralism and Christianity*. Duquesne Studies, Theological Series 11. Pittsburgh, Pa.: Duquesne University Press -Louvain: Nauwelaerts, 1971.

French translation, *Structuralisme et Christianisme.* Paris: Mame, 1973.

1201 Schiwy, Günther. "Strukturalismus in Paris." *Stimmen der Zeit,* August 1967, pp. 91-104.

1202 Schiwy, Günther. *Der französische Strukturalismus: Mode, Methode, Ideologie.* Reinbeck bei Hamburg: Rowohlt, 1969, 249p.

1203 Schiwy, Günther. "Neue Ergebnisse des Strukturalismus." *Wissenschaft und Weltbild,* 25 Jahrg., Nr. 2, April-Juni 1972, pp. 113-122.

Scholte, Bob. see 82

Scholte, Bob. "Claude Lévi-Strauss." see 723

1204 Scholte, Bob. "Comments to the essays of Part Three: 'Structuralism as ethno-logic," see ROSSI.

1205 Schwimmer, Erik. "Comments to the essays of Part Two: "The practice of structural analysis." see 23

Sebag, Lucien. see 957

1206 Segre, C. "Risposta a un questionairo sullo strutturalismo (compilato da C. Segre)." *Paragone,* no. 182, April 1965.

1207 Sierksma, Fokke. "Met en tegen Lévi-Strauss." *Tirade* (Antwerp), vol. VII, 1963, pp. 306-330.

Simonis, Yvan. see 961

1208 Simonis, Yvan. "Silence du structuralisme, silence de la religion." *Project,* novembre 1967.

Simonis, Yvan. see 48

Simonis, Yvan. see 785

Simonis, Yvan. see 761

Sperber, Dan. "Le structuralisme en anthropologie." see 735

Suret-Canale, J. see 962

Les Temps Modernes. see 1283

1209 Thion, Serge. "Structurologie," *Aletheia*, no. 4, mai 1963, pp. 219-227.

1210 Tornos, Andres M. "Lévi-Strauss y su estructuralismo." *Razon y Fé*, tomo CLXXVIII, fasc. 1-2, July-August 1968, pp. 59-78.

Urmeneta, Fermín de. see 619

1211 Uscatescu, George. *Aporias del estructuralismo*. Madrid: Instituto de Estudios Politicos, 1971,178p.

1212 Uscatescu, George. *Genesi e vicende dello strutturalismo*. Pisa: Giardini, 1972, 135p.

1213 Tullio-Altan, C. "Lo strutturalismo di Lévi-Strauss e la ricerca antropologica." see 740

1214 Tullio-Altan, C. "Strutturalismo e funzionalismo in Lévi-Strauss." *Studi di Sociologia*, vol. IV, 1966, pp. 369-386.

Verstraeten, Pierre. see 86

1215 Verstraeten, Pierre. "Lévi-Strauss ou la tentatioh du néant." *Les Temps Modernes*, 19e année, no. 206, juillet 1963, pp. 66-109; and *Ibid.*, nos. 207-208, août-septembre 1963, pp. 507-552.
Spanish translation, *Problemas del estructuralismo*. Buenos Aires: Eudecor, Dist. Tres Americas, 1967, 240p.

1216 Volpe, Galvano della. "Marxismo contro strutturalismo." *Rinascità*, no. 44, November 20, 1965, pp. 36-37.

1217 Viet, J. *Les Méthodes structuralistes dans les sciences sociales*. The Hague, Paris: Mouton, 1965.

1218 Wahl, François et al. *Qu'est-ce que le structuralisme?* Paris: Editions du Seuil, 1968. [Ducrot, Todorov, Safouan]

1219 Watte, Pierre. "Où va la philosophie? Il? Etes-vous structuraliste?" *La Revue Nouvelle*, 23e année, tome XLV, no. 6, 15 juin 1967.

1220 Wald, Henri. "Structure, structural, structuralism." *Diogenes*, no. 66, Summer 1969, pp. 15-24.

1221 Weinrich, H., and M. Wandruezka. "Der Erling des
     Strukturalismus. Diskussion aktueller. Probleme."
     Zeitschrift für Romanische Philologie, vol. LXXXIV,
     1968, pp. 98-109.

1222 Wilden, Anthony. "Structuralism as epistemology of
     closed systems." see Rossi

1223 Weinrich, Harald. "Strukturalismus." *Merkur*, 23.Jhrg.,
     Heft 6, Nr. 254, Juni 1969, pp. 593-595.

     Yale French Studies. see 1284

     Zimmermann, Marc Jay. see 529

     Zehraoui, Absene. see 866

STRUCTURAL AND FUNCTIONAL

     Kobben, A. J. F. see 1159

     Pouwer, Jan. "The structural and functional approach
     in cultural anthropology." see 719

1224 Pouwer, Jan. "The structural-configurational approach:
     a methodological outline," in ROSSI.

1225 Rivière, Peter. "Structural and functional." *New Society*,
     vol. XI, no. 383, January 29, 1970, pp. 188-189

     Tullio-Altan, C. see 1214

1226 Anonymous. "Structure and society." *The Times Literary
     Supplement*, no. 3318, September 30, 1965, pp. 863-865.

     Aubenque, Pierre. see 873

     Barbut, Marc. see 964

1227 Bastide, Roger, ed. *Sens et usages du terme structure
     dans les sciences humaines*. The Hague: Mouton, 1962.
     Spanish translation,*Sentidos y usos del termino
     estructura en las ciencias del hombre*. Buenos Aires:
     Editorial Paidos, 1971.

1228 Boudon, Raymond. *A quoi sert la notion de structure: Essai sur la signification de la notion de structure dans les sciences humaines*. Paris: Gallimard, 1968.
English translation, *The uses of structure*. London: Heinemann, 1971.
Italian translation, M. G. Losano, *Strutturalismo e scienze umane*. Torino: Einaudi, 1970.

Coult, A. D. "The structuring of structure." see 647

1229 Deleuze, Gilles. "De la structure," in *Logique du sens*. Paris: Editions de Minuit, 1969.

Dyson-Hudson, Neville. see 556

Eco, Umberto. see 971

Fisher, John B. see 514

Friedrich H. see 1141

Goddard, D. see 656a

Gardner, Howard. see 553

Gioanola, Elio. see 1024

Girard, René. see 922

1230 Greimas, A.-J. "Structure et histoire." *Les Temps Modernes*, 22e année, no. 246, 1966, pp. 815-827.

Godelier, Maurice. see 600

1231 Guaraldi, Antonella. "Per un surrealismo logico." *Revue Internationale de Philosophie*, 19e année, nos. 73-74, fasc. 3-4, 1965, pp. 442-448.

1232 Hernández, Carmen Maria de. "Origen y significado de las estructuras en Lévi-Strauss." *Revista de Filosofía de la Universidad de Costa Rica*, vol. XI, no. 32, January-June 1973, pp. 53-82.

1233 Jalley-Crampe, Michèle. "La notion de structure mentale cans les travaux de Claude Lévi-Strauss." *La Pensée*, no. 135, septembre-octobre 1967, pp. 53-62.

Lagadec, Claude. see 801

Lanteri-Laura, G. see 802 and 803

1234 Lupasco, S. *Qu'est-ce qu'une structure?* Paris: Christian Bourgeois, 1967.

Makarius, Raould. "Lévi-Strauss et le structures inconscientes de l'esprit." see 682

1235 Malavassi, V. Guillermo. "Bricolage sobre naturaleza y estructura." *Revista de Filosofía de la Universidad de Costa Rica*, vol. XI, no. 32, January-June 1973, pp. 13-32.

1236 Martano, Giuseppe. "'Struttura' disumanizzante." *Logos* (Italia), 1972, pp. 189-194.

Mouloud, Noël. see 758

1237 Mourelos, G. "La notion de structure dans la philosophie moderne." [in Greek] *Annales d'Esthétique*, vol. VIII, 1969, pp. 119-136.

1238 Paci, Enzo. "Il senso delle strutture in Lévi-Strauss." *Paragone*, February 1966, no. 42, pp. 114-125.

1239 Paci, Enzo. "Sul concetto di struttura in Lévi-Strauss." *Giornale Critico della Filosofia Italiana*, vol. XLIV, 1965, pp. 483-503.

1240 Paci, Enzo. "Il senso delle strutture in Lévi-Strauss." *Revue Internationale de Philosophie*, 19e année, nos. 73-74, fasc. 3-4, 1965, pp. 300-313.

1241 Paci, Enzo. "Il senso delle parole: struttura." *Aut Aut*, no. 73, 1963.

Paci, Enzo. see 596

Remotti, Francesco. see 975

1242 *Revue Internationale de Philosophie.* "La notion de structure," numéro spécial, 19e année, nos. 73-74, fasc. 304, 1965.

1243 Rothenstreich, Nathan. "On Lévi-Strauss' concept of structure." *Review of Metaphysics*, vol. XXV, March 1972, pp. 489-526.

158   STRUCTURAL AND FUNCTIONAL

    Rossi, Ino. see 220

    Rubio Carracedo, José. see 584

    Schrag, Calvin O. see 1059

    Sebag, Lucien. see 810

SURREALISM

    Steinwachs, Gisela. see 512

SYMBOL

    Crumrine, N. Rose. see 1069

    Ferraro, Guido. see 414

1244 Fessard, G. "Symbole, surnaturel, dialogue," in *Démythisation et morale*. *Archivio di Filosofia*, Paris: Aubier-Montaigne, 1965.

    Van Haeperen, Joseph. see 85

SYMBOLISM AND SYMBOLIST

    Boon, James A. see no. 1.

1245 Boon, James A. "Surface affinities: Contents and interests shared by Lévi-Strauss and Symbolists," pp. 17-37 in no. 1.

1246 Heusch, Luc de. "Anthropologie structurale et symbolisme." *Cahiers Internationaux de Symbolisme*, vol. II, 1963, pp. 51-66.

SYSTEM

1247 Remotti, Francesco. "La concezioni dei sistemi in Lévi-Strauss." *Quaderni di Sociologia*, vol. XVII, nos. 1-2, 1968, pp. 31-56.

1248 Wilden, Anthony. *System and Structure*. London: Tavistock, 1972.

TECHNIQUE

    Heusch, Luc de. see 799

TIME

Barnes, J. A. "Time flies like an arrow." see 629

Gellner, Ernest. "Time and theory in social anthropology." see 651

Gorer, Geoffrey. "Time and the primitive mind." see 321

TOTEMISM

1249 Mendelson, E. Michael. "The 'Univited Guest': Ancilla to Lévi-Strauss on totemism and primitive thought," in Edmund R. Leach, ed., *The Structural study of myth and totemism.* London: Tavistock Publications, 1967, pp. 119-140.

TYPOLOGY

Muntz, Peter. see 523

UNCONSCIOUS

1250 Charrier, J.-P. *L'Inconscient et la psychanalyse.* Paris: Presses Universitaires de France, 1968, pp. 98-99.

Crumsrine, N. Rose, and Barbara Jane Macklin. see 1069

1251 Forni, Guglielmo. "Claude Lévi-Strauss: dal dubbio antropological all metafisica dell'inconscio," in *Strutturalismo filosofico.* Padova: Ed. Gregoriana, 1970, pp. 163-173.

1252 Forni, Guglielmo. "La 'metafisica dell'inconscio' di Lévi-Strauss," in *Il Soggetto e la storia.* Bologna: Il Mulino, 'Saggi no. 114', 1972, 260p.

1253 Hesnard, A. *L'Oeuvre de Freud et son importance pour le monde moderne.* Préface de Maurice Merleau-Ponty. Paris: Payot, 1960, pp. 286-289.

1254 Kasakoff, Alice. "Lévi-Strauss' idea of social unconscious." see Rossi, no. 23

Makarius, Raoul, and Laura Makarius. "Lévi-Strauss et les structures inconscientes de l'esprit." see 682 Reprinted as "Tristes structures," in 44.

160　UNCONSCIOUS

1255　Renzi, Emilio. "Sulla nozione di inconscio in Lévi-Strauss." *Aut Aut*, no. 88, July 1965, pp. 55-61. Portuguese translation, "Sobre a noção do inconsciente em Lévi-Strauss," in Luiz Costa Lima, *O Estruturalismo de Lévi-Strauss*. Petropolis, Vozes, 1969, pp. 107-113.

1256　Rossi, Ino. "Unconscious in the anthropology of Claude Lévi-Strauss." *American Anthropologist*, vol. LXXV, February 1973, pp. 20-48.

　　　Rossi, Ino. see 23

1257　Rossi, Ino. "The intellectual antecedents of Lévi-Strauss' notion of unconscious," in 23.

UNIVERSALITY

1258　Verstraeten, Pierre. "Universalité naturelle et culturelle chez Lévi-Strauss." *Annales de l'Institut de Philosophie*, 1969, pp. 59-107.

VALUE

1259　Reynolds, Larry T. and Janice M. Reynolds. "The givens of Claude Lévi-Strauss. A value analysis in the sociology of knowledge." *Journal of Value Inquiry*, vol. II, Spring 1968, pp. 22-30.

VIKING MEDAL

1260　Anonymous. "Six selected as candidates for 1965 Viking medal." *American Anthropologist*, vol. LXVII, February 1965, p. 73.

WOMEN

　　　McNelly, Cleo. see 259

REVIEWS THAT HAVE DEVOTED SPECIAL ISSUES TO
LEVI-STRAUSS AND STRUCTURALISM

1261 *Aletheia,* "Le structuralisme," no. 4, mai 1966, pp. 187-241. [Articles by Barthes, Thion, Lévi-Strauss, Godelier, Axelos]

1262 *Alternative,* vol. X, 1967, "Strukturalismusdiskussion (mit Bibliographie)"

1263 *Alternative,* vol. XI, 1968, "Strukturalismus und Literaturwissenschaft."

1264 *Annales (Economies--Sociétés--Civilisations),* 19e année, no. 6, novembre-decembre 1964, pp. 1085-1115. [Articles by R. Barthes, Raphael Dividal, Edmund Leach. An excellent set of articles.]

1265 *L'Arc,* "Claude Lévi-Strauss," no. 26, 1965. [Articles by Pingaud, Genette, de Heusch, Lévi-Strauss, Deliège, Pouillon. Notes by Guiart, Gardin, Clastres]

1266 *Aut Aut,* "Claude Lévi-Strauss," no. 88, July 1965. [Articles by A. Bonomi, P. Caruso, E. Renzi, etc.]

1267 *Bulletin de la Société française de Philosophie,* "Le langage et l'immanence," no. 1, janvier-mars, 1965.

1268 *Cahiers de Philosophie,* "L'anthropologie," no. 1, janvier 1966.

1269 *Cahiers Internationaux de Symbolisme,* "Le structuralisme," nos. 17-18, 1969. [Articles by Durand, Piaget, Gonseth and Rudhardt]

1270 *Cahiers pour l'Analyse,* "Lévi-Strauss dans le XVIIIe siècle," no. 4, 1966. [Essays by Derrida and Mosconi]

1271 *Communications,* "L'analyse structurale du récit," no. 8, 1966.

1272 *Esprit, "La Pensée Sauvage* et le structuralisme," no. 322, novembre 1963, pp. 543-627. [Articles by Cuisenier, Ruwet, Gaboriau, Ricoeur, followed by a discussion with Lévi-Strauss]

REVIEWS

1273 *Esprit*, "Structuralismes: idéologie et méthode," 35e année, no. 360, mai 1967, pp. 769-976. [Articles by Domenach, Cuisenier, Bertherat, Conhil, Dufrenne, Ricoeur, Burgelin, Ladrière]

1274 *Esprit*, "Le mythe aujourd'hui," no. 4, 1971. [Articles by Barthes, Calvino, Rabant, Ramnous, Lévi-Strauss, Boyer, etc.]

1275 *Kursbuch*, no. 5, May 1966, "Strukturalismus."

1276 *Meddelelser fra Danskloererforeningen*. No. 1, 1971, "Claude Lévi-Strauss."

1277 *Le Monde, [des Livres]*, no. 8339, 5 novembre 1971, pp. 19-21.

1278 *Nouvelle Revue de Psychanalyse*, "Incidences de la psychanalyse," no. 1, Spring 1970.

1278a *La Pensée*, "Structuralsime et marxisme," no. 135, octobre 1967. [Articles by Mouloud, Dubois, Cohen, Deschamps, etc.]

1279 *Revista de Filologia Espanola*, "Problemas y principios del estructuralismo linguistico," vol. XVI, 1967.

1280 *Revista de Filosofía de la Universidad de Costa Rica*, vol. XI, no. 32, January-June 1973.

1281 *Revue Internationale de Philosophie*, "La notion de structure," nos. 73-74, fasc. 3-4, 1965. [Articles by Granger, Martinet, Mouloud, Francastel, Paci, etc.]

1282 *Revue de l'Enseignement Supérieur*, "Les sciences ethnologiques," vol. III, 1965.

1282a *Renascità*

1283 *Les Temps Modernes,* "Problèmes du structuralisme," no. 246, 1966. [Articles by Pouillon, Barbut, Greimas, Godelier, Bourdieu, Macherey and Ehrmann]

1284 *Yale French Studies*, "Structuralism," nos. 36-37, 1966. [Essays by Martinet, Lévi-Strauss, Scheffler, Lacan, Ehrmann, Riffaterre, Lewis, etc.]

SECTION 7: APPENDIX: ADDITIONAL ITEMS

APPENDIX: ADDITIONAL ITEMS

BOOKS

1290 Badcock, C. R. *Lévi-Strauss. Structuralism and Sociological Theory.* London: Hutchinson, 1975, 126p.

1291 Barksdale, E. C. *The Dacha and the Duchess. An application of Lévi-Strauss's theory of myth in human creativity to works of nineteenth-century Russian novelists.* New York: Philosophical Library, Inc., 1974.

1292 Carreras, Alberto. *El estructuralismo de Lévi-Strauss.* Valencia: Universidad; Facultad de Filosofía y Letras, 1972, 13p. [es tirada aparte de *Saitabi*, 1972, pp. 23-35]

1293 Del Ninno, M. *L'Analisi dei miti in Claude Lévi-Strauss: Lessico metodologico.* Quaderni del Circolo Semiologico Siciliano, 6, 1975.

1294 Klein, Sh., et al. *Modelling Propp and Lévi-Strauss in a meta-symbolic simulation system.* Computer Sciences Department, University of Wisconsin, Madison, 1974.

1295 Leach, Edmund R. *Culture and Communication.* The Logic by which symbols are connected. New York: Cambridge University Press, 1976. [*Les Mythologiques*]

1296 Merquior, J. G. *A Estética de Lévi-Strauss.* (Biblioteca Tempo Universitario, 40.) Rio de Janeiro: Tempo Brasileiro, 1975.

1297 Muntz, Peter. *When the 'Golden Bough' Breaks. Structuralism or Typology?* London-Boston: Routledge and Kegan Paul, 1973.

1298 Prado Júnior, Caio. *Estruturalismo de Lévi-Strauss e marxismo de Louis Althusser.* São Paulo: Editora Brasiliense, 1971, 108p.

CHAPTERS AND/OR SECTIONS IN BOOKS

1299 Bauman, Zygmunt. *Culture as praxis*. London: Routledge and Kegan Paul, 1973, 198p.

1300 Bloch, Maurice, ed. *Marxist Analyses and social anthropology*. New York: John Wiley and Sons, 1975.

1301 Bohannon, Saul J. and Mack Glazer, eds. *High Points in Anthropology*. New York: Alfred A. Knopf, 1973.

1302 Bühl, W. L. *Funktion und Struktur* (Nymphenburger Texte zur Wissenschaft Modelluniversitat, 20). München: Nympehnburger Verlagshandlung, 1975.

1303 Chiari, Joseph. "Structuralism," pp. 161-187 in *Twentieth Century French thought from Bergson to Lévi-Strauss*. London: Paul Elek, and New York: Gordion Press Inc., 1975, 207p.

1304 Domenach, Jean-Marie. *Le Sauvage et l'ordinateur*. Paris: Editions du Seuil, 1976.

1305 Douglas, Mary. *Natural symbols. Explorations in cosmology*. London: Barrie and Rockliff/The Cresset Press, 1970. Also Harmondsworth, Middlessex: Penguin Books, 1973.

1306 Georgi, Robert. *Le Temps freudien du verbe*. Lausanne: L'Age d'Homme, 1973, 164p.

1307 Lowell, Robert. "Lévi-Strauss in London" [a poem], in *History*. London: Faber and Faber, 1973.

1308 Murphy, Robert E. "Lévi-Strauss," pp. 177-205 (and passim) in *The Dialectics of Social Life: Alarms and excursions in anthropological theory*. New York-London: Basic Books, Inc., 1971.

1309 Needham, Rodney. *Remarks and Inventions. Skeptical essays about kinship*. London: Tavistock Publications, 1974.

1310 Needham, Rodney, ed. *Rethinking Kinship and marriage*. London: Tavistock Publications, 1971. (pp. 125-129, 172-179 and passim)

1311 Nutini, Hugo G. *San Bernardino Contla. Marriage and family structure in a Tlaxcalan Municipio.* Pittsburgh, Pa.: University of Pittsburgh Press, 1968 [pp. 378-383 on concept of 'structure'].

1312 Oppitz, M. *Notwendige Beziehungen. Abriss der Strukturalen Anthropologie.* (Suhrkamp Taschenbuch Wissenschaft, 101). Frankfurt am Main: Suhrkamp, 1975.

1313 Petterlini, A. *Filosofia e antropologia. Richerche metodologische.* Verona: Fiorini, 1975, 153p.

1314 Pettit, Philip. *The Concept of structuralism: A critical analysis.* Dublin: Gill and Macmillan, 1975, 117p.

1315 Poster, Mark. "Sartre and structuralism," pp. 306-340 in *Existential Marxism in postwar France.* Princeton, N.J.: Princeton University Press, 1975.

1316 Régnier, André. *La Crise du langage scientifique.* Paris: Anthropos, 1974, 402p.

1317 Said, Edward. *Beginnings. Intention and Method.* New York: Basic Books, 1975.

1318 Schaff, Adam. "Le structuralisme en tant que courant intellectuel," pp. 9-45 in *Structuralisme et marxisme.* Traduit du polonais par Claire Brendel. Paris: Editions Anthropos, 1974, pp. 9-45.

1319 Tagliacozzo, G., ed. *Giambattista Vico, Galiani, Joyce, Lévi-Strauss, Piaget.* Roma: Armando Armando Editore, 1975.

1320 Védrine, Hélène. *Les philosophies de l'histoire, Déclin ou crise?* Paris: Payot, 1975.

DISSERTATIONS

1321 Pace, Allen David, Jr. "The bearer of ashes: Claude Lévi-Strauss and the rpoblem of cultural relativism." Ph.D. dissertation, Yale University. *Dissertation Abstracts International*, vol. XXXVI, no. 11, May 1974, p. 7164-A.

168 APPENDIX

ARTICLES IN PERIODICALS

1322   Anonymous. "The Waste Land and the Hot House? Notes on
       a Lecture by Lévi-Strauss," *Royal Anthropological
       Institue News*, no. 12, January-February, 1976.

1323   Anonymous. "Taller men wear longer trousers." *Economist*,
       vol. CCLI, no. 6817, April 20, 1974, pp. 123-124.
       [Louis Althusser]

1324   Anonymous. "Un ethnologue de la culture. Entretien avec
       Claude Lévi-Strauss." *La Nouvelle Critique*, no. 61,
       1973, pp. 27-36.

1325   Anonymous. "Institut: M. Claude Lévi-Strauss candidat
       à l'Académie Française." *Le Monde*, no. 8733, 10 février
       1973, p. 25.

1326   Anonymous. "The anti-structuralists." *Times Literary
       Supplement*, no. 3750, January 18, 1974, p. 58.

1327   Anonymous. "Myths and supermyths." *Economist*, vol.
       CCXLVII, no. 6765, April 21, 1973, pp. 114-115.
       [*From Honey to Ashes*]

1328   Bergson, Philip. *"Tristes Tropiques*, by Claude Lévi-
       Strauss. Translated by John and Doreen Weightman."
       Oxford Literary Review, Spring Term 1974, p. 5.

1329   Bonilla, Luis. "Ciencias sociales." *Estafeta Literaria*,
       núm. 539, 10 mayo 1974, pp. 1711-1712. [*El Futuro de
       los estudios del parentesco*]

1330   Boon, James A. and David M. Schneider. "Kinship vis-a-
       vis Myth: Contrasts in Lévi-Strauss' approach to cross-
       cultural comparison." *American Anthropologist*, vol. 76,
       no. 4, December 1974, pp. 799-817.

1331   Bostoen, H. "Het mensbeeld van Claude Lévi-Strauss."
       Bijdragen, vol. XXXV, 1974, pp. 82-99. [L'Homme
       chez Claude Lévi-Strauss, 99-100]

1332   Bostoen, H. "Wijsgerige vragen over de antopologie van
       Claude Lévi-Strauss." *Bijdragen*, vol. XXXV, 1974,
       pp. 186-200. [Résumé: Questions philosophiques au
       sujet de l'anthropologie lévi-straussienne, 201]

APPENDIX   169

1333   Brown, Edward J.   Review of James A. Boon, *From Symbolism
       to structuralism*. (See no. 1)   *Clio*, vol. 4, June 1975,
       pp. 416-419.

1334   Bulhof, Ilse N. "Structure and Change in Welhelm
       Dilthey's Philosophy of History." *History and Theory*,
       vol. XV, 1976, pp. 21-32.

1335   Burkhart, John E. "Lévi-Strauss, structural anthropolo-
       gist." *Listening*, vol. X, Fall 1975, pp. 32-43.

1336   Clavel, Maurice. "La pomme et le pissenlit." *Le Nouvel
       Observateur*, no. 502, 24-30 juin 1974, pp. 60-61.

1337   Clément, Catherine. "Le rire de Demeter." *Critique*,
       no. 323, avril 1974, pp. 306-325. [*L'Homme nu*]

1338   DaVia, Guiseppe. "Lo strutturalismo." *Osservatore
       Romano*, anno CVIX, no. 284, 9-10 dic. 1974, p. 3.

1339   de Araúgo, Ma. L.   *"Mythologiques IV." Rivista da
       Faculdade de Letras*. Serie de Filosofía (Porto),
       vol. I, 1971, pp. 275-282; and vol. II, 1972, pp. 107-
       122.

1340   De Meireles, José Luis. "Antopologia estructural: A
       proibicão do incesto segundo Lévi-Strauss." *Revista
       Portuguesa de Filosofia*, vol. XXXI, Julio-sept. 1975,
       pp. 268-283.

1341   Demetz, Peter. "Literary scholarship: past and future."
       Comparative Literature Studies, vol. 10, no. 4,
       December 1973, pp. 364-373.

1342   Dennis, Ph. A. "Lévi-Strauss in the Kindergarten:
       The Montessori preschooler as bricoleur." *International
       Review of Education*, [The Hague] vol. XX, no. 1, 1974.

1343   Donato, Eugenio. "Structuralism. The aftermath."
       Sub-Stance, no. 7, Fall 1973, pp. 9-26.

1344   Eckert, Charles W. "The English cine-structuralists."
       Film Comment, vol. IX, no. 3, May-June 1973, pp. 46-51.

1345   Faucci, Dario. "Vico, Rousseau, Lévi-Strauss," pp. 200-
       202 in Per l'edizione nazionale di Vico. A cura di
       Umberto Bosco et al. *Bolletin C. St. Vichiani*, vol. III,
       1973, pp. 200-202.

APPENDIX

1346 Goddard, David. "Philosophy and structuralisme."
Philosophy of Social Science, vol. V, June 1975,
pp. 103-123.

1347 Gorer, Geoffrey. "Tour de force." *Observer*, [*Tristes
Tropiques*] no. 9,520, January 13, 1974, p. 25.

1348 Gramont, Sanche de. "No hay sociedades superioreres."
Revista de Occidente, vol. XXXVIII, núm. 113-114,
agosto-sept. 1972, pp. 215-232.

1349 Hammon, Philippe. "Narrative semiotics in France."
Style, vol. VIII, no. 1, Winter 1974, pp. 30-45.

1350 Hanhardt, John G., and Charles H. Harpole." Linguistics,
structuralism and semiology. Approaches to the cinema
with a bibliography." *Film Comment*, vol. IX, no. 3,
May-June 1973, pp. 52-59.

1351 Harris M. "Lévi-Strauss et la palourde." *L'Homme*,
vol. XVI, no. 2, 1976.

1352 Heinrichs, H. J. "Die Besinnung auf das Allgemeine. Zu
dem Werk von Claude Lévi-Strauss." *Psyche. Zeitschrift
für Psychoanalyse und ihre Anwendungen*, Heft 2-XXX,
1976.

1353 Kaplan, M. "A note on Nutini's 'The ideological bases
of Lévi-Strauss' structuralism!" *American Anthropologist*, vol. LXXVI, 1974, pp. 62-65.

1354 Keesing, Roger M. "Transformational linguistics and
structural anthropology." *Cultural Hermeneutics*,
vol. II, 1974, pp. 243-266 [Chomsky and L-S].

1355 Laffly, Georges. "La réception de Claude Lévi-Strauss
à l'Académie." *Ecrits de Paris*, no. 339, septembre
1974, pp. 95-103.

1356 Leach, Edmund. "Vico e Lévi-Strauss sull'origine dell'
umanità." *Rassegna Italiana di Sociologia* (Bologna),
vol. XIII, no. 2, 1972, pp. 221-233.

1357 Le Clézio, J. M. G. "Claude Lévi-Strauss: *L'Homme nu.*"
Cahiers du Chemin, no. 21, 15 avril 1974, pp. 171-184.

1358 LeGoff, Jacques, and Pierre Vidal-Naquet. "Lévi-Strauss
      en Broceliande." *Critique*, no. 325, juin 1974, pp. 541-
      571. [*Anthropologie structurale deux*]

1359 Magana Esquivel, Antonio. "El hombre y su lenguaje."
      Hispano Americano, núm. 1335, 4 dic. 1974, p. 72
      [On Octavio Paz, *Claude Lévi-Strauss o el neuvo festin
      de Esopo*]

1360 McCormack, William C. Review of Peter Munz, "*When the
      Golden Bough Breaks: Structuralism or Typology.*"
      American Anthropologist, vol. LXXVIII, no. 1, March
      1976, p. 144.

1361 Murphy, Robert F. "Remarkable feast." *New Republic*,
      vol. CLXX, no. 20, May 18, 1974, pp. 23-24. [*Tristes
      tropiques*]

1362 Petrus, Leon C. "The word as metaphor. An inter-
      disciplinary theory." *Soundings*, no. 3, Fall 1972,
      pp. 269-291.

1363 Pierre, José. "Dans les masques présentés par Lévi-
      Strauss, José Pierre a vu de drôles de choses."
      La Quinzaine Littéraire, no. 224, 1-15 janvier, 1976,
      pp. 16-17, 30. [*La Voie des Masques*]

1364 Rétif, A. "*La Pensée Sauvage, Le Totémisme aujourd'hui.*"
      Etudes, tome CCCXV, 1962, pp. 427-428.

1365 Rheims, M. "*La Voie des masques.*" *La Nouvelle Revue des
      Deux Mondes*, mars 1976, pp. 588-598.

1366 Richmann, Michele. "G. Bataille, *Death and Sensuality*
      . . . Lévi-Strauss, *The Elementary Structures of
      Kinship.*" *Diacritics*, vol. VI, no. 1, Spring 1976,
      pp. 46-53.

1367 Rosenberg, Aubrey. "The temperamental affinities of
      Rousseau and Lévi-Strauss." *Queen's Quarterly*,
      vol. LXXXII, no. 4, Winter 1975, pp. 543-555.

1368 Rossi, Ino. Review of *Structural Anthropology, Volume II*,
      --Boon and Korn." *American Anthropologist*, vol. LXXVIII,
      no. 1, March 1976, p. 145.

1369 Rossi, Ino. Review of Raoul and Laura Makarius, *Structuralisme ou ethnologie*. *American Anthropologist*, vol. LXXVII, no. 4, December 1975, pp. 931-933.

1370 Salazar Cardenas, Rafael. "El hombre total J. P. Sartre, Claude Lévi-Strauss ." *Libro Annual* (ISEE, México), vol. II, 1973-1974, pp. 181-191.

1371 Salovesh, Michael. "Baiting a master and his masterwork." *Review in Anthropology*, vol. I, no. 3, August 1974, pp. 414-424. [Review of Francis Korn, see no. 11]

1372 Soto Verges, Rafael. "Literatura mágica." *Estafeta Literaria*, núm. 545, 10 agosto, 1974, pp. 4-7.

1373 Sperber, Dan. "The Myth behind the mask. *La Voie des masques*." *Times Literary Supplement*, 12 March 1976, no. 3, 861, p. 286.

1374 Steiner, George. "The lost garden." *New Yorker*, vol. L, no. 15, June 3, 1974, pp. 100-108. [*Tristes Tropiques*, Durkheim]

1375 Strenski, Ivan. "Reductionism and structural anthropology." *Inquiry*, vol. XIX, no. 1, Spring 1976, pp. 73-89.

1376 Sturrock, John. "Systems and brothers." *New Review* (London), vol. I, no. 4, July 1974, pp. 77-78.

1377 Thomas, L. L., and J. Z. Kronenfeld and D. B. Kronenfeld. "Asdiwal crumbles: A critique of L vi-Straussian myth analysis." *American Anthropologist*, vol. LXXVIII, no. 3, 1976.

1378 Urrutia, Benjamin. "Lévi-Strauss and Mormonism." *American Anthropolgist*, vol. LXXVI, no. 2, June 1974, p. 342. [*Les Structures élémentaires de la parenté*]

1379 Vogt, W. Paul. "The use of studying primitives: A note on the Durkheimians, 1890-1940." *History and Theory*, vol. XV, 1976, pp. 33-44.

1380 Werblowsky, R. J. Z. "Structure and Archetype." *The Journal of the Ancient Near Eastern Society of Columbia University*, vol. V, 1973.

1381 White, Hayden V. "Historicism, History, and the Figurative Imagination." *History and Theory*, vol. XIV, 1975, pp. 48-67.

1382 Wieting, S. G. "Myth and symbol analysis of Claude Lévi-Strauss and Victor Turner." *Social Compass* (Louvain), vol. XIX, no. 2, 1972, pp. 139-154.

1383 Witte, H. *"Mythologiques I."* Cahiers du Symbolisme, no. 7, 1965, pp. 83-84.

1384 Zimmerman, Marc. "Theoretical bases of the Marxist-Structuralist Encounter." *New German Critique*, no. 7, Winter 1976-76.

PART TWO

BIBLIOGRAPHY OF THE WRITINGS OF
CLAUDE LEVI-STRAUSS

1936

1400 "Contribution à l'étude de l'organisation sociale des Indiens Bororo." *Journal de la Société des Américanistes*, vol. XXVIII, fascicule 2, pp. 269-304.

1401 "Entre os selvagems civilizados." *O Estado de São Paulo*.

1402 "Os mais vastos horizontes do mundo." *Filosofia, Ciências e Letras*, vol. I, pp. 66-69 (São Paulo).

1937

1403 "A civilisação chaco-santiaguena." *Revista do Arquivo Municipal*, vol. IV, (São Paulo), 28p.

1404 "La sociologie culturelle et son enseignement." *Filosofia, Ciencias e Letras*, (São Paulo), vol. II.

1405 "Poupées Karaja." *Boletim de la Sociedade de Etnografia e de Folklore*, (São Paulo), vol. I.

1406 "Indiens du Brésil (Mato-Grosso)." Mission Claude et Dina Lévi-Strauss. Guide-catlogue de l'exposition (21 janvier-3 février 1937). Muséum National d'Histoire Naturelle, Musée de l'Homme, Paris, pp. 1-14.

1942

1407 "Fards indiens." *VVV*, vol. I, no. 1, pp. 33-35.

1408 "Souvenir of Malinowski." *VVV*, vol. I, no. 1, p. 45.

1943

1409 "The art of the Northwest Coast at the American Museum of Natural History." *Gazette des Beaux-Arts* (New York), pp. 175-182.

1410 "Guerre et commerce chez les Indiens d'Amérique du Sud." *Renaissance* (Revue trimestrielle publiée par l'Ecole Libre des Hautes Etudes, New York), vol. I, fascicule 1-2, pp. 122-139.

1411 "The social use of kinship terms among Brazilian Indians." *American Anthropologist*, vol. XLV, no. 3, July-September, pp. 398-409.

1412 Review of Leo Simmons, *Sun Chief*. *Social Research*, no. 10, pp. 515-517.

1944

1413 "On dual organization in South America." *America Indigena* (Mexico), vol. IV, pp. 37-47.

1414 "The social and psychological aspects of chieftainship in a primitive tribe: The Nambikwara of Northwestern Mato-Gross." *Transactions of the New York Academy of Sciences*, series II, vol. VII, no. 1, pp. 16-32. Reprinted in Ronald Cohen and John Middleton, eds., *Comparative Political Systems*. New York: The Natural History Press, 1967.

1415 "Reciprocity and hierarchy." *American Anthropologist*, vol. XLVI, no. 2, pp. 266-268.

1945

1416 "L'analyse structurale en linguistique et en anthropologie." *Word* (Journal of the Linguistic Circle of New York), vol. I, no. 2, pp. 1-21. [Reprinted in *Anthropologie structurale*, chapter II.]

1417 "Le dédoublement de la représentation dans les arts de l'Asie et de l'Amérique." *Renaissance* (New York), vol. II-III, 1944-1945, pp. 168-186. [Reprinted in *Anthropologie structurale*, chapter XIII.]

1418 "L'oeuvre d'Edward Westermarck." *Revue de l'Histoire des Religions*, tome CXXIX, nos. 1, 2 and 3, pp. 84-100.

1946

1419 "French sociology," in *Sociology in the Twentieth Century*, edited by G. Gurwitch and Wilbert E. Moore, pp. 503-537. New York: Philosophical Library, Inc. French translation, *La Sociologie au XXe siècle*. Paris: Presses Universitaires de France, 1947, pp. 513-545.

1420 "The name of the Manbikwara." *American Anthropologist*, vol. XLVIII, no. 1, pp. 139-140.

1421 "La technique du bonheur." *Esprit*, no. 127, pp. 643-652. [Special number dedicated to 'L'homme américain' (Written in 1944)]

1947

1422 "La théorie du pouvoir dans une société primitive," in *Les Doctrines politiques modernes*, pp. 41-63. New York: Brentano.

1423 "Sur certaines similarités morphologiques entre les langues chibcha et nambikwara." *Actes du XXVIIIe Congrès International des Américanistes*, Paris, pp. 185-192.

1424 "Le serpent au corps rempli de poissons." *Actes du XXVIIIe Congrès International des Américanistes*, Paris, pp. 633-636. [Reprinted in *Anthropologie structurale*, chapter XIV, pp. 295-299. German translation, "Die Shlange mit dem Korper voller Fische," *Strukturale Anthropologie*, pp. 292-296 (Translated by Hans Naumann). English translation, *Strucural Anthropology*.]

1948

1425 *La Vie familiale et sociale des Indiens Nambikwara*. Paris: Société des Américanistes, Gonthier, 132p. Italian translation by P. Caruso, *La Vita familiare e sociale degli Indiani Nambikwara*. Torino: Einaudi, 1970.

180 BIBLIOGRAPHY

1426 "The Tupi-Kawahib," in *Handbook of South American Indians*, edited by J. Steward, Bureau of American Ethnology, Smithsonian Institution, Washington, vol. III, pp. 299-305.

1427 "The Tribes of the Upper Xingu River," in *Ibid.*, vol. III, pp. 321-348.

1428 "The Nambicuara," in *Ibid.*, vol. III, pp. 361-369.

1429 "The Tribes of the Right Bank of the Guaporé River," in *Ibid.*, vol. III, pp. 371-379.

1949

1430 *Les Structures élémentaires de la parenté*. Paris: Presses Universitaires de France, 640p. (Prix Paul Pelliot). Reedited 1967, Paris: Mouton.
Italian translation, *Le Strutture elementari della parentela*, trad. di A. M. Cierse e L. Serafini. Milano: Feltrinelli, 1969.
English translation by J. H. Bell, J. R. von Sturmer, and R. Needham, *The Elementary Structures of Kinship*. Boston: Beacon Press, 1969, 512p.
German translation of ch. I, "Natur und Kultur," in W. E. Mühlmann und E. W. Müller (Hrsg), *Kulturanthropologie*. Köln-Berlin, 1966.

1431 "L'efficacité symbolique." *Revue de l'Histoire des Religions*, tome CXXXV, no. 1, pp. 5-27. Reprinted in *Anthropologie structurale*, chapter X, pp. 205-227. German translation, "Die Wirksamkeit der Symbole," pp. 204-226 in *Strukturale Anthropologie*.

1432 "Histoire et ethnologie." *Revue de Métaphysique et de Morale*, 54e année, nos. 3-4, pp. 363-391. Reprinted as Introduction to *Anthropologie structurale*, pp. 3-33, "Introduction: Histoire et ethnologie."
German translation, "Einleitung: Geschichte und Ethnologie," pp. 11-40 in *Strukturale Anthropologie*.

1433 "La politique étrangère d'une société primitive." *Politique Etrangère*, no. 2, May, pp. 139-152.

BIBLIOGRAPHY 181

1434 "Le sorcier et sa magie." *Les Temps Modernes*, 4e année, no. 41, pp. 3-24. Reprinted, chapter IX in *Anthropologie structurale*, pp. 183-203.
German translation, "Der Zauberer und seine Magie," pp. 183-203.
English translation, "The sorcerer and his magic," in John Middleton, ed., *Magic, Witchcraft and Curing*. New York: The Natural History Press, 1967.

1950

1435 "Introduction à l'oeuvre de Marcel Mauss," in M. Mauss, *Sociologie et anthropologie*. Paris: Presses Universitaires de France, pp. IX-LII. 3rd ed. 1966. Italian translation by F. Zannino, *Teoria generale della magia e altri saggi*. Torino: Einaudi, 1965.

1436 "Marcel Mauss." *Cahiers Internationaux de Sociologie*, vol. VIII, pp. 72-112.

1437 "The use of wild plants in Tropical South America," in *Handbook of South American Indians*, edited by J. Steward, Bureau of American Ethnology, Smithsonian Institution, Washington, vol. III, pp. 465-486.

1438 "Préface," to Katherine Dunham, *Danses d'Haiti*. Paris: Fasquelle.

1439 "Préface," to C. Berndt, *Women's Changing Ceremonies in Northern Australia*. *Cahiers de l'Homme*, vol. I, no. 1, pp. 3-8.

1440 "Documents rama-rama." *Journal de la Société des Américanistes*, tome XXXIX, pp. 84-100.

1441 "Sur certains objets en poterie d'usage douteux provenant de la Syrie et de l'Inde." *Syria*, tome XXVII, fascicule 1-2, pp. 1-4.

1951

1442 "Avant-propos," *Bulletin International des Sciences Sociales*, Paris: UNESCO, (numéro spécial consacré à l'Asie du Sud-Est), vol. III, no. 4, pp. 825-829.

1443 "Les sciences sociales au Pakistan," in *Ibid.*, vol. III, no. 4, pp. 885-892.

1444 "Language and the analysis of social laws." *American Anthropologist*, vol. LIII, no. 2, pp. 155-163.
Reprinted in chapter 3, pp. 63-75 of *Anthropologie structurale*, "Langage et société."
German translation, "Sprache und Gesellschaft," in *Kursbuch*, 5, 1966; and in *Strukturale Anthropologie*, pp. 68-79.

1952

1445 *Race et histoire*. Paris: UNESCO, 52p. Reedited, Paris: Gonthier, 1967. Reprinted in *Anthropologie structurale II*, pp. 377-422.
Italian translation by P. Caruso, *Razza e storia e altri studi di antropologia*. Torino: Einaudi, 1967.
German translation by Traugolt Konig, *Rasse und Geschichte*. Frankfurt am Main: Suhrkamp, 1972, 102p.

1446 "Social structure." Wenner-Gren Foundation International Symposium on Anthropology, New York. Reprinted, pp. 524-558 in *Anthropology Today*, prepared under the chairmanship of A. L. Kroeber. Chicago: University of Chicago Press, 1953. Also reprinted, "Structure sociale," in *Bulletin de Psychologie*, vol. VI, no. 7, 1953, pp. 358-390. Also chapter XV, "La notion de structure en ethnologie," pp. 303-351 in *Anthropologie structurale*.
German translation, "Die Strukturbegriff in der Ethnologie," pp. 299-346 in *Strukturale Anthropologie*.

1447 "Kinship systems of three Chittagong Hill tribes." *Southwestern Journal of Anthropology*, vol. VIII, no. 1, pp. 40-51.

1448 "Miscellaneous notes on the Kuki." *Man*, vol. LI, no. 284, pp. 167-169.

1449 "La notion d'archaisme en ethnologie." *Cahiers Internationaux de Sociologie*, vol. XIII, pp. 3-25. Reprinted, chapter VI, pp. 113-132 in *Anthropologie structurale*.
German translation "Der Begriff des Archaismus in der Ethnologie," pp. 115-134 in *Strukturale Anthropologie*.

1450 "Le Père Noël supplicié." *Les Temps Modernes*, 7e année, no. 77, pp. 1572-1590.
Abridged English translation, "Where does Father Christmas come from," in *New Society*, 19, 1963, pp. 6-8.
Italian translation in *Razza e storia e altri studi di antropologia*, a cura di P. Caruso. Torino: Einaudi, 1967.

1451 "Les structures sociales dans le Brésil central et oriental." *Proceedings of the 29th International Congress of Americanists*, vol. III. Reprinted in Sol Tax, ed., *Indian Tribes of Aborininal America*, Chicago: University of Chicago Press, 1952, pp. 302-310.
Reprinted, chapter VII, pp. 133-145 of *Anthropologie structurale*.
German translation, "Die sozialen Strukturen in Zentral- und Ostbrasilien," pp. 135-147 in *Strukturale Anthropologie*.

1452 "Le syncrétisme religieux d'un village mogh du territoire de Chittagong." *Revue de l'Histoire des Religions*, tome CXLI, 1951-1952, no. 2, pp. 202-237.

1453 "La visite des âmes." *Annuaire de l'Ecole Pratique des Hautes Etudes*. (Ve section--Sciences religieuses), 1951-1952, pp. 20-23.

1454 "Toward a general theory of communication." Paper submitted to the International Conference of Linguists and Anthropologists, Bloomington, University of Indiana (mimeographed).

1953

1455 "Chapter One," in Results of the Conference of Anthropologists and Linguists, in *Supplement* to *International Journal of American Linguistics*, vol. XIX, no. 2, April, pp. 1-10. (Translated and adapted, chapter IV, pp. 77-91, "Linguistique et anthropologie," in *Anthropologie structurale*.)
German translation "Sprachwissenschaft und Anthropologie," pp. 80-94 in *Strukturale Anthropologie*.

1456 "Panorama de l'ethnologie, 1951-1952." *Diogène*, vol. II, pp. 96-123.
German translation, "Überblick über die Ethnologie." *Diogenes. Internationale Zeitschrift für Philosophie und Wissenschaft*, vol. I, 1953-1954, pp. 230-256.

1457 "Recherches de mythologie américaine (1)." *Annuaire de l'Ecole Pratique des Hautes Etudes* (Sciences religieuses), 1952-1953, pp. 19-21.

"Social structure." see 1346

"Structure sociale." *Bulletin de Psychologie*, vol. VI, no. 5, pp. 358-390. see 1952

1954

1458 "L'art de déchiffrer les symboles." *Diogène*, no. 5, pp. 128-135.
German translation, "Die Kunst, Symbole zu deuten." *Diogenes*, vol. II, 1954-1955, pp. 684-688.

1459 "Place de l'anthropologie dans les sciences sociales et problèmes posés par son enseignement." *Les Sciences Sociales dans l'Enseignement Supérieur*, Paris: UNESCO, 32p. Reprinted, chapter XVII, pp. 377-418 in *Anthropologie structurale*.
German translation, "Die Stellung der Anthropologie in den "Sozialwissenschaften und die daraus resultierenden Unterrichtsprobleme," pp. 369-408 in *Strukturale Anthropologie*.

1460 "Qu'est-ce qu'un primitif?" *Le Courrier*, UNESCO, nos. 8-9, pp. 5-7.

1461 "Recherches de mythologie américaine (2)." *Annuaire de l'Ecole Pratique des Hautes Etudes* (Section des Sciences religieuses), 1953-1954, pp. 27-29.

1955

1462 *Tristes Tropiques.* Paris: Plon, 462p. Later published in pocket book edition, Paris: Union Générale d'Editions, Collection 10-18, nos. 12-13. New edition 1974.
English translation by John Russell, *A World of Wane.* London: Hutchinson, 1961. [Chapters 14, 15, 25, 34 of the French edition are omitted in this translation.] New translation by J. Weightman, London: Cape, 1973-- New York: Atheneum, 1974, *Tristes Tropiques,* 1st American edition. New York: Criterion Books, 1961. Abridged German translation by Suzanne Heintz, *Traurige Tropen.* Köln: Verlag Kiepenheuer and Witsch, 1960. Italian translation by B. Garufi, *Tristi Tropici.* Milano: Il Saggiatore, 1960.

1463 "Diogène couché." *Les Temps Modernes,* no. 110, pp. 1187-1220.

1464 "Les mathématiques de l'homme." *Bulletin International des Sciences Sociales,* (numéro spécial sur les mathématiques), vol. VI, no. 4, pp. 643-653. Reprinted in *Esprit,* vol. XXIV, no. 10, pp. 525-538.
German translation, "Die Mathematik vom Menschen," *Kursbuch,* 8, 1965, pp. 176-188.
Spanish translation, "Las matematicas del hombre," in *Estructuralismo e epistemologia.* Selecc. de José Sazbon. Trad. j. Castorina e.a. Buenos Aires: Ed. Nueva Visión, 1970. Coll. "El pensamiento estructuralista, no. 10.

1465 "Rapports de la mythologie et du rituel." *Annuaire de l'Ecole Pratique des Hautes Etudes* (Sciences religieuses), 1954-1955, pp. 25-28.

1466 "Les structures élémentaires de la parenté." *La Progenèsa,* Centre International de l'Enfance (Travaux et Documents VIII). Paris: Masson, pp. 105-110.

1467 "The structural study of myth." *Journal of American Folklore*, vol. LXVIII, no. 270, pp. 428-444.
French translation with some modifications, "La structure des mythes," chapter XI, pp. 226-255 in *Anthropologie structurale*.
German translation, "Die Struktur der Mythen," pp. 226-254 in *Strukturale Anthropologie*.

1956

1468 "The family," pp. 261-285 in *Man, Culture and Society*, edited by Harry L. Shapiro. London, New York: Oxford University Press, pp. 261-285.
Italian translation by P. Caruso, in *Razza e storia e altri studi di antropologia*, pp. 143-177. Torino: Einaudi, 1967.

1469 "Les organisations dualistes existent-elles." *Bijdragen tot de Taal-, Land-, en Volkenkunde*, vol. CXII, no. 2, pp. 99-128. (In Honor of Prof. J. P. B. Josselin de Jong). Reprinted, chapter VIII, pp. 147-180 in *Anthropologie structurale*.
German translation, "Gibt es dualistische Organisationen?" pp. 148-180 in *Strukturale Anthropologie*.

1470 Review of Georges Balandier, "*Sociologie des Brazzavilles noires*." *Revue Française de Sciences Politiques*, vol. VI, no. 1, pp. 177-179.

1471 "Le droit au voyage." *L'Express*, 21 septembre.

1472 "La fin des voyages." *L'Actualité Littéraire*, no. 26, pp. 29-32.

1473 "Jeux de société." "*United States Lines*." *Paris Review* (special number on games).

1474 "Les prohibitions du mariage." *Annuaire de l'Ecole Pratique des Hautes Etudes*, (Sciences religieuses), 1955-1956, pp. 39-40.

1475 "Sorciers et psychanalyse." *Le Courrier*, UNESCO, July-August, pp. 8-10.

1476 "Structure et dialectique," pp. 289-294 in *For Roman Jakobson. Essays on the Occasion of his Sixtieth Birthday*. The Hague: Mouton. Reprinted, chapter XII, pp. 257-266 in *Anthropologie structurale*. German translation, "Struktur und Dialektik," pp. 255-264 in *Strukturale Anthropologie*.

1477 "Les trois humanismes." *Demain*, no. 35, August 9-15, p. 16. Reprinted in *Anthropologie structurale II*, "Réponses à des enquêtes," pp. 316-338.

1478 "Sur les rapports entre la mythologie et le rituel (séance du 26 mai 1956). *Bulletin de la Société Française de Philosophie*, no. 3, pp. 100-109. (Discussion: Diop, Dumont, Goldmann, Lacan, Leiris, Merleau-Ponty, Métraux, Mme. D. Paulme, Tubiana, J. Wahl, pp. 109-123)

1957

1479 Review of R. Briffault and B. Malinowski, "*Marriage: Past and Present.*" *American Anthropologist*, vol. LIX, no. 5, pp. 902-903.

1480 "Recherches récentes sur la notion d'âme." *Annuaire de l'Ecole Pratique des Hautes Etudes* (Sciences Religieuses), 1956-1957, pp. 16-17.

1481 "Le symbolisme cosmique dans la structure sociale et l'organisation cérémonielle des tribus américaines." *Serie Orientale Roma*, vol. XIV, pp. 47-56. Institut pour l'Etude de l'Orient et de l'Extrême-Orient, Rome.

1482 "These cooks did not spoil the broth." *Le Courrier*, UNESCO, 10, pp. 12-13.

1483 "The principle of reciprocity: the essence of life," pp. 74-84 in L. Coser, and B. Rosenberg, eds. *Sociological Theory. A book of readings*, New York, 1957.

1958

1484 *Anthropologie structurale.* Paris: Plon, 454p.
Contains:
I. Introduction: Histoire et ethnologie, pp. 3-36
LANGAGE ET PARENTE
II. L'analyse structurale en linguistique et en anthropologie, pp. 37-62
III. Langage et société, pp. 63-76
IV. Linguistique et anthropologie, pp. 77-92
V. Postface aux chapitres III et IV, pp. 93-110
ORGANIZATION SOCIALE
VI. La notion d'archaisme en ethnologie, pp. 113-132
VII. Les structures sociales dans le Brésil central et oriental, pp. 133-146
VIII. Les organisations dualistes existent-elles? pp. 147-180
MAGIE ET RELIGION
IX. Le sorcier et sa magie, pp. 183-204
X. L'efficacité symbolique, pp. 205-226
XI. La structure des mythes, pp. 227-256
XII. Structure et dialectique, pp. 257-267
ART
XIII. Le dédoublement de la représentation dans les arts de l'Asie et de l'Amérique, pp. 269-294
XIV. Le serpent au corps rempli de poissons, pp. 295-302
PROBLEMES DE METHODE ET D'ENSEIGNEMENT
XV. La notion de structure en ethnologie, pp. 303-352
XVI. Postface au chapitre XV, pp. 353-376
XVII. Place de l'Anthropologie dans les sciences sociales et problèmes posés par son enseignement, pp. 377-418

Translations:
English: C. Jacobson and B. Grundfest Schoepf, *Structural Anthropology.* New York: Basis Books, 1963. Also Doubleday Anchor Books, 1967.
German: Hans Naumann, *Strukturale Anthropologie.* Frankfurt am Main: Suhrkamp, 1967.
Italian: Paolo Caruso, *Antropologia strutturale.* 3rd ed. Milano: Mondadori, 1966, 1968.
Spanish: *Antropologia estructural.* Buenos Aires: Eudeba, 1969, 2a ed.

1485 "Préface" to M. Bouteiller, *Sorciers et jeteurs de sorts*. Paris: Plon, pp. I-IV.

1485a Review of R. Firth, ed., *Man and Culture: An Evaluation of the Work of B. Malinowki,*" *Africa*.

1486 "Dis-moi quels champignons." *L'Express*, april 10.

1487 "Documents tupi-kawahib," in *Miscellanea Paul Rivet*, Mexico.

1488 "Le dualisme dans l'organisation sociale et les représentations religieuses," in *Annuaire de l'Ecole Pratique des Hautes Etudes* (Sciences religieuses), 1957-1958 and 1958-1959.

1489 "Un monde, des sociétés." *Way Forum*, March. "One world, many societies." *Way Forum*, March.

1959

1490 "Amérique du Nord et Amérique du Sud." *Le Masque*, Musée Guimet, Paris.

1491 --Article, "Mauss, Marcel," in *Encyclopaedia Britannica*, vol. XIV, 1133a.

1492 --Article, "Passages Rites," in *Encyclopaedia Britannica*, vol. XVII, 433b-434a.

1493 "Le masque." *L'Express*, no. 443.

1494 "Préface" to Don C. Talayesva, *Soleil Hopi*. Paris: Plon, I-X.
Italian translation by L. Pellisari, *Capo Sole*. Milano: Bompiani, 1969.

1495 "La geste d'Asdiwal." *Annuaire de l'Ecole Pratique des Hautes Etudes* (Sciences religieuses), 1958-1959, pp. 3-43. Reprinted in *Les Temps Modernes*, no. 179, March 1961. Reprinted in *Anthropologie structurale II*, pp. 175-233.
English translation, "The Story of Asdiwal," in Leach, ed., *The Structural Study of Myth*, pp. 1-47. London: ASA Monograph, no. 5, 1967.

BIBLIOGRAPHY

German translation, "Die Sage von Asdiwal," in C. A.
Schmitz, ed., *Religions-Ethnologie*. Frankfurt am
Main, 1964, pp. 154-195.

1960

1496 "Four Winnebago myths. A structural sketch," in *Culture
and History*. Essays in Honor of Paul Radin, edited by
S. Diamond. New York: Columbia University Press,
pp. 351-362. Reprinted in John Middleton, ed., *Myth
and Cosmos*. New York: The Natural History Press,
1967. Reprinted in *Anthropologie structurale II*,
"Quatre mythes Winnebago," pp. 235-249.
Italian translation by P. Caruso in *Razza e storia
e altri studi di antropologia*. Torino: Einaudi,
1967, pp. 179-194.

1497 "Ce que l'ethnologie doit à Durkheim." *Annales de
l'Université de Paris*, T. XXX, no. 1, pp. 47-52.
Reprinted in *Anthropologie structurale II*, pp. 57-62.

1498 "Le dualisme dans l'organisation sociale et les représentations religieuses." *Annuaire de l'Ecole Pratique
des Hautes Etudes* (Sciences religieuses), 1959-1960.

1499 "Méthodes et conditions de la recherche ethnologique
française en Asie," in *Colloque sur les Recherches*.
Paris: Fondation Singer-Polignac.

1500 "Les trois sources de la réflexion ethnologique." *Revue
de l'Enseignement Supérieur*, Paris, pp. 43-50.

1501 "Compte rendu d'enseignement (1959-1960)." *Annuaire du
Collège de France*. *Leçon inaugurale* faite le mardi,
5 janvier 1960. Collège de France. Chaire d'Anthropologie sociale. Paris. Annuaire du Collège de
France. Paris. Reprinted in *Anthropologie structurale II*, pp. 11-44, "Le champ de l'anthropologie."
English translation by Sherry Artner Paul and Robert
Paul, under the title, "The Scope of Anthropology,"
in *Current Anthropology*, vol. VII, no. 2, 1966,
pp. 112-123. Published in Book form, *The Scope of
Anthropology*. London: Cape, 1968. The original
French text appeared in *Aut Aut*, no. 88, July 1965,
pp. 8-41.

Italian translation by P. Caruso, "Elogio dell'
antropologia," in *Razza e storia e altri studi di
antropologia*, pp. 47-82. Torino: Einaudi, 1967.
Spanish translation by Carlos R. Giordano, *Elogio
de la antropologia*. Cordoba: Ed. *Cuadernos de Pasado
y Presente*, no. 2, 1968.
Portuguese translation, "Aula inaugural," pp. 45-77
in Luis Costa Lima, *O Estruturalismo de Lévi-Strauss*.
Petropolis: Vozes, 1969.

1502 "L'anthropologie social devant l'histoire." *Annales*, no. 4.

1503 "Interview avec J.-P. Weber." *Le Figaro Littéraire*, May 14.

1504 "On manipulated sociological models." *Bijdragen tot de Taal-, Land-, en Volkenkunde*, vol. CXVI, no. 1, pp. 45-54. Reprinted, "Sens et usage de la notion de modèle," in *Anthropologie structurale II*, pp. 89-101.

1505 "La structure et la forme. Réflexions sur un ouvrage de Vladimir Propp." *Cahiers de l'Institut des Sciences Economiques Appliquées* (Recherches et dialogues philosophiques et économiques, 7), no. 99, March, pp. 3-36. Reprinted in *Anthropologie structurale II*, pp. 139-173. Also in "Analyse morphologique des contes russes," *International Journal of Slavic Linguistics and Poetics*, vol. III, 1960, pp. 122-149. Italian translation in V. Propp, *Morfologia della faba*, a cura di G. Bravo. Torino: Einaudo, 1966, pp. 165-199.

1506 "Le problème de l'invariance en anthropologie." *Diogène*, 31, pp. 23-33.

1961

1507 "La chasse rituelle aux aigles." *Annuaire de l'Ecole Pratique des Hautes Etudes*, (Sciences religieuses), 1959-1960.

1508 "La crise moderne de l'anthropologie." *Le Courrier*, UNESCO, vol. XIV, no. 11, pp. 12-17.

1509 "Le métier d'ethnologue." *Les Annales. Revue mensuelle des lettres françaises*, nouvelle série, July, no. 129, pp. 5-17.

1510 "La geste d'Asdiwal." *Les Temps Modernes*, see 1959.

1511 Résumé des cours de 1960-1961. *Annuaire du Collège de France*, 61e année.

1512 "Comptes rendus divers." *L'Homme*, vol. I.

1513 *Entretiens avec Claude Lévi-Strauss*, ed. par Georges Charbonnier. Paris: Plon-Julliard.
English translation, *Conversations with Claude Lévi-Strauss*. London: Jonathan Cape, 1969.
Italian translation by A. Rosso Cattabiani, *Primitivi e civilizzati*. (Problemi attuali). Milano: Rusconi, 1970, 2e ed.
German translation by Alfred Kuoni and Katrin Reinhardt, *Primitive und Zivilisierte*. Nach Gesprächen aufgezei aufgezeichnet von G. Charbonnier. Zürich: Verlag der Arche, 1972.
Spanish translation, *Arte, linguaje, etnologia*. Entervistas con Georges Charbonnier. La Habana: Instituto del Libro, 1970, 189p. Also translated by Francisco Gonzalez Aramburu. Mexico: Siglo Veintiuno Editores, 1968.

1514 "Les Nombreux visages de l'homme." *Le Théâtre dans le Monde*, vol. X, no. 1.
English translation, "The Many Faces of man." *World Theater*, vol. X, no. 1, 1961.

1962

1515 *Le Totémisme aujourd'hui*. Paris: Presses Universitaires de France.
English translation by Rodney Needham, *Totemism*. Boston: Beacon Press, 1963, Penguin, 1973.
Italian translation by D. Montaldi, *Il totemismo oggi*. Milano: Feltrinelli, 1964.
German translation by Franz H. Naumann, *Das Ende des Totemismus*. Frankfurt am Main: Suhrkamp, 1968.
Polish translation, by Aniela Steinsberg, *Totemizm*. Warsaw: Panstwowe Wydawnictwo Naukowe, 1968.

1516 *Le Pensée sauvage.* Paris: Plon, 392p.
English translation by *The Savage Mind.* Chicago: Chicago University Press, 1966.
German translation by Franz H. Naumann, *Das Wilde Denken.* Frankfurt am Main: Suhrkamp, 1968.
Italian translation by P. Caruso, *Il pensiero selvaggio.* Milano: Il Saggiatore, 1964.
Polish trnaslation by Andrzej Zajaczkowski, *Mysl Nieoswojona.* Warsaw: Panstwowe Wydawnictwo Naukowe, 1969.

1517 "La antropologia, hoy: entrevista a Claude Lévi-Strauss, con Eliseo Veron." *Cuestiones de Filosofia,* vol. I, nos. 2-3, Buenos Aires.

1518 "The bear and the barber." The Henry Myers Memorial Lecture. Reprinted from *The Journal of the Royal Anthropological Institute,* vol. XVIII, Part I, 1963, pp. 1-11.

1519 "*Les Chats* de Charles Baudelaire (in collaboration with R. Jakobson)." *L'Homme,* vol. II, no. 1, pp. 5-21.
English translation by Katie Furness-Lane, "Charles Baudelaire's 'Les Chats', pp. 202-221 in Michael Lane, ed., *Introduction to Structuralism.* New York: Basic Books, 1971.
German translation in *Alternative 62/63,* 1968, pp. 156-170. Also in *Sprache im technischen Zeitalter,* 29, 1969, pp. 1-19. Reprinted in *Il Corpo,* no. 1, 1965.

1520 "Crowds." *New Left Review,* no. 15, pp. 3-6. Translation of chapter XV, "Foules," of *Tristes Tropiques.*

1521 "Jean-Jacques Rousseau, fondateur des sciences de l'homme," l'homme," in *Jean-Jacques Rousseau.* Université ouvrière et faculté des lettres de l'Université de Genève, Coll. Langages. Neuchâtel: La Baconnière, pp. 239-248. Reprinted in *Anthropologie structurale II,* pp. 45-56.
Italian translation by P. Caruso, in *Razza e storia e altri studi di antropologia,* pp. 83-96. Torino: Einaudi, 1967. Reprinted, "Rousseau, père de l'ethnologie." *Le Courrier,* UNESCO, vol. XVI, no. 3, 1963, pp. 10-15. Also as "Ethnologue avant l'heure." *Les Nouvelles Littéraires,* November 29, 1962 [special number on Rousseau]

1522 "Comptes rendus divers." *L'Homme*, vol. II.

1523 "Les limites de la notion de structure en ethnologie,"
pp. 40-45 in R. Bastide, ed., *Sens et usages du terme structure* (Coll. Janua Linguarum), vol. XVI. The Hague.
Italian translation by L. Basso Lonzi in *Usi e significati* del termine struttura. Milano: Bompiano, 1965, pp. 37-43.
Spanish translation by B. Dorriots, *Sentido y usos del termino struttura*, Buenos Aires: Paidos, 1968.

1524 "Sur le caractère distinctif des faits ethnologiques."
Revue des Travaux de l'Académie des Sciences morales et politiques, vol. CXV, 4e série, Paris, pp. 211-219.

1525 "Compte rendu d'enseignement (1961-1962). *Annuaire du Collège de France*.

1963

1526 "The bear and the barber." see 1962

1527 "Marques de propriété dans deux tribus sud-américaines (in collaboration with N. Belmont)." *L'Homme*, vol. III, no. 3, 102-108.

1528 "Résumés des cours de 1962-1963." *Annuaire du Collège de France*, 63e année.

1529 "Les discontinuités culturelles et le développement économique et social." *Table Ronde sur les prémices sociales de l'industrialisation*, Paris, UNESCO, 1961. Reprinted in *Anthropologie structurale II*, pp. 365-376.

1530 "Rousseau, père de l'ethnologie." see 1962

1531 "Interview de Claude Lévi-Strauss avec Paolo Caruso."
Aut Aut, no. 77, September, pp. 27-45. Reprinted in P. Caruso, *Conversazioni con C. Lévi-Strauss, M. Foucault, J. Lacan*. Milano: Mursia, 1969.

1532 "Réponse à quelques questions." *Esprit*, no. 322,
 November, pp. 628-653. [special number dedicated to
 La Pensée sauvage et le structuralisme"]
 English translation, "A confrontation [with P. Ricoeur,
 M. Gaboriau, J.-P. Faye, K. Axelos, et al.] *New Left
 Review*, no. 62, July-August 1970, pp. 57-74.
 Portuguese translation, "Respostas a algumas questões,"
 pp. 192-220 in Luiz Costa Lima, *O Estruturalismo de
 Lévi-Strauss*. Petropolis: Vozes, 1969.

1964

1533 *Mythologiques I: Le cru et le cuit*. Paris: Plon, 402p.
 English translation by John and Doreen Weightman,
 The Raw and the Cooked. New York: Harper and Row,
 1969.
 Italian translation by A. Bonomi, *Il Crudo e il
 cotto*. Milano: Il Saggiatore, 1966.
 German translation by Eva Moldenhauer, *Mythologica I:
 Das Rohe und das Gekochte*, Frankfurt am Main:
 Suhrkamp, 1970.

1534 "Alfred Métraux, 1902-1963." *Annales de l'Université de
 Paris*, no. 1.

1535 "Alfred Métraux, 1902-1963." *Journal de la Société des
 Américanistes*.

1536 "Hommage à Alfred Métraux." *L'Homme*, vol. IV, no. 2.

1537 "Compte rendu d'enseignement (1963-1964)." *Annuaire du
 Collège de France*.

1538 "Critères scientifiques dans les disciplines sociales et
 humaines." *Revue Internationale des Sciences Sociales*,
 vol. XVI, no. 4, Paris, UNESCO. Reprinted in *Anthropologie structurale II*, pp. 339-364. Reprinted in
 Aletheia, no. 4, May 1966, pp. 189-212. special
 number on Structuralism
 English translation, "Criteria of science in the social
 and human disciplines." *International Social Science
 Journal*, no. 4, 1964.
 Italian translation by P. Caruso, in *Razza e storia e
 altri studi di antropologia*, pp. 265-291. Torino:
 Einaudi, 1967.

Spanish translation, "Criterios cientificos en las disciplinas sociales y humanas," in R. Barthes, et al., *Approximacion al estructuralismo*. Trad. por Mercedes Riani and Victoria Julia. Buenos Aires: Ed. Galarna, 1967.

1539 "Reciprocity, the essence of social life," pp. 36-48 in *The Family: Its Structure and Functions*, R. L. Coser, ed. New York: St. Martin's Press.

1540 "Sur quelques problèmes posés par l'étude des classifications primitives," in *Mélanges Alexandre Koyré*, vol. II, "L'Aventure de l'esprit", *Histoire de la Pensée*, vol. XIII, pp. 335-345. Reprinted in *La Pensée sauvage*, pp. 79-89.

1965

1541 "Compte rendu d'enseignement (1964-1965)." *Annuaire du Collège de France*.

1542 "Entretien avec Claude Lévi-Strauss (en collaboration avec M. Delahaye et J. Rivette)." *Les Cahiers du Cinéma*, tome XXVI, no. 4.

1543 "Les sources polluées de l'art." *Arts-Loisirs*, April 7-13.

1544 "The future of kinship studies." The Huxley Memorial Lecture for 1965. *Proceedings of the Royal Anthropological Institute of Great Britain and Ireland*, pp. 13-22.

1545 "Présentation d'un laboratoire d'anthropologie sociale." *Revue de l'Enseignement Supérieur*, vol. III.

1546 "Le triangle culinaire." *L'Arc*, no. 26, pp. 19-29. Also in Yvan Simonis, *Claude Lévi-Strauss ou la passion de l'inceste. Introduction au structuralisme*. Paris: Aubier-Montaigne, 1968, pp. 225-234. English translation, "The culinary triangle," *Partisan Review*, vol. XXXIII, Fall, 1966, pp. 586-595. German translation, "Das kulinarische Dreck." *Frankfurter Allgemeine Zeitung*, March 26, 1966.

1547 "Strutturalismo e critica," resposta a un questionario compilato da Cesare Segre," *Paragone*, no. 182, Reprinted in *Catologo generale 1958-1965*. Milano: Il Saggiatore. Reprinted in *Anthropologie structurale II*, pp. 316-338.

1548 "Réponse à un questionnaire sur 25 témoins de notre temps." *Le Figaro Littéraire*, no. 1023, November 25. Reprinted in *Anthropologie structurale II*, pp. 316-338.

1549 "Entretien avec Tanneguy de Quénetain." *Réalités* (Paris), January.
Italian translation in *'ABC'* (Milano), February 1965.

1550 "L'umanità si avvicina a se stessa." Entretien avec P. Caruso. *Rinascità*, supplemento culturale, no. 5, Roma, May 29. Reprinted in P. Caruso, *Conversazioni con C. Lévi-Strauss, M. Foucault, J. Lacan*. op. cit. 1963, 6th item.

1551 "L'art en 1985," *Arts*. Reprinted in *Anthropologie structurale II*, pp. 316-338.

1552 "Civilisation urbaine et santé mentale." *Les Cahiers de l'Institut de la vie*; Reprinted in *Anthropologie structurale II*, pp. 316-338. [All 4 in sections entitled: "Réponses à des enquêtes"]

1966

1553 "Anthropology: Its achievements and future." *Current Anthropology*, vol. VII, April, pp. 124-127. *Nature*, vol. CCIX, January 1.

1554 "L'oeuvre du Bureau of American Ethnology et ses leçons." Traduit de l'anglais (*Knowledge about Man*, New York: Simon and Schuster), reprinted in *Anthropologie structurale II*, pp. 63-75.

1555 *Mythologiques II: Du Miel aux cendres*. Paris: Plon, 453p.
English translation by John and Doreen Weightman, *From Honey to Ashes*. London: Jonathan Cape, 1973-New York: Harper and Row, 1974.

198   BIBLIOGRAPHY

> Italian translation by A. Bonomi, *Dal Miele alle ceneri*. Milano: Il Saggiatore, 1970.
> Spanish translation, *De la miel a las cenizas*. México: Fondo de Cultura Economica, 1971.

1556 "Compte rendu d'enseignement (1965-1966)." *Annuaire du Collège de France*.

1557 "Interview" accordée aux *Cahiers de Philosophie* (numéro spécial: Anthropologie). January, no. 1.

1558 "The disappearance of man." *The New York Review*, July 28.

1559 "Interview of Claude Lévi-Strauss with P. Caruso." *Atlas*, April, pp. 245-246.

1560 "Interview of Claude Lévi-Strauss with George Steiner." *Encounter*, April, pp. 32-38.

1561 "Entretien avec Claude Lévi-Strauss de Raymond Bellour." *Les Lettres Françaises*, no. 1125, March 31. see 1967

1562 "A propos d'une rétrospective." *Arts*. Reprinted in *Anthropologie structurale II*, pp. 316-338.

1967

1563 "Vingt ans après." *Les Temps Modernes*, no. 256, 23e année, pp. 385-406. Préface to the revised and corrected reedition of *Les Structures élémentaires de la parenté*. The Hague-Paris: Mouton. see 1947 for translations.

1564 "Le sexe des astres," in *Mélanges offerts à Roman Jakobson pour sa 70e année*. The Hague: Mouton, pp. 1163-1170. Reprinted in *Anthropologie structurale II*, pp. 251-261.
English translation, "The Sex of the heavenly Bodies," in M. Lane, ed., *Structuralism A Reader*. London: Cape, 1970, pp. 330-379. New York: Basic Books, 1971, pp. 330-339. [Translation by Phillip Brew]

1565 "The particular task of anthropology." in Gloria B.
Levitas, ed., *Culture and Consciousness. Perspectives
in the Social Sciences.* New York, pp. 308-312.
Reprinted in *Anthropologie structurale*, pp. 397-401.

1566 "Compte rendu d'enseignement (1966-1967)." *Annuaire du
Collège de France.*

1567 "Présentation du laboratoire d'anthropologie sociale."
Sciences, no. 47.

1568 "A contre-courant," entretien avec Guy Dumur. *Le Nouvel
Observateur*, no. 115, janvier 25-31, pp. 30-32.

1569 "Entretiens de Gilles Lapouge avec Claude Lévi-Strauss."
Le Figaro Littéraire, February 2.

1570 "Interview of P. Caruso with Lévi-Strauss," in *Paese
Sera-Libri*, January 20. Reprinted in P. Caruso,
*Conversazioni con C. Lévi-Strauss, M. Foucault, J.
Lacan.* op cit., 1963, 6th item.

1571 "A propos de 'Lévi-Strauss dans le XVIIIe siècle'."
Cahiers pour l'Analyse, no. 8.

1572 "Entretien avec Claude Lévi-Strauss de Raymond Bellour."
Les Lettres Françaises, no. 1165, January 12, p. 7,
and *Ibid.*, no. 1187, June 15, 1967. Reprinted in
Le Livre des autres. Paris: Edition de l'Herne, 1971,
pp. 145-161.
German translation, "Claude Lévi-Strauss: 'Wie arbeite
der menschliche Geist? Eine Gespräch mit Raymond
Bellour," pp. 75-88 in Adelbert Reif (Hrsg), *Antworten
der Strukturalisten.* Hamburg: Hoffmann und Campe,
1973.

1573 "The Nambicuara of Northern Mato Grosso," in R. Cohen
and J. Middleton, (eds.), *Comparative Political
Systems.* New York: The National History Press.

1574 "Les clefs du mystère humain. Un entretien de Eugene
Gwell avec Claude Lévi-Strauss." *Le Patriote
Illustré* (Bruxelles), no. 35, 27 août, p. 3045, col. 3.

1575 "Entretien avec Claude Lévi-Strauss (Françoise Mallet)."
Le Magazine Littéraire, no. 4, February 1967, pp. 42-
44.

1968

1576 *Mythologiques III: L'Origine des manières de table.*
Paris: Plon.

1577 "Hommage aux sciences de l'homme." *Information sur les Sciences Sociales*, vol. VII, no. 2, pp. 7-11.

1578 "Religions comparées des peuples sans écriture." *Problèmes et Méthodes d'Histoire des religions.* Mélanges publiés par la section des sciences religieuses à l'occasion du centenaire de l'Ecole Pratique des Hautes Etudes, Paris, Presses Universitaires de France, pp. 1-7. Reprinted in *Anthropologie Structurale II*, pp. 77-85.

1579 "La grande aventure de l'ethnologie." *Le Nouvel Observateur*, no. 166, January 17.

1580 "Vivre et parler. Un débat entre François Jacob, Roman Jakobson, Claude Lévi-Strauss et Philippe l'Héritier." *Les Lettres Françaises*, no. 1221, February 14 and 21. German translation, "Leben und Sprechen. Eine Diskussion unter Leitung von Michel Tréguier," pp. 45-70 in Adelbert Reif, ed., *Antworten der Strukturalisten*. Hamburg: Hoffmann und Campe, 1973.
see 1967

1581 "Entretien." *Fiera Letteraria*, March 14.

1582 "Le structuralisme n'est pas une philosophie'. Entretien avec Claude Lévi-Strauss de Absene Zehraoui." *Témoignage Chrétien*, no. 1241, 18 avril 1968, pp. 17-18.

1583 "Exchange between Lévi-Strauss and Hiatt," in R. Lee and I. Devore, eds., *Man the Hunter*. Chicago: Aldine Publishing Co., 1968, pp. 210-212.

1584 "Le structuralisme sainement pratiqué ne prétend pas formuler une nouvelle conception du monde et même de l'homme'." *Le Monde*, January 12.

1585 "Sur les divers usages du structuralisme. Réponse à Gadoffre." *Le Monde*, 14 novembre.

1586 "Entrevue radiodiffusée avec Michel Tréguer, dans la série *'Un Certain Regard'* hiver 1968. Reprinted in Catherine Backes-Clément, *Claude Lévi-Strauss ou la structure et le malheur*. Paris: Seghers, Collection 'Philosophes de tous les temps,' no. 66, 1970, pp. 172-188.

1970

1587 "Les champignons dans la culture. A propos du livre de M. R.-G. Wasson." *L'Homme*, vol. X, no. 1, January-March, pp. 5-16. Reprinted in *Anthropologie structurale II*, pp. 262-280.

1588 "La théorie." *VH 101*, no. 2. [Contains short articles by Barthes, Lévi-Strauss, Soller, Benveniste, Robbe-Grillet, etc.]

1589 "We no longer know how to bring our children into the world we have built'." (Interview with Lévi-Strauss, edited by C. Dreyfus). *Mademoiselle*, vol. LXXI, August, pp. 236-237, 324.

1590 "An interview with Claude Lévi-Strauss (Wendy Moonan, et al.)." *University Review*, vol. X, p. 21.

1591 "Myth and meaning." *The Sunday Times*, no. 7694, November 15, 1970, p. 27. [Interview]

1971

1592 *Mythologiques IV: L'homme nu.* Paris: Plon.

1593 "Comment ils [les mythes] meurent." *Esprit*, vol. XXXIX, pp. 684-706. Reprinted, "Comment meurent les mythes," in *Science et conscience de la société.* Mélanges en l'honneur de Raymond Aron, 2 vols. Paris: Calmann-Levy. Reprinted in *Anthropologie structurale II*, pp. 301-315.
English translation, "How myths die," F. C. T. Moore. *New Literary History*, vol. V, Winter 1974, pp. 269-281.

1594 "Rapports de symétrie entre rites et mythes de peuples voisins, pp. 161-178 in Th. O. Beidelman, ed., *The Translation of Culture. Essays to honor E. E. Evans-Pritchard*. London: Tavistock Publications. Reprinted in *Anthropologie structurale II*, pp. 281-300. Also in *Le Magazine Littéraire*, no. 58, November 1971, pp. 30-31, 56-65.

1595 "Le temps du mythe." *Annales*, nos. 3-4, Paris, vol. XXVI, pp. 533-540.

1596 "Bolero de Maurice Ravel." *L'Homme*, revue française d'anthropologie, vol. XI, no. 2.

1597 "Race et culture." *Revue Internationale des Sciences Sociales*, vol. XXIII, no. 4, Paris, UNESCO, pp. 608-625.

1598 "The deduction of the crane," in P. Maranda and E. Kongas Maranda, eds., *Structural Analysis of Oral Tradition*. Philadelphia: University of Pennsylvania Press.

1599 "Interview with Claude Lévi-Strauss by Edwin Newmann." W.N.B.C. Television, *Speaking Freely*. September 17, pp. 1-23.

1600 "*L'Express* va plus loin avec Claude Lévi-Strauss." (Interview). *L'Express*, no. 1027, March 15-21, pp. 60-66.

1601 "Le problème ultime des sciences de l'homme consistera un jour a ramener la pensée à la vie." *Le Magazine Littéraire*, no. 58, November, pp. 22-29.

1602 "A visit to Lévi-Strauss by John Weightman." *Encounter*, vol. XXXVI, no. 2, pp. 38-42.

1603 "Interview with Claude Lévi-Strauss." *Diacritics*, vol. I, no. 1, Fall 1971, pp. 44-50.

1604 "Préface" à Lucien Sebag, *L'Invention du monde chez les Indiens pueblos*. Paris: François Maspero, Bibliothèque d'anthropologie, 1971, 506p.

1605 "Entretien: Claude Lévi-Strauss et les *Mythologiques*: 'Réconcilier le sensible et l'intelligible." *Le Monde* [*des Livres*], no. 8339, 5 novembre 1971, pp. 17-20.

1606 "L'anthropologie pour quoi faire? Lévi-Strauss invité du dimanche." *Les Lettres Françaises*, no. 1392, June 30-July 6, p. 18. (Interview with Pierre Daix)

1607 "Entretien de Pierre Daix avec Claude Lévi-Strauss sur *Les Mythologiques*. 1- La signification des mythes américains." *Les Lettres Françaises*, no. 1406, October 13-October 20, pp. 3-4.
German translation, "Die Bedeutung der amerikanischen Mythen: Ein Gespräch mit Pierre Daix," pp. 89-104 in Adelbert Reif, Hrsg., *Antworten der Strukturalisten*, 1973.

1608 "Entretien de Pierre Daix avec Lévi-Strauss sur *Les Mythologiques*. II--Structuralisme, humanisme, matérialisme." *Les Lettres Françaises*, no. 1407, October 20-26, pp. 6-7.

1609 "Entretien avec Lévi-Strauss (Jean Pouillon): L'homme habillé par le mythe." *Les Nouvelles Littéraires*, 49e année, no. 2297, October 1, pp. 14-15.
German translation, "Der Mensch, bekleider durch den Mythos. Ein Gespräch mit Jean Pouillon," pp. 105-110 in Adelbert Reif, Hrsg., *Antworten der Strukturalisten*, 1973.

1610 "De quelques rencontres." *L'Arc*, no. 46, 1971, pp. 43-47. [Special number devoted to Merleau-Ponty]

1972

1611 "La mère des fougères," in *Langues et techniques, nature et société*. Mélanges offerts à André G. Haudricourt. 2 vols. Paris: Klincksieck.

1612 "Structuralism and ecology." Gedersleeve lecture delivered at Barnard College, March 28. *Barnard Alumnae*, Spring 1972, pp. 6-14. Reprinted in *Social Sciences Information*, (Paris: UNESCO), vol. XII, no. 1, 1973.

1613 "Marcel Detienne, Les jardins d'Adonis." *L'Homme*, revue française d'anthropologie, vol. XII, no. 4.

1614 "François Jacob et Claude Lévi-Strauss face à face." [Interview]. *Le Figaro Littéraire*, no. 1338, January 7, 1972, pp. 13, 16.

1615 "A conversation with Claude Lévi-Strauss: The father of structural anthropology takes a misanthropic view of lawless humanism." (With A. Akoun et al.). *Psychology Today*, vol. V, no. 12, 1972, pp. 37-39, 74-82.

1973

1616 *Anthropologie structurale II*. Paris: Plon, 450p.
Contains:
"Le champ de l'anthropologie," (Leçon inaugurale), pp. 11-44
"Jean-Jacques Rousseau fondateur des sciences de l'homme," pp. 45-56
"Ce que l'ethnologie doit à Durkheim," pp. 57-62 (*Annales* 1960)
"L'Oeuvre du Bureau of American Ethnology et ses leçons," pp. 63-75
"Religions comparées des peuples sans écriture," pp. 77-85
"Sens et usage de la notion de modèle," pp. 89-101 ('On Manipulated models, 1960)
"Réflexions sur l'atome de parenté," pp. 103-135 (*L'Homme*, 1973)
"La structure et la forme," pp. 139-173 (Cahiers de l'INSEA, 1960—*Int Jr. of Slavic Linguistics*, 1960)
"La Geste d'Asdiwal," pp. 175-233

"Quatre mythes Winnebago," pp. 235-249
"Le sexe des astres," pp. 251-261
"Les champignons dans la culture," pp. 262-280
"Rapports de symétrie entre rites et mythes des
  peuples voisins," pp. 281-300 (1971)
"Comment meurent les mythes," pp. 301-315 (1971)
"Réponses à des enquêtes: "Les trois humanismes"
  (Demain 1956); "Structuralisme et critique
  littéraire (*Paragone* 1965); "A propos d'une
  rétrospective (*Arts* 1966); "L'art en 1985 (*Arts*
  1965); "Civilisation urbaine et santé mentale"
  (*Les Cahiers de l'Institut de la Vie* 1965);
  "Témoins de notre temps" (*Le Figaro Littéraire*
  1965), pp. 316-338
"Critères scientifiques dans les disciplines sociales
  et humaines," pp. 339-364 (*Revue Int. des Sciences
  Sociales*, 1964)
"Les discontinuités culturelles et le développement
  économique et social," pp. 365-376 (*Information sur
  les Sciences sociales*, Paris: Mouton, 1963)
"Race et histoire," pp. 377-422 (*La Question raciale
  dans le monde moderne*, Paris: UNESCO, 1952)

English translation, *Structural Anthropology, Volume
II*, translated by Monique Layton. New York: Basic
Books, Inc., 1976.

1617 "Religion, langue et histoire: A propos d'un texte de
  Ferdinand de Saussure," in *Mélanges en l'honneur de
  Fernand Braudel*, 2 vols. Toulouse: Privat.

1618 "L'atome de parenté." *L'Homme*, vol. XIII, no. 3.
  Reprinted, "Réflexions sur l'atome de parenté," in
  Anthropologie structurale II, pp. 103-135.

1619 "Claude Lévi-Strauss," in Madeleine Chapsal, *Les
  Ecrivains en personne*, pp. 153-167. Paris: René
  Julliard, Union Générale d'Editions. (Interview)

1620 "Le problème des sciences humaines au Collège de
  France." *La Nouvelle Revue des Deux Mondes*, Paris.

1621 "Dieu existe-t-il?" in Christian Chabanis, e.a., *Dieu
  existe-t-il? Non . . . répondent . . . . Claude Lévi-
  Strauss.* Paris: Fayard, 1973, 412p.

1974

1622 *Discours de réception à l'Académie française* prononcé le jeudi 24 juin 1974. Paris: Institut de France, 1974.

1623 "Comment travaillent les écrivains: Claude Lévi-Strauss (J.-L. de Rambures, interview)." *Le Monde*, juin 21.

1624 "Des intellectuels, pourquoi faire? Réponse de Claude Lévi-Strauss." *Le Monde*, 15 novembre.

1625 "Intervista con Lévi-Strauss (Nicolà Gasbarro e Francesco Maiello)." *Il Ponte*, XXX, 1974, pp. 65-77.

1626 *Race, Science and Society* by Claude Lévi-Strauss [and others]. New York: Columbia University Press, 1974, 370p. [*The Race Question in Modern Society*, 1956]

1975

1627 *La Voie des masques*. 2 vol. Collection "Les Sentiers de la création." Genève: Skira.

1628 "Propos retardataires sur l'enfant créateur." *La Nouvelle Revue des Deux Mondes*, janvier.

1629 "Un ethnologue dans la ville." *Le Figaro*, March 7 and May 9.

1630 "De Chrétien de Troyes à Richard Wagner." Programme de *'Parsifal'*, *Bayreuther Festspiele*.

1631 "Mythe et oubli," in Julia Kristeva, volume collectif d'hommages à Emile Benveniste," Paris: Editions du Seuil.

1632 Article "Antropologia," in *Enciclopedia Italiana*. Extracts republished in *Diogène*, no. 90, April-June.

1633 "Histoire d'une structure," in *Explorations in the Anthropology of Religion. Essays in honour of Jan Van Ball*, edited by W. E. A. Van Beek and J. H. Scherer. *Verhandelingen van het Koninklikk Instituut voor Taal-, Land-, en Volkenkunde*, 74. The Hague: Martinus Nijhoff, 1975, pp. 71-78.

1634 *Compte rendu d'enseignement.* Annuaire du Collège de France, 75e année.

1976

1635 "Cosmopolitisme et exogamie" (dans un volume d'hommages à la mémoire de Roger Bastide). Paris: Editions Gauthier-Villars.

1636 "Une Préfiguration anatomique de la gémellité (dans un volume de mélanges offerts à Germaine Dieterlen). Paris: Editions Hermann.

1637 "Structuralisme et empirisme." *L'Homme, revue française d'anthropologie*, vol. XVI, no. 2.

1638 "Hommage à Jean Piaget" (dans un volume d'hommages à Jean Piaget pour son 80e anniversaire). Stuttgart: Ernst Klett Verlag.

1639 Compte rendu de: Jean de Lery, *Voyage fait en la terre du Brésil* (1580). Nouvelle édition, Genève: Droz, 1975. (Pour un numéro spécial du *Time Literary Supplement* consacré à l'Amérique du Sud, à paraître en juillet 1976.)

INDEX

INDEX 211

Abbagnano, Nicolà 234, 351
Abdel-Malek, A. 941
Abel, Lionel 9, 327, 566
Abel, Peter 867
Adams, John W. 23, 281
Aguilar de Alfaro, Adelita 1070
Akoun, A. A. et al. 830
Aletheia 1261
Albérès, René Marill 1099
Alternative 1262, 1263
Amar, André 1101
Améry, Jean 898, 1017
Amodio, L. 1100
Amoros, Celia 352
Anderson, E. N. Jr. 353
Anderson, Robert 300
Annales 1264
Anonymous 178, 179, 238, 239
  283, 354-370, 492, 533,
  550, 567, 601-602, 620-624,
  831-832, 979, 980, 1046-
  1054, 1061, 1102, 1226, 1260
Anquetil, Gilles 493
Arc (l') 1265
Ardener, Edwin 872
Arnaud, A.-J. 894
Aron, Raymond 87, 240, 500
Aubenque, Pierre 873
Audiberti, J. 88, 504
Auger, Pierre 969
Aut Aut 1266
Auzias, J.-M. 518, 1103
Axelos, Kostas 524, 942
Azancot, L. 371

Backès-Clément, Catherine 24,
  57, 73, 89, 90, 91, 92,
  372-377, 505, 625, 1018
Badiou, Alain 970
Bakker, Reinout 93, 1104
Balandier, Georges 94, 95,
  241, 626, 766
Balashov, N. 1105
Balliu, Julien 961
Bamberger, Joan 378
Banaji, Jacrus 627

Banton, Michael 976
Barbut, Marc 964
Barden, G. 379
Barnes, J. A. 628-629
Barthes, R. 284, 301, 507, 630,
  1106, 1107
Bartolomei, Giangaetano 513
Basehart, Harry 1089
Bastide, Roger 97, 242, 302,
  767, 1227
Bataille, Georges 98, 180,
  244
Baudry, Jean-Louis 285, 303
Beattie, J. J. M. 631, 1068
Beauvoir, Simone de 181, 1031,
  1032
Beck, B. 245
Bell, J. H. 99, 632
Bellour, Raymond 33, 344, 380-
  381, 833-836
Bender, Donald 633
Bendow, Burton 15, 634
Benjamin, Geoffrey 100
Benoist, Jean-Marie 382, 1108
Bermejo, José Maria 900
Berndt, Ronald M. 101, 635
Bernabei, F. 606-607
Bersani, Jacques, et al. 917,
  918
Bersani, Leo
Berting, J. 182
Besançon, A. 792
Bettinini, Gianfranco 750
Bharati, Agiehananda 265, 266
  636
Bidney, D. 286, 304, 383
Bierwisch, M. 1109
Blanchot, Maurice 102
Blanquart, P. 1110, 1111
Boehm, R. 532, 1009
Boisdeffre, Pierre de 919
Bonomi, Andrea 75, 637, 1019,
  1112
Boon, James A. 1, 106, 306,
  384, 541-542, 561, 596, 982,
  1005, 1245,
Boudon, Raymond 1228
Bourdieu, Pierre 871, 1020

INDEX

Bourdillon, Michael 385, 981
Boussard, Léon 545
Bouteiller, M. 267
Brain, Robert 103
Brandi, Cesare 752
Braudel, F. 793
Broderick, Alan H. 305
Broekman, Jan M. 1113
Brogger, J. 638
Brosse, Jacques 104, 105, 386-388
Bryson, Norman 107, 246
Buchler, Ira N. 183, 185, 868-869, 870, 983
Bulletin de la Société française de Philosophie 1267
Bulmer, Ralph 186, 639
Burgess, Anthony 287, 288, 389
Burling, Robbins 640
Burridge, K. O. L. 289

Cacciari, M. 817
Cahiers pour l'Analyse 1270
Caillois, Roger 111, 112
Calogeras, R. C. 290, 390
Caltofen, Segura R. 247
Cantoni, R. 108
Carracedo, José Rubio (see Rubio)
Cardoletti, P. 268
Caronna, G. 109, 269
Carpenter, Edmund 307
Cartier-Bresson, H. 1035
Caruso, Paolo 27, 58, 69, 110, 113, 235, 308, 391-392, 568, 837-840, 943, 1033
Castel, R. 815
Castello, Vidal Abril 1115
Cattabiabi, A.
Caws, Peter 9, 393, 1118
Cebik, L. B. 1115
Cereda, Guiseppe 270
Chabanis, Christian, et al. 746
Chambers, Ian 508
Chapsal, Madeleine 841
Charbonnier, Georges 4, 28, 59

Charrier, J.-P. 1119, 1250
Chatel de Brancion, Paul 114
Chatelet, François 394, 1062, 1120
Chomsky, Noam 875
Chapra, S. 309
Cixous, Hélène 395
Clastres, Pierre 73, 115, 642
Cockburn, Alexander 116
Cohen, Percy S. 396, 646
Colby, Benjamin N. 643-644
Colette, Jacques 248, 310, 311, 397
Conley, Tom 985
Conn, W. E. 312, 751
Cordero, Rodrigo 189, 291
Cornwell, John 398
Corti, Maria and Cesare Segre 753, 1006
Corvez, Maurice 49, 1122, 1123
Cotroneo, Girolamo 944
Coult, Allan D. 647
Courchay, C. 648
Courtes, Jean 31, 73
Cousteix, P. 399
Cox, C. B.
Cranston, Maurice W. 521
Crémant, Roger 1124
Cressant, Pierre 32
Crozier, Michel 117
Crumrine, N. Rose 23, 1069
Cruz, Juan Cruz 402
Cuisenier, Jean 189, 313, 400, 649, 1125
Culler, Jonathan 2, 401, 876, 1030

Daix, Pierre 403-404, 569, 843, 1126, 1127, 1128
Damisch, H. 769
D'Amico, Robert 794, 1129
Davenport, William 1090
Davy, G. 190
Davy, John 405
Deas, Malcolm 249

INDEX   213

de George, Richard   1130
de Grève, M.   36
de Ipola, Emilio Rafael (see Ipola)
de Josselin de Jong (see Josselin)
Delahye, M.   844
Deleuze, Gilles   118, 1229
Delfendahl, Bernard   34, 650
Deliège, Célestin   73, 406, 977
Deligiorgis, Stravos   1021
Deluy, Henry   1034
De Man, Paul   119
Denant, Antoine   877
Dening, Gregory   407
Derrida, Jacques   55, 120, 121, 122, 562, 754
Detienne, M.   408
Detweiler, Robert   920
Devereux, G.   651
Devyver, A.   42
De Vita, R.   965
Diamond, Stanley   23, 652, 653, 654, 1131
Dicaro, A.   958
Dieguez, Manuel de   1071
Dinneen, Francis P.   901
Domenach, J.-M.   409, 1132
Donato, Eugenio   250, 410, 878, 921
Dorfles, Gillo   608
Douglas, Mary   271, 282, 411
Dreyfus, Catherine   846
Dubois, Jean   903
Dufrenne, Mikel   522, 1133, 1134
Dumasy, Annegret   53, 517, 530-531, 537a, 540, 560, 570
Dumont, Louis   191
Dumur, Guy   847
Dundes, A.   655
Durand, Gilbert   345
Durbin, Marshall   902
Duvignaud, Jean   251, 609, 879
Dyson-Hudson, Neville   556

Eco, Umberto   123, 124, 971, 1135, 1136
Edeline, Francis   880
Edmont, Michel-Pierre   656
Esbroeck, Michel van   786
Esprit   986, 1272, 1273, 1274
Esteva Fabrigat, Claudio   413, 657
Ethier-Blais, Jean   549
Etiemble, R.   252

Fages, J.-B.   38, 1137, 1138
Fanizza, Franco   658, 1072
Ferraro, G.   414
Ferrata, Giansiro   509
Ferrier, Jean-Louis   47
Ferry, Jacqueline F.   125
Fessard, G.   787, 1139, 1244
Fialkowski, Aldine   788
Fiedler, Leslie A.   1063a
Finas, Lucette   25
Fisher, John B.   514
Fisher, John L.   659
Finley, M. I.   795
Flam, Leopold   1022
Fleischmann, Eugène   55, 967
Florenne, Yves   315
Fontaine de Visscher, Luce   881
Forge, Anthony   192, 1036
Forni, Guglielmo   1251, 1252
Fortes, Meyer   193, 194, 292
Fortini, F.   316
Fouchet, Max-Pol   253
Fowlie, Wallace
Fox, Robin   195, 293, 294, 295
Frandon, I.-M.   346
Francovich, Guillermo   1140
Frank, J. N.   126
Freedman, M.   29
Freedman, R. L.   415
Friedrich, H.   1141
Funt, David Paul   1142
Furer-Baimendorf, C. von   272
Furet, François   896-897

Gaboriau, Marc 318, 796
Gadoffre, Gilles 347
Gallini, C. 196
Galimberti, A.
Gallagher, Patrick 319
Galzingna, M. 62
Garcia, Tobas 320
Gardner, Howard 7, 416, 417
  551, 552, 553, 987
Gasbarro, Nicola 850
Gasché, Rodolphe 54, 317, 519,
  592
Gatti, Luis 1143
Gaudet, Pierre 418
Geertz, Cilfford 128
Geertz, Hildred 650a
Gellner, Ernest 651a
Genet, (J. Flanner) 1037
Genette, Gerard 73, 1144
Geras, N. M. 1023
Gerber, Rudolph J. 1146
Giannotti, G. 652a
Giacon, C. 1024, 1045
Gibson, Mickey 419, 653a
Gilsenan, M. 654a
Gioanola, Elio 1025
Girard, René 922, 923
Glusksmann, A. 420, 571, 1147
Glucksmann, Miriam 8
Goddard, D. 655a, 656a
Godelier, Maurice 595, 797,
  945, 946
Goldmann, Lucien 572, 947,
  948, 1148
Gonzalez, O. 129, 1149
Goody, J. 197
Gorer, Geoffrey 321
Goodenough, Ward H. 657a
Gordon, Sigfredo 421
Gramont, Sanche de 9, 130
Granai, G. 770
Granger, Georges 972, 1073,
  1074
Green, André 798
Greimas, A.-J. 422, 593, 1230
Grenet, P. 1150
Gritti, J. 819
Gruppi, Luciano 949

Guaraldi, Antonella 1231
Guerrieri, A. M. 131, 1038
Guerin, G. 423
Guiart, Jean 73, 132, 771,
  772, 1039
Guier, Jorge Enrique 198,
  827
Guillen, Claudio 924
Gurvitch, Georges 1091
Gusdorf, Georges 538, 773,
  1075
Gwell, Eugène 849
G. P.-M.

Hamilton-Peterson, James 30
Harris, Marvin 658a
Hart, C. W. M. 199
Hartman, Geoffrey H. 1152
Hartmann, Klaus 573
Hauck, Gerhard 659a
Haudricourt, A. 660, 904
Hays, H. R. 133
Hayes, Nelson E. and T. M. 9
Hayman, David 925
Henriques, Fernando 424
Hernandez, Carmen Maria de
  1232
Hess, John 425
Hesnard, A. 1253
Heusch, Luc de 39, 73, 200
  201, 202, 254, 426, 661,
  799, 828, 950, 1246
Hodgson, Godfrey 134, 427
Hoffman, Hans 662
Homans, George C. 203
Hughes, H. Stuart 9, 135,
  1088
Hultkrantz, O. 428
Hund, Wulf O. 1153
Hund, William B. 764
Huxley, Francis 9, 136, 137
Hyde, Gordon 1154
Hymes, D. H. 663, 905, 906,
  907
Hiatt, R. 851

Ipola, Emilio de 77, 768
Izard, Michel 429, 988

Jacob, André 800
Jacob, François 852
Jacques, François 664, 1040
Jaeggi, Urs 1155
Jager, M. 138
Jahoda, G. 1096
Jallat, Jeannine 963
Jalley Crampe, Michèle 1233
Jameson, Fredric 1156
Jeanson, Francis 574
Jelenski, K. A. 255
Jesi, F. 430
Johansen, Suend 575
Josselin de Jong, P. E. de 10, 206

Kahn, Jean-François 1157
Kalisky, René 926
Kampits, Peter 1158
Kamstra, J. H. 783
Kang, Shin-Pyo 665, 749
Kasakoff, Alice 666, 1254
Kaufmann, Herbert 604
Kermode, Frank 927, 1055
King, A. R. 432
Kirk, G. S. 433
Köbben, A. J. F. 939, 1159, 1160
Kockelmans, Joseph 434, 789, 1010
Kongas, Elli-Kajia 667, 974
Korn, Frances 11, 12, 207, 208
  208, 668, 940, 973
Kortmulder, K. 205
Krader, Lawrence 23, 1075a
Krause-Jensen, E. 1161
Kukukdjian, George 853
Kuper, Adam 669
Kursbuch 1275

Lacapra, Dominick 520
Lacroix, Jean 139, 256, 322,

Ladrière, Jean 1076, 1163
Laffly, Georges 605
Lafrance, Guy 494
Lagadec, Claude 801
Laing, R. D. 273
Lampo, Mireille 78
Lancelotti, Mario A. 274
Lane, Michael 1164
Langlois, Jean 50, 1026
Lanteri-Laura, G. 576, 802, 802a
Lanza, Riccardo 60
Lapierre, J. William 1097
Lapouge, Gilles 437, 854
Lassudrie-Duchene, B. 670
Lavers, Annette 5, 438
Leach, Edmund R. 6, 9, 13, 14, 22, 40, 55, 70, 140, 141, 142, 143, 209, 323, 324, 325, 439, 440-441-442, 597, 671-675, 882-883, 989, 990, 991, 992, 1166
LeBlond, Jean-Maris 1077
Lee, K. 526
Lefebvre, Henri 144-145, 165, 803, 884, 1167
Lefeuvre, Michel 545
Lefort, Claude 210, 211, 676
Leiris, Michel 257
Lemaire, A. H. F. 1168
Lepenies, Wolf 55, 146, 543, 820, 1169
Levin, David Michael 577, 780
Lévi-Strauss, Claude 546, 1007
Licciardello, Pasquale 677
Lienhardt, Godfrey 16, 443, 678-679
Lima, Luiz Costa 75
Lipsius, Frank 257, 258
Littlejohn, James 18, 212
Locher, G. W. 148, 804
Lopez Martin, Alfonso 1170
Lounsbury, Floyd 20, 213
Luporini, Cesare 501
Lupasco, S. 1234
Lyotard, Jean-François 147

216 INDEX

L., J.

Maci, Guillermo 886
Macksey, Richard 3, 151, 885
MacRae, Donald 444
Magliola, Robert 1011
Magana Esquivel, A. 445
Mainberger, Gonsalv K. 1171
Makarius, Laura (see Makarius, Raoul)
Makarius, Raoul 44, 296, 680-689, 774, 821, 1172
Malavassi, V. Guillermo 446, 1235
Mallet, Francine 855
Maquet, Jacques 23, 993
Maranda, Pierre 69--693, 1041, 1092
Marc-Lipiansky, Mireille 41, 495
Marchan, Simon 610
Maria, Roger 26
Mariani, E. 1174
Marin, L. 557
Matarasso, M. 326
Maybury-Lewis, David 9, 214, 449, 450
McNelley, Cleo 259
McGinn, T. 765
Medina, Angel 805
Mehlmann, Jeffrey 79, 152, 527, 534
Meijer, P. W. M. de 554
Melenk, H. 510, 1173
Mendelson, E. Michael 1249
Mepham, John 448, 1078
Mercier, P. 694
Merleau-Ponty, Maurice 544
Merquior, J. G. 598, 1175
Metais, G. 215
Mettra, Claude 451, 1056
Miceli, S. 452
Michelson, A. 611
Miguelez, Roberto 775
Milet, Albert
Milet, André 45, 1176
Millet, Louise 1177

Miotto, A. 695
Molnar, Thomas 149
Montes, Santiago 71, 696
Moonan, Wendy 856
Moore, F. C. T. 216
Moore, O. K. 887
Moore, Tim 17
Mora, Fernando 895
Moravia, Sergio 61, 150, 560, 1079
Morawski, Stefan 612
Morazé, Charles 327, 806
Morelle, Paul 453-544, 1057, 1058
Morisani, Ottavio 613
Morot-Sir, Edouard 756
Mosconi, J. 757
Mougin, Georges 9, 348, 908-909
Mouloud, Noël 758-759, 888, 1080
Mounin, Noël
Mourelos, G. 1237
Muller, Jean-Claude 217, 697
Muntz, Peter 523, 698
Murdock, George P. 699, 1093
Murphy, David 153
Murphy, R. F. 154, 951

Nadel, Siegfried F. 1094
Nagel, Herbert 55, 528
Nannini, Sandro 1042
Nathhorst, Bertel 994
Needham, Rodney 19, 218, 327a, 700
Nethold, Anna-Maria 594
Nettl, Peter 328
Newman, Edwin 857
Nodelman, Sheldon 614
Nutini, Hugh G. 9, 515, 535a 701-704, 760, 822-823, 1081

Olsen, Michel 930
Oppitz, Nichael 260
Orans, Martin 705

Ortigues, Edmond 706

Paci 75, 599, 707-709, 712,
  1012, 1013, 1014, 1178,
  1238, 1239, 1240, 1241
Panoff, Michel 455
Parain, Brice 155, 710
Parain-Vial, Jeanne 615, 807,
  824
Pautasso, S. 816
Pawowski, T. 913
Paz, Octavio 21, 46, 72
Pensée (La) 1278a
Pepper, G. 275
Peristiany, J. 218a
Pettit, Philip 599, 600
Philip, Jim 329
Piaget, Jean 1179, 1180, 1181
Picon, Gaëtan 261
Pieri, Sergio 954
Piguet, Jean-Claude 330, 578
Pingaud, Bernard 73, 74, 579,
  580, 1182, 1183, 1184
Pinto, Evelyne 456, 931
Pirson, Pierre 711
Piselli, Francesco 616
Pividal, Raphael 156, 331
Pochtar, Ricardo 457, 781,
  889
Poirier, J. 776
Pocock, D. F. 157
Pollman, Leo 932
Pompeo Faracovi, Ornella 953
Poole, Roger C. 297, 547, 890-
  891, 1185
Pouillon, Jean 73, 158, 219,
  458, 460-461, 581-582, 714-
  716, 858, 955-956, 995, 1187
Posner, Charles 713
Poster, Mark 503
Pouwer, Jean 23, 459, 717-719,
  996, 1224
Prado, Bento 563
Prastaro, A. M. 1186
Preti, Giulo 564, 1083
Psathas, George 1015
Puccetti, Roland 899

Puddu, M. R. 1082

Queiroz, M. I. Pereira de 745

Radice, R. 66
Rambures, J.-L. 859
Ravera, M. 65
Ravis, G. 809
Rayfield, J. R. 720
Régis, Louis-M. 462
Régnier, André 784
Reif, Adelbert 1188
Remotti, Francesco 63, 64,
  777, 975, 1247
Renaud-Vernet, O. 463, 997
Renzi, Emilio 75, 1255
Revel, Jean-François 159, 332-
  333-334, 464-465, 511
Reynolds, Larry 1098, 1259
Richard, Philippe 466-467
Ricoeur, Paul 75, 790-791,
  1190
Rideau, Emile 1189
Riffaterre, Michel 349
Ritter, Hans Henning 55, 565
Rivelaygue, Jacques 1027
Riviere, Claude 496
Rivière, Peter 1225
Robey, David 1191
Robert, Jean-D. 43
Robinson, Marguerite S. 721
Rodinson, M. 236, 779, 1066,
  1067
Ronfani, V. 1084
Rosen, Lawrence 23, 583
Rossi, Ino 23, 80, 220, 825,
  933, 966, 1256, 1257
Rosner, K. 617
Rouboud, J. 516, 911
Rothenstreich, Nathan 1243
Roy, Claude 160, 468
Roudiez, Leon S. 559
Rubio Carracedo, José 497,
  584, 747, 826, 1192
Rucinski, Brunon J. 1194
Runciman, W. G. 1193

Ruwet, Nicolas   75, 469, 912-914
Ruyer, Raymond   585, 722, 755

Sahlins, Marshall D.   161
Said, Edward   162, 1196
Saint-Phalle, Thérèse de   470
Salisbury, A. A.   221
Salman, D. H.   471, 998
Saltini, Vittorio   539, 782
Sansom, Basil   276
Sartre, Jean-Paul   223, 586-587
Scarduelli, Pietro   67
Schaff, Adam   1197
Schechner, R.   222, 829
Scheffler, H. W.   224, 1198
Schintholzer, Birgit   81
Schiwy, Günter   978, 1199, 1200, 1201, 1202, 1203
Schmidt, Alfred   56, 68
Schneider, David M.   727
Schrag, Calvin O.   1059
Schuwer, C.   226, 474
Schober, Rita   935
Scholes, Robert   350, 555, 588, 934
Scholte, Bob   9, 37, 52, 82, 225, 472-473, 536, 723-724-725-726, 728, 1204
Schwimmer, Erik   23, 1004, 1205
Sebag, Lucien   474a, 475, 810, 957, 959, 999
Segre, C.   1206
Selby, Henry A.   729
Sève, Lucien   960
Servier, J.   163
Seymour-Smith, Martin   164, 476
Shalvey, Thomas J.   83, 477, 1000
Shankmann, Paul   478
Sharpe, Eric J.   730
Sierksma, Fokke   166, 1207
Simone, F.   165, 1043
Simonis, Yvan   23, 48, 84, 732, 761, 785, 961, 1060, 1208

Singerman, Ora   335
Sini, C.   280
Slamet-Velsink, Ina E.   227, 733
Smith, Pierre   479, 1001
Solomini, Maria Ponzo   731
Solotaroff, T.   168
Sommerfelt, Alf   915
Sontag, Susan   9, 169, 278, 279
Soto, Verges, Rafael   1086
Sousberghe, Louis de   228
Southwold, Martin   481, 734
Sperber, Dan   537, 735
Stack   336
Steiner, George   480, 860
Stern, Alfred   1029
Steinwachs, Gisela   512
Stuck, Heiner   298
Sturtevant, William C.   736
Suret-Canale, J.   962
Swanson, Guy E.   737

Tagliaferri, Aldo   618
Tally-Crampe, Michele   968
Tanneguy de Quenétain   861
Tarn, Nathaniel   170
Tax, Sol   738
Tennekes, J.   739,
Thion, Serge   1209
Tibaldi, G.   589, 813
Topolski, Jerzy   814
Tornos, Andres M.   1210
Torrance, John   483, 1002
Tournier, Michel   1044
Toybnee, Philip   172
Tréguier, Michel   862-863
Trotignon, Pierre   173
Tullio-Altan, C.   740-741-742, 916, 1213, 1214
Turnbull, Colin M.   337
Turner, T.   482

Urmeneta, Fermín de   619
Uscatescu, Jorge   893, 1211, 1212

Valeri, Valerio 171
van Haeperen, Joseph 85
van Loon, J. F. Glastra 762
Védrine, Hélène 590, 812
Veltmeyer, Henry 502
Vercier, Bruno 262
Vernant, Jean-Pierre 229
Verón, Eliseo 864
Verstraeten, Pierre 86, 1216, 1258
Vidal-Naquet, P. 811
Vidich, Arthur J. 558
Viet, J. 1217
Vita, Luis Washington 338
Vogt, Evon C. 743
Volpe, Galvano, Della 1217

Waehlens, Alphonse de 1016, 1028
Wagner, Roy 230
Wahl, François 1218
Wahl, Jean 484
Wald, Henri 1220
Waldberg, Patrick 1045
Wallace, A. F. C. 231
Ward, B. E. 744
Warner, Lloyd W. 232
Warnock, Mary 339
Watte, P. 1219
Weightman, John 174, 175, 485, 865, 1063
Weinrich, H. 488, 936, 1003, 1221, 1223
Wells, Rulon 1087
Wetterich, N. E. 1165
White, H. 233
White, Hayden 815
Wilden, Anthony 23, 535, 763, 1222, 1248
Willems, E. 263
Willis, R. G. 486, 487
Wilson, Carter 489
Wood, Michael 1064
Worsley, Peter 299, 340
Wunderlich, D. 341

Yalman, N. 342, 491
Young, L. M. 490
Yurick, Sol 176, 938

Zehraoui, Absene 866
Zéraffa, Jean 937
Ziegler, Jean 591
Zimmermann, Marc Jay 529
Zimmermann, Robert L. 177, 343

Ref
Z
8504.35
L36